GUIDE TO PASSING THE PSI REAL ESTATE Exam

4TH EDITION

Lawrence Sager

Dearborn
Real Estate Education

While a great deal of care has been taken to provide accurate and current information, the ideas, suggestions, general principles and conclusions presented in this text are subject to local, state and federal laws and regulations, court cases and any revisions of same. The reader is thus urged to consult legal counsel regarding any points of law—this publication should not be used as a substitute for competent legal advice.

Publisher: Diana Faulhaber
Development Editor: Anne Huston
Managing Editor: Ronald J. Liszkowski
Art and Design Manager: Lucy Jenkins

Published by Real Estate Education Company®,
a division of Dearborn Financial Publishing, Inc.®
155 North Wacker Drive
Chicago, IL 60606-1719
(312) 836-4400
http://www.REcampus.com

Printed in the United States of America.

01 02 10 9 8 7 6 5 4

Library of Congress Cataloging-in-Publication Data

Sager, Lawrence.
    Guide to passing the PSI real estate exam / Lawrence Sager. — 4th ed.
        p. cm.
    ISBN 0-7931-3849-3
        1. Real estate business—United States—States—Examinations, questions,
etc.   I. Title

HD1381.5.U5 S24   2000
333.33'0973—dc21

                                                                00-044557

CONTENTS

The growing complexity of the real estate business has been accompanied by an increased emphasis on real estate education. Evidence for this emphasis is the trend toward state requirements for both prelicense and continuing education. Accordingly, many states currently employ professional testing organizations to aid them in the development and administration of licensing examinations. One of these organizations is PSI Licensing Examination Services, Glendale, California, which has developed widely used licensing exams for real estate professionals.

The focus of this study guide is preparation for PSI's licensing examinations. Of the existing books devoted to preparing for real estate licensing exams, this is the first study guide geared specifically to the new format of the PSI examination. The PSI exam is distinctive and challenging. As such, it warrants the specialized focus of *Guide to Passing the PSI Real Estate Exam*.

This book is intended to guide prospective licensees in their preparation for the exam. It is intended to *direct* effort. The study aids presented will help the student make the best use of his or her preparation time. It is hoped that this study guide will enable the prospective salesperson or broker to achieve success not only on the licensing exam but ultimately in the dynamic field of real estate.

My thanks to all those who participated in the preparation of this text. I am especially grateful for the comments and advice of: John Morgan, Morgan Testing Services, Waterford, CT, R. Patrick Diamond, Gulf South Real Estate Institute, Inc., Lake Charles, LA; Mary Otis, Northern Virginia Association of Realtors, Fairfax, VA; Andrew G. Pappas, CT Community Technical Colleges; and William Selsberg, Norwalk Community Technical College, Norwalk, CT.

My thanks also to the Real Estate Education Company staff: Diana Faulhaber, Anne Huston, and Ron Liszkowski.

This book is dedicated to my wonderful wife, Adrienne, for all of her support and encouragement.

Lawrence Sager is a licensed real estate broker, certified residential appraiser, and REALTOR®. He holds a master's degree in urban land economics from the University of Illinois and is Real Estate Coordinator at the Madison Area Technical College. His writings have appeared in numerous publications on real estate and related fields.

Sager has acted as research consultant for Madison Area Technical College, the University of Wisconsin and other public and private organizations. He is a Certified Fair-Housing trainer and has served as president of the Community Reinvestment Alliance, Madison, Wisconsin. He has worked with the Wisconsin Real Estate Examining Board as a course writer and as the assistant executive secretary in the certification of educational programs for real estate licensure. He is a member of the Professional Standards Committee of the REALTORS® Association of South Central Wisconsin as well as the Appraiser Application Advisory Committee of the Wisconsin Department of Regulation and Licensing and the Advisory Committee on Continuing Assessor Education of the Wisconsin Department of Revenue. He is the author of *Guide to Passing the Real Estate Exam (ACT)*, *Wisconsin Real Estate: Practice and Law*, and the 1980 and 1983 editions of the *Wisconsin Real Estate Manual*. He is also the author of *Guide to Passing The PSI Real Estate Exam Software* and a CD ROM on *Real Estate Law and Practice in Wisconsin*. Sager also serves as an expert witness in the areas of real estate practice and law as well as competency of real estate licensees.

Use of
the Manual

The aim of this manual is to prepare you on as many levels as possible to pass the real estate licensing examination compiled by the PSI Licensing Examination Services, in Glendale, California. The *Guide* addresses two primary aspects of test taking:

1. the structure and format of the exam and

2. the content of the exam.

The organization of the *Guide* follows these two basic concerns. In addition to suggesting the most efficient use of this manual, Part 1 provides specific information about the PSI organization, testing procedures, and the test itself. Part 2, "Examination Strategies," is intended to familiarize you with the *format* of the questions in the PSI exam and suggests a strategy for optimizing test scores. Several studies have shown that given two examinees of equal ability and subject knowledge, the one who is more familiar with the form and style of the test will consistently score better than the other. Accordingly, Part 2 discusses the mechanics and the strategies of a test. It explains, for example, the parts of a question and how a typical question is developed. It illustrates how to analyze a question for clues to the right answer and how to determine what skills the question is intended to measure. Particular attention is given to the types of questions used by PSI in its real estate licensing examinations.

Exam content receives the foremost emphasis in the remaining parts of the *Guide.* Part 3 presents a strategy for optimizing test results by using the diagnostic exams and formats of concepts presented in Parts 4 to 12, 14, and 15. Part 13 is a test of real estate mathematics.

Finally, Part 16, "Salesperson Examinations," and Part 17, "Broker Examinations," afford an opportunity to take sample 80 and 100-question exams to measure your knowledge and the test-taking skills you have gained. The Glossary is a handy reference list of real estate terms and definitions.

EXAMINATION INFORMATION AND BACKGROUND

PSI's Real Estate Licensing Examination is prepared by a committee of test-development specialists, outstanding educators in real estate, and representatives from U.S. licensing jurisdictions. This committee has devised the national and, in some cases, the state portions of both the broker and the salesperson licensing exams.

The most important step in building the PSI examination is preparing the blueprint for the exam. Committee members define the test outline in detail: what subject matter should be covered, how many questions should be devoted to each topic, what abilities should be tested, how difficult or easy the questions should be. Using the completed test specifications as a guide, PSI item writers in the field submit a first draft of questions, which is reviewed and revised by other panels of experts for legal and factual accuracy. Their revision then is reviewed by additional panels of real estate practitioners to assess the difficulty of questions as part of an additional validation process.

Alternative forms of the salesperson and broker examinations are compiled. To protect exam security, the questions and their presentation in each section differ from one alternate test to another. Because the examinations cover the same content and are equally difficult, the system is fair to all examinees.

The salesperson exam contains from 110 to 150 multiple-choice questions. Ample time is allowed to complete the test.

The exam has two parts. The first part is an 80-question or 100-question test that measures your understanding of real estate practices and principles common to all the participating jurisdictions. Discussions in Part 2 of the *Guide* provide a breakdown of the divisions of the national test and their relative importance in the exam.

The second part of each exam (30 to 50 questions) is the state test. The questions focus on real estate regulations and practices and state statutes that are unique to each jurisdiction. More information on the content of this part of the exam can be obtained from your real estate commission.

All questions on the salesperson examinations are multiple choice, with four alternatives. (Formats are discussed in detail in Part 2, "Examination Strategies.") Objective or multiple-choice questions are advantageous because they can accurately test several different levels of an applicant's knowledge in a limited amount of time and can be scored quickly.

Each correct answer counts as one point; no credit—nor penalty—is given for wrong answers. This means that it will benefit you to answer all the questions on the exam as best you can. The answer sheet should be free of all marks except filled-in ovals and identifying information; marking more than one answer to a question counts as a wrong answer. The example below illustrates the correct way to fill in an answer:

> • How many alternatives does a PSI exam question have?
>   1. Three   Sample Answer Spaces
>   2. Four
>   3. Five   (1) (**2**) (3) (4)
>   4. Six

You must pass both the national section and the state section of the test. The required percentage of correct answers varies from one licensing commission to another; this information is available from your local jurisdiction. PSI policy is to send all examinees their score reports. Each of these reports indicates the examinee's scores on each of the two major sections of the exam (national and state), as well as on the various content areas in each major section. The scores represent the examinee's performance on a scale of 0–100. At present, PSI does not allow an applicant to review her or his examination.

On the day of your real estate exam, take your test center admission ticket, personal identification, several number-two pencils, an eraser, and a watch to the testing center. Many jurisdictions allow examinees to use silent, battery-powered calculators although these calculators cannot have alphabetic keypads or paper tape. Slide rules also are allowed, but you should be able to work the math problems without such aids. No other paper or aids should be taken to the test site.

Standard instructions and procedures are part of the written exam booklet and probably will be read to you by a test supervisor before you begin the exam. When you get your test booklet, read the directions completely. When you receive your answer sheet from the test supervisor, be sure to enter your identifying information on it properly. Otherwise, the report of your score could be delayed or lost.

Approximately half of the states using PSI currently are having their examinees take the exam by computer. Taking the PSI examination by computer is simple; neither computer experience nor typing skills is required for taking the test, which requires you to use fewer than 12 keys. Upon being seated at the computer terminal, you will be prompted to confirm your name, identification number, and the examination for which you are registered.

An introduction to the computer and keyboard will appear on the screen prior to your starting the exam. The time allowed for this introduction will not count as part of your exam time.

The introduction includes a sample screen display telling you to press "1", "2", "3", or "4" to select your answer or to press "?" to mark for a later review. You then press "enter" to record your answer before moving on to the next question. You may change your answer as often as you like before pressing enter. Note that during the examination, the time remaining for your examination will be displayed at the top of the screen and updated as you record your answers. After you have answered every question in the examination, if you have time remaining you will be given the opportunity to review all of the questions in the examination. You also will have the choice of reviewing only those questions that you marked for review or ending your examination and seeing your results. You may change your answers during the review options. You may repeat the review options as time allows.

SALESPERSON EXAMINATION

The content order in Parts 4 through 14 of this text follows the organization of the basic areas of PSI's national salesperson test:

1. Property ownership
2. Land use controls and regulations
3. Valuation and market analysis
4. Financing
5. Laws of agency
6. Mandated disclosures
7. Contracts
8. Transfer of property
9. Practice of real estate
10. Mathematics
11. Specialty areas

Parts 4 to 12 and 14 end with a brief examination of the topics covered in each section. These pretests, called "diagnostic tests," will help you determine your particular strengths and weaknesses and thus indicate which section of the examination needs additional review. They will identify the specific real estate concept, terminology, or application that you do not fully comprehend. The answers for each pretest are keyed to the page with the information you need to know for that subsection. The concepts-to-understand outlines that immediately precede their associated pretests are useful as a general review. In addition, in conjunction with the pretest they can help you identify your problem topics quickly and accurately. The recommended procedure for using these sections is to take the pretests, then check your answers against the answer key provided at the end of the pretest. If your evaluation of your wrong answers indicates that you misunderstand the topic, review the outline that follows. If necessary, consult other texts for additional clarification. If your evaluation on the pretest indicates that you understand the concept but missed the question because of its structure, then reread Part 2, "Examination Strategies." If the math is a problem, check Part 13 for a basic real estate mathematics review.

As a final check on your knowledge, read the "Study and Review Checklist" in Part 3. When you feel sufficiently prepared, turn to the 80 or 100-question sample exam in Part 16 (for salesperson) or Part 17 (for broker). These exams closely approximate an actual PSI exam in content and format. They offer an opportunity to test your knowledge and test-taking skills thoroughly. The answer key and its explanations will help you identify your problem topics, based on the results of your diagnostic pretests and the sample exam. Consider consulting real estate principles and practice texts if you missed a significant number of questions that relate to a specific topic.

PSI Test Specifications for Salespeople

In the national portion of the real estate licensing examination for salespersons, PSI has defined its testing priorities as follows:

- **Property Ownership** makes up 13 percent of the test. This segment covers general topics such as classes of property, land characteristics, encumbrances, types of ownership, and descriptions of property.

- **Land-Use Controls and Regulations** makes up 10 percent of the test. This segment covers the kinds of restrictions that can limit property use, including public restrictions, such as zoning ordinances and building and housing codes, and private restrictions, such as those identified in deed restrictions.

- **Valuation and Market Analysis** makes up 7 percent of the test. This segment covers the methods used to estimate value as well as how economic and financial conditions affect real estate values.

- **Financing** makes up 13 percent of the test. This segment covers a knowledge of financing alternatives and practices of financial institutions.

- **Laws of Agency** makes up 11 percent of the test. This segment covers topics such as buyer and seller agency, subagency, termination of agency, and compensation.

- **Mandated Disclosures** makes up 4 percent of the test. This segment covers property disclosure forms, inspection, and material facts.

- **Contracts** makes up 13 percent of the test. This segment covers topics such as listing contracts, purchase agreements, counteroffers, amendments, cancellation agreements, leasing agreements, options, and land contracts for deed.

- **Transfer of Property** makes up 7 percent of the test. This segment covers topics such as title insurance and deeds.

- **Practice of Real Estate** makes up 7 percent of the test. This segment covers fair housing laws and advertising.

- **Mathematics** makes up 11 percent of the test. This segment tests the ability to calculate land and building areas, real estate commissions, mortgage payments and prorations. It also measures your understanding of the ability to work with percentages.

- **Specialty Areas** makes up 4 percent of the test. This segment covers topics such as property management and common interest ownership properties.

BROKER EXAMINATION

The broker exam is comprised of 100 to 150 questions (80 to 100 in the national test and, usually, 25 to 50 in the state test) and lasts up to five hours. Part 17 of the Guide, "Broker Examinations," contains a discussion of the broker exam, one 80-question and one 100-question sample exam. The answer key that follows includes discussions of the answers and references to the page numbers that cover the topics. Wisconsin's broker exam (100 questions) includes a broker management section, covered in Part 15.

The "Study and Review Checklist" in Part 3, the diagnostic tests and concepts-to-understand outlines in Parts 4 to 12, as well as Parts 14 and 15, the math review in Part 13, and the sample exams in Parts 16 and 17 should be of considerable study value to the prospective broker in preparing for the exam.

PSI Test Specifications for Brokers

In the national portion of the real estate licensing examination for brokers, PSI includes the same categories covered in the salesperson exam, with the exception of Wisconsin. The difference between the two national tests is the proportion of questions in each category. The distribution in the broker exam is as follows:

- **Property Ownership** (10 percent)

- **Land-Use Controls and Regulations** (10 percent)

- **Valuation and Market Analysis** (7 percent)

- **Financing** (13 percent)

- **Laws of Agency** (11 percent)

- **Mandated Disclosures** (3 percent)

- **Contracts** (13 percent)

- **Transfer of Property** (9 percent)

- **Practice of Real Estate** (8 percent)

- **Mathematics** (10 percent)

- **Specialty Areas** (6 percent)

The state supplement exam for brokers contains approximately 25 to 50 questions and is based on a state's statutes, rules, and contractual forms. Some of the states, such as Wisconsin, develop their own broker exams, in cooperation with PSI.

PART 2

Examination Strategies

The PSI real estate examinations are achievement tests that candidates must pass before they can work as salespeople or brokers in their states. An achievement test measures an individual's proficiency in a given field. The ultimate objective of the license exam is to maintain the standards of the industry and to protect the public from persons not qualified to practice real estate sales and brokerage. The exam, therefore, tests

- the knowledge applicants have gathered through license-preparation courses and individual study and

- the ability of the applicants to use that knowledge in real estate applications.

GUIDELINES FOR PREPARING FOR THE EXAM

Mental and Physical Preparation

Multiple-choice tests demand a special type of mental preparation. While memorizing definitions, terms, and formulas, keep in mind that some questions also will require you to apply your knowledge to novel situations. Concentrate on real estate principles as you study, and try to *apply the principles and facts to real-life situations*.

An excellent method of preparing for an exam is to take similar tests prior to the actual exam. You can gain important percentage points simply by being an experienced test taker. The more similar to the actual exam the practice test is in content and format, the more you will benefit. This is the strategy behind the presentation of the diagnostic tests and the salesperson and broker exams in this manual. Taking the sample tests under actual test conditions (see Part 1 for details) will improve both your knowledge of the subject and your psychological readiness.

You will earn a better score if you are in top physical and mental shape the day of the test. It is a good idea to review your notes within the 48 hours before the exam. Get your normal amount of rest the night before the exam; it *is not* wise to stay up all night in a panic-stricken effort to cram. Eat normally, but do not have a heavy meal before going to the test.

Your *attitude* is at least as important as your metabolic state. You should be prepared, determined and positive. A small amount of anxiety is natural—it can even help you do your best—but too much anxiety is a handicap. Try to remain calm before and during the exam—do not worry about results at this point. Panic is irrational and self-defeating; it will only decrease your score.

Build your confidence by finding out ahead of time how to get to the test location, as well as availability of parking and by arriving a few minutes early. Bring all the appropriate materials. Find a seat at the front of the room, if possible, so you can hear the instructions clearly. Identify the test supervisors in case you have a question or problem later.

Do not *anticipate* the difficulty of the exam. There are bound to be some test candidates working themselves into a panic with last-minute cramming. Do not let their behavior affect you.

Following Directions

One of the major causes of incorrect answers is carelessness. Listen attentively to the test supervisor's instructions. Try not to let your eagerness to start the test make you miss the general rules.

Remember, if you are using an answer sheet, the scorer registers only pencil marks; it cannot tell the difference between a stray mark and an intended answer. An answer will not be counted unless the pencil mark is fairly dark and in the correct place. Keep your responses within the oval, but fill the space entirely. Do not write your answers on scratch paper and then transfer them to the answer sheet all at one time. This procedure invites errors and wastes valuable test-taking time.

Read all written directions carefully, then follow them *exactly*. A sample worked-out problem usually is provided. Even if you think you are familiar with that type of problem, *never* skip the instructions. If you are using an answer sheet, place the answer sheet to the right of the exam booklet if you are right-handed, to the left if you are left-handed. When you actually begin the exam, read carefully, not quickly. Be sure that you understand each question completely before answering. Each question should be read twice to make sure of the question being asked.

A major cause of test errors is simply failure to think. Many tests measure judgment and reasoning, as well as factual knowledge. Always try to choose the *best* answer to a question; more than one alternative may be partially correct. Do not look for trick questions; choose the most logical answer to the premise of each question. Statistically, your first answer is likely to be the correct answer so do not change it unless you are absolutely sure you have made an incorrect answer.

Words used in the questions will have their standard meanings unless they are special real estate terms. It sometimes helps to rephrase a question if you are not sure of the answer. For example, you may suspect that **4** is true in the following item:

> ● In holding a deposit delivered with an offer, which of the following would be the best place to put the money, provided you had no instructions to the contrary?
> 1. In your office safe
> 2. In a neutral depository in the buyer's name
> 3. In your checking account
> 4. In a neutral depository

By rephrasing mentally, "The best place to put a deposit delivered with an offer would be in a neutral depository," you can clarify your thoughts about **4** being the correct answer. Be careful, though, not to change the meaning of the question when you rephrase it.

Pacing

Work through the exam at a comfortable rate. You are allowed ample time to finish the 120 to 150-question exam; however, you should work as rapidly as you can without sacrificing accuracy. Budget your time before you begin the exam. If you are not taking the test on a computer, keep a watch handy. Plan on having more than half the questions answered before half the exam time has elapsed. NOTE: With the computer you do not have to waste time shading-in your answers—and your results are immediate. In Iowa, for example, you have 2½ hours to take the test.

You may want to take a short break halfway through the exam. If you are ahead of schedule, you can afford to look up from your paper; take several deep, slow breaths; stretch your legs; relax in your seat; and rest for a minute or two. This breaks physical and mental tension and helps prevent mistakes.

As you work through the exam, answer the easy questions first—they are worth the same number of points as the hard ones, and they will build your confidence. Mark difficult items and time-consuming calculation problems and return to them later. You may find clues in later questions; or, if time runs out, you will have all the sure points. Do not give hurried answers just because you are intimidated by the number of questions. Most objective items are not very time-consuming. Do not become discouraged if the exam seems difficult. No one is expected to get a perfect score.

DEVELOPING TEST QUESTIONS

The PSI exams are the result of a collaboration by real estate experts and educators. How the tests for salespeople and brokers are organized and how many questions are associated with each topic of the exam were covered in Part 1, "Use of the Manual." This section discusses the mechanics of test building.

Both the broker and the salesperson exams are completely multiple choice. Each test usually includes two types of questions. The first type tests your knowledge of general real estate, and the second tests your ability to apply this knowledge to specific real estate situations. The parts of a typical multiple-choice question are shown in the examples below:

> ● When a claim is settled by a title insurance company, the company acquires all rights and claims of the insured against any person who is responsible for the loss. This is called
> 1. escrow.   3. certificate of title.
> 2. abstract of title.   4. subrogation.

The Stem

The first step in developing a question is to write the *stem,* or *lead.* The stem provides all the information necessary to determine the correct response. It usually does not include irrelevant or extraneous information; the exceptions generally are items dealing with mathematics.

The stem can be an incomplete statement, as in the preceding example, or a question.

> • A lease provides a minimum rent of $250 per month plus 5 percent of annual gross income over $100,000. If the tenant did $145,000 in business last year, what total rent was paid?
> 1. $3,000   3. $4,500
> 2. $5,250   4. $7,250

The answer is **2.** Although the direct question lead tends to be somewhat less ambiguous than the incomplete statement, it usually is slightly longer and contains fewer clues to the correct response.

The Alternatives

The alternatives then are written, with the correct, keyed response embedded among the choices. In the PSI exam, the alternatives are presented in a multiple-choice format. The multiple-choice format, as illustrated in the preceding example, supplies four separate alternative answers. In this format, you are asked to consider four possible answers, alone and in combination. Study the following example:

> • Listing agreements include which of the following?
> 1. An open listing only
> 2. An exclusive-right-to-sell listing only
> 3. An open listing and an exclusive-right-to-sell listing
> 4. A contract for deed

The answer is **3.** The purpose of distractors is to differentiate between well-prepared examinees and those who do not know the subject. Test developers often use popular misconceptions or even true statements that do not apply to the stem as distractors. Questions that do use true statements as distractors test not only your knowledge but also your judgment concerning the relevance of that knowledge. The difficulty of a question depends on the quality, or plausibility, of the distractors. In the worst case, where you have no idea which answer may be correct, the chance of answering it correctly is 25 percent because, theoretically, one out of four questions could be answered correctly just by guessing. The question is much easier, and the odds of guessing correctly much higher, if one or two responses can be immediately eliminated.

SAMPLE QUESTIONS

The questions on the exam are not set up to trick you. You will, however, encounter several exam questions on the broker's exam that are more complex than the majority of the questions. Such questions are usually in a situational (story) format. You will need to read each question carefully to know exactly what is being asked before you begin to formulate your answer.

Examples of questions that seem to be the most difficult for examinees are illustrated in this section. These include questions involving superfluous facts, reading comprehension, multistep math, value judgments, and best answer.

Superfluous Facts

Exam questions frequently contain superfluous facts that are not needed to answer the questions. For example:

> • A family paid $50,000 for their home five years ago, making a $10,000 down payment. Their monthly payment, including interest at 7¾ percent, is $286. The interest portion of their last payment was $225.27. What was the approximate loan balance before their last payment?
> 1. $29,480.64
> 2. $34,880.52
> 3. $44,283.87
> 4. None of the above

The answer is **2.** The only facts needed to answer this question are the amount of the last interest payment and the rate of interest. To solve, simply multiply the amount of the monthly interest, $225.27, by 12. Then divide the result by the interest rate, 0.0775, to get the approximate loan balance.

Reading Comprehension

Another type of question you may find on the test requires that you read each word extremely carefully for comprehension. For example:

> • Closing of a transaction for a residential property is set for April 19, 1996. The seller has a three-year insurance policy that expires June 25, 1997. The seller has prepaid a three-year premium of $555. The buyer is to take over the policy as of the date of closing. The amount credited to the buyer at closing is
> 1. $185.00.
> 2. $202.99.
> 3. $231.25.
> 4. None of the above

The answer is **4.** because the prorated amount of the prepaid insurance would be *debited* to the buyer.

Multistep Math

A type of question that frequently appears on PSI exams involves mathematics problems that require several steps. For example:

> • A woman bought a house at exactly the appraised value. She negotiated a loan through a savings-and-loan association at 75 percent of the appraised value. The interest rate was 9 percent. The first month's interest was $405. What was the approximate selling price of the property?
> 1. $54,000
> 2. $60,000
> 3. $72,000
> 4. None of the above

The answer is **3.** To answer this question, first multiply $405 by 12 to get the approximate annual interest ($4,860). Then divide $4,860 by the interest rate, 0.09, to get the amount of the loan ($54,000). Finally, divide $54,000 by 0.75 to find the appraised value ($72,000), which is the same as the purchase price. Sometimes, a candidate who understands the mathematical process can use the answer key and work backward.

$$\$72,000 \times 75\% \ (0.75) = \$54,000 \times 9\% \ (0.09) = \$4,860 \div 12 \text{ months} = \$405$$

Value Judgments

A few questions on the exam may require you to make value judgments. For example:

- A broker listed a small house for $86,000, obtaining an executed sales contract on it within six weeks at $85,000. The broker learned there was an existing $75,000 first mortgage and a $5,000 second mortgage on the property. The broker knew the real estate could be refinanced on a new $70,000 first-mortgage loan. The holder of the second mortgage told the broker he was willing to discount his $5,000 note, selling it for $4,500. The buyer has $20,000 cash and qualifies for a new $70,000 first-mortgage loan. The broker should
  1. say nothing to the seller about refinancing and allow the transaction to close.
  2. tell the seller the second mortgage can be paid off at a $500 discount.
  3. tell the holder of the second mortgage the property is sold and, therefore, he or she should demand the full amount of $5,000.
  4. buy the second mortgage himself at the $500 discount.

The answer, of course, is **2.** As an agent of the seller, the broker must act in the seller's best interest.

Best Answer

You will frequently be asked to choose the best answer from alternatives when the ideal answer is not present. For example:

- A broker listed a beachfront home at $263,000. Three weeks later, the broker was fortunate to obtain a full-price offer on the beach house. Stopping by the house after the sales contract was executed and in force, the broker was appalled to see a large foundation crack. Two days later the broker noticed the crack had been carefully repaired. The broker knew the seller was unaware of the crack because she had extremely poor eyesight. The broker suspected that the crack had been fixed by the seller's son-in-law, a building contractor. The broker should
  1. disclose the fact of the crack to the buyer.
  2. immediately cancel the sales contract.
  3. keep quiet about the crack because it has been repaired.
  4. confront the son-in-law with his suspicions and threaten to sue.

The best alternative available here is **1**. It would be ideal to inform the seller of the crack, requesting permission to inform the buyer, but that alternative does not appear here. Note that this question also asks you to make a value judgment.

HOW TO ANALYZE A QUESTION

Apparent Content

In general, the PSI exams are designed to measure your real estate knowledge and skills. Multiple-choice questions can test much more than your recall of specific facts. The PSI exam will, in fact, test how well you understand a given concept; whether you can apply rules to real-life situations; and how well you can analyze, synthesize, and evaluate information, then arrive at a correct conclusion. If you can determine what ability the question is trying to measure, it will help you become a more effective test taker. The levels of skill the PSI exam seeks to measure are illustrated by the following examples:

> *Example 1*
> - How many acres are there in a section?
>   1. 16   3. 200
>   2. 36   4. 640

The answer is **4**. This is an example of *recall*, or recognition. The point of the question is to find out if you know this fact about sections—logic does not help much in determining the answer. The *factual question* is the easiest type to recognize.

> *Example 2*
> - Brokers owe their primary fiduciary duty to which of the following?
>   1. The principal   3. The public
>   2. The lender   4. The real estate commission

The answer is **1**. This type of question seeks to measure your understanding of the concept of fiduciary duty—and who it involves. *Comprehension questions* such as this often require you to identify real estate principles, laws, or practices.

> *Example 3*
> - An investor leases a 20 unit apartment building for a net monthly rental of $5,000. If this figure represents a 7.5 percent return on investment, what is the original cost of the property?
>   1. $80,000   3. $800,000
>   2. $200,000   4. None of the above

The answer is **3**. Multiply the monthly rental by 12 to get the rental income ($60,000). Then divide $60,000 by 7.5 percent (0.075) to get the investment cost ($800,000). *Application questions* such as this are one level higher than comprehension questions. They ask you to use recall or understanding to solve a new real estate-related problem. Knowledge of real estate laws, regulations, principles, and practices must be applied to concrete situations encountered on the job. Math problems are usually of this type.

> *Example 4*
> • Which of the following types of financing would be the most appropriate for a young veteran who has just used most of his savings to complete his degree in engineering and now would like to buy a house for his family?
>   1. A conventional mortgage   3. A VA mortgage
>   2. An installment contract   4. An FHA mortgage

The correct answer is **3.** At this point you are being tested not only on the concept of financing but also on your ability to weigh each of the options and come up with the best answer. *Analysis items* gauge your ability to identify parts of a whole, understand the relationships among the parts or identify the way that these elements are organized. You may have to differentiate between reasons and conclusions or indicate the relative importance of causes or factors. This question involves more than recall, for all the options are true. You must take your thinking one step further.

> *Example 5*
> • Which of the following types of listing agreements affords the broker the most protection?
>   1. An open listing   3. A net listing
>   2. An exclusive-agency listing 4. An exclusive-right-to-selling listing

The correct answer is **4.** *Evaluation questions* such as this one test your ability to determine the best solution or to judge value in some manner. Often you must use recall, comprehension, analysis, *and* synthesis to arrive at the answer.

Studies show that items testing the lower levels of cognition (recall or recognition) are easier than application, comprehension, and higher-level questions. However, items testing the higher cognitive functions often can be solved by using general intelligence rather than specific real estate knowledge. Your score can be improved simply by exercising logic. You can turn this to your advantage by reasoning through difficult problems using the following seven steps:

1. Read the items carefully to determine the general subject the item is testing and exactly what is asked.

2. Reread the question for essential facts and qualifiers.

3. Eliminate answers that you know are incorrect.

4. Rephrase the problem (often helpful).

5. Determine what principles or formulas are necessary and how to solve the problem.

6. Apply relevant information to arrive at a solution.

7. Reread the question and check the answer.

Try this item for practice:

> • If an offer to purchase is received under certain terms and the seller makes a counteroffer, what is the prospective purchasers' legal position?
>   1. They are bound by the original offer.
>   2. They must accept the counteroffer.
>   3. They are relieved of the original offer.
>   4. They must split the difference with the seller.

The answer is **3.** How do you use the seven steps to arrive at that answer? In step 1, you determine that the subject is whether an offer is binding under certain circumstances. In step 2, you reread the question to determine that the prospective purchasers make an offer and the seller makes a counteroffer. In step 3, you eliminate any obviously incorrect answers—in this case, response **4.** Step 4 suggests rephrasing the problem: "If the buyers make an offer under certain terms and the seller makes a counteroffer, the buyers. . . ." Step 5 is performed so automatically for this type of question that you may not be conscious that you are doing it. You need to know that an offer is not binding on the prospective purchasers once a counteroffer has been made. In step 6 you determine that alternative **3** is correct. Step 7 ensures that you have understood the question and have marked the right answer.

Although this logical process may seem long or complicated, your mind will accomplish it automatically within a few seconds once you train yourself to think or reason through questions.

Functional Content

There are two basic approaches to answering test questions. Thus far in this section, we have concentrated on one approach—determining the *apparent content* of the item, that is, the real estate facts being tested. To answer questions using the apparent content approach, you must draw on your knowledge of real estate and follow the logical problem-solving processes described earlier. You will answer most of the questions on the PSI license exam on the basis of their apparent content.

There may be a few questions, however, whose answers you will be unsure of based on the apparent content. Questions also can be analyzed on the basis of their *functional content*. The functional content of a test item consists of clues and cues that are inadvertently built in by the test developer and tend to lead you to the correct answer. Making a *psychological* as well as a *logical* analysis can lead you to the correct answer to a question, or at least can improve the guessing odds. These subtle clues and cues are called *specific determiners*, which are signs unrelated to actual subject-matter knowledge that lead you to infer that a particular answer is correct or incorrect. This section discusses 11 different types of specific determiners and illustrates common functional content patterns. (An asterisk indicates the correct answer.)

1. *Length of alternative responses*—There is a tendency for item writers to express the correct response more carefully and in greater detail than the distractors. Therefore, the correct answer often is longer than the other alternatives. For example:

- If property is held by two or more owners as tenants in common, one owner's interest would pass on his or her death to which of the following?
  1. The remaining owners
  - 2. The heirs or whoever is designated in the decedent's will as the devisee
  3. The surviving owner and/or her or his heirs
  4. The state

2. *Grammatical clues*—The correct response sometimes is more consistent grammatically or semantically with the stem, although test developers try to avoid this. The following items point out some clues of which to be aware.

- A person agrees to buy the seller's land for $30,000. The buyer deposits the purchase price with a third party and the seller deposits the deed with the third party. The third party is instructed to record the deed when the seller delivers good title to the land. The third party is to pay the seller $30,000 less agreed tax proration when the buyer has good title. This procedure is called an
  1. provisional sale.   3. power of attorney.
  2. sale upon condition.   • 4. escrow.

A or *an* in the stem can indicate whether the correct answer starts with a consonant or with a vowel.

- Who are the parties involved in a warranty deed?
  1. Mortgagor   3. Exchangee
  2. Exchanger   • 4. Grantor and grantee

As shown in the above question, the stem may imply a singular or a plural response, thus helping you narrow the range of possible answers. Awkward phrasing of one or more alternatives suggests that they are distractors.

3. *Qualifiers and absolute words*—Alternative responses often contain qualifying words and phrases that are clues to their correctness or incorrectness. Qualifiers that lessen the strength of the statement usually are found in true or correct statements. Such qualifiers include *generally, may, often, should, tend to,* and *usually.* Absolute words usually are found in incorrect responses. These include *absolute, absolutely, all, alone, always, completely, doubtless, entirely, forever, indefinitely, indisputable, infallible, infinite, irrefutably, must, never, no, none, only, positive, quite, shall, sole, totally, unchangeable, undeniable, undoubtedly, unequivocal, unquestionable, wholly,* and *without exception.* Study the following example.

> ● A real estate broker acting as the agent of the seller
>   • 1. should render faithful services to the seller.
>   2. can always make a profit, if possible, in addition to commission.
>   3. must agree to a change in price without the seller's approval.
>   4. can accept a commission from the buyer without the seller's approval.

4. *Repetition of phrases or word matching*—An obvious specific determiner is the repetition of a key phrase in both the stem and the correct answer. In some cases, synonyms for key words in the stem will appear in the correct answer.

> ● Which of the following represents a failure to perform or fulfill a contract?
>   1. Defect   3. Subordination
>   2. Delinquency   • 4. Breach of contract

More subtle cues are provided by verbal associations (word matching) that you make naturally and must recognize consciously.

> ● Which of the following is a capitalization rate?
>   • 1. A factor used to estimate a property's value from its annual net income
>   2. A percentage of gross annual income
>   3. Income from an investment property
>   4. The amortization of an investment

You can eliminate all answers except **1** and **2** simply by realizing that a *rate* can be a factor **(1)** or a percentage **(2)** but cannot be a dollar amount **(3)** or a concept **(4)**.

5. *Homogeneity of alternatives*—Questions usually are designed so that the four responses are homogeneous; that is, they share similar features. If one answer strikes you as odd or dissimilar, study it carefully. It may be the correct choice.

> ● Which of the following would *NOT* be a party to a trust deed transaction?
>   1. Beneficiary   3. Trustor
>   • 2. Mortgagor   4. Trustee

6. *Generality of responses*—Sometimes the correct response is more general and inclusive than any distractor. Such "soft" statements almost have to be true because they are so general.

> ● Licensed real estate salespeople are expected to be expert in which of
>   the following?
>   ● 1. Appraisal   3. Basic real estate principles
>   2. Investment   4. Construction

7. *All of the above and none of the above*—Any question that offers "all of the above" as
   an option has a useful functioning content pattern. If you know that at least two of
   the other responses are correct, you can deduce that "all of the above" is the right
   answer, even if you are unfamiliar with the remaining responses. Conversely, if you
   know that one of the options is incorrect, you can eliminate both that option and
   "all of the above," improving your odds of guessing. "None of the above" is rarely
   a correct response, except occasionally in math problems. PSI tends to use "none of
   the above" in its math problems, so that they cannot be calculated backward from
   the answers. PSI also tends to avoid "all of the above" in exam questions.

8. *Synonymous distractors*—Whenever you read two alternatives that have the same
   meaning, you know that neither is correct. Synonymous distractors are a trap that
   test developers fall into when they are hard-pressed for a fourth alternative.

> ● An owner had a wet bar installed in a home. This is considered
>   1. an improvement.   3. a chattel.
>   ● 2. a fixture.   4. personal property.

Answers **3** and **4** have the same meaning; neither is correct.

9. *Opposite alternatives*—After writing the keyed response, a test developer may
   include its opposite as a distractor. Therefore, if opposites appear among the alternatives, one may be the correct answer. Study responses **1** and **2** below.

> ● Who usually bears the cost of the sales commission?
>   1. The buyer   3. The broker
>   ● 2. The seller   4. The mortgage lender

In some cases, responses that exclude each other will cover the entire range of possibil-
ities. You then can be even more certain that one of the pair is correct.

10. *Overlapping answers*—When one response to a question with a single correct
    answer includes or overlaps another response, you should realize that either both
    are correct or both are incorrect. This narrows your choices significantly.

> ● The duties of a broker to the principal include
>   1. care.   3. appraisal.
>   ● 2. care and obedience.   4. notice.

In questions asking for the best answer, one of the overlapping alternatives usually is correct.

11. *Vague pronouns*—Because test developers write the correct response first, they always use the correct noun in it. Later, when they write the distractors, they may unthinkingly use pronouns with the correct response as the antecedent rather than the question stem. A simple example follows:

> - A woman lists with a broker for $50,000. A minority group member makes an offer of $45,000, but the broker does not present the offer. Which of the following is true?
>   - 1. She is a victim under the Federal Fair Housing Act of 1968.
>   2. The fact that the offer was not presented is a violation of RESPA.
>   3. The offer was so low that there was no need to present it to the seller.
>   4. An offer does not always have to be presented to the seller.

If you encounter an item like this, the correct answer will be the one that has a proper pronoun referent or that contains the noun itself.

The benefit of specific determiners is not that they help you pass the exam without knowing the material or that they lead you to the correct answer every time. Their value is that they help you focus on likely responses and eliminate other answers. Mental alertness should supplement your real estate knowledge. Multiple-choice tests are intended to test your knowledge of what is not correct as well as what is correct, so do not hesitate to reason your way through difficult items using elimination.

Rational guessing is related more to problem solving and judgment than to luck. The PSI real estate licensing exam is designed to reward correct responses, not to penalize examinees for incorrect guesses. Make sure, therefore, that you have answered every question before turning in the exam.

EXAM STRATEGY

Many people study diligently and simply show up at the examination site without having given any thought to a strategy for taking the test. To maintain your confidence, poise and positive mental attitude, you should start the examination with a game plan for taking the test.

We suggest that you develop your own strategy for completing the test. An example of an exam strategy follows:

Unless testing is computer-generated, start with the state examination. It is the shorter test, comprising 40 to 50 questions. Read each question once to determine the particular subject matter of the question. Carefully underline key words. Read the question a second time, and concentrate on determining the correct response. If you are uncertain of the correct answer, eliminate obviously incorrect responses. If you still are uncertain of the single best answer, circle the question number in the test booklet or ask the computer to record the number for future review of the choice selected and move on to the next question. You should be aware that states such as Connecticut do not allow you to return the completed exam. The entire state exam should be completed in this fashion even if, hypothetically, you have answered only 8 of 40 questions. Then move to the national exam, again answering the questions you know and skipping the questions you are uncertain about. By doing this, you divide the test into two parts:

1. the part you know, which you answer quickly and efficiently and remove from further consideration, and

2. the part you do not know but have managed to isolate, to which you can devote the remainder of your test time.

If math is your strength, you should next complete the math. There will be approximately ten math questions on the exam. After completing the math (on a mental high), your strategy is to go back to the state portion, then the national portion, and make a second pass through the exam. Do this until both tests have been completed.

Multiple-choice items often test not only your knowledge of specific points but also your ability to relate other information to the point. Many important topics have more than one question allotted to them. The correct answer to one question often can be found in some portion of another, so jot down the numbers of the questions that you think contain clues. This will help you in rechecking answers or answering questions you skipped.

If math is not your strength, do not let yourself be intimidated by the calculation problems. A good approach to math questions is to estimate the answer before actually working the problem. Figure neatly and carefully—this reduces error; then compare your answer with your original estimate. If they are different, you may have misplaced a decimal or used the wrong equation. If you cannot tell from the problem what equation to use, make up a simple, similar problem and determine the equation from that. If you cannot solve a problem, or if you obtain an answer that is not one of the options, check to see if you used all the figures given in your calculations. If you cannot solve a math problem in the usual way, you sometimes can find the correct solution by working backward from the given answers.

Math problems often use varying units that must be converted. You may have to change income per month to income per year before applying a formula, or you may have to convert square feet to acres before proceeding with a calculation.

If you really have no idea how to solve a math problem and must guess blindly, eliminate the two most extreme numerical answers and mark one of the remaining choices. This tactic is not always correct, but the odds favor it.

After completing every question on the exam, proofread your answer sheet if you are taking the exam with an answer key. Make sure that your answers are next to the correct numbers, that you did not misread any of the questions, and that you marked the answer you intended for each item. By using extra time to correct any careless mistakes, you may boost your score significantly. *Do not change an answer unless you are sure the new one is correct. Studies show that an examinee's first response usually is correct and that changes will decrease the score.*

By developing an exam strategy similar to this, you will be in command—not the exam.

PART 3

A Strategy For Studying

This chapter gives you a strategy for studying and incorporating the diagnostic tests and outlines of concepts to understand in Parts 4 through 14. Next is the "Study and Review Checklist," which you can use as an easy reference to see if you are familiar with the subjects covered on the PSI examination.

Parts 4 through 14 correspond to testing areas on the PSI exam for salesperson: "Property Ownership," "Land Use Controls and Regulations," "Valuation and Market Analysis," "Financing," "Laws of Agency," "Mandated Disclosures," "Contracts," "Transfer of Property," "Practice of Real Estate," "Mathematics," and "Speciality Areas." Part 15, "Brokerage Management," is included for those taking the broker exam in Wisconsin. Each part begins with an "Outline of Concepts to Understand" for the subject area. The "Outline of Concepts" is followed by a "Review List" of items you should be familiar with for the subject area. Each part ends with the "Diagnostic Test," its "Answer Key," and a test score box. Take the pretest and analyze your results before reviewing the content outline. If your progress score suggests that you need improvement, use the test results to establish your priority areas for study.

Keep in mind that the outline format of the concepts is designed primarily to organize your real estate knowledge concisely. If you are having difficulty with a particular topic, consult real estate practice and theory texts for a comprehensive explanation of the topic. *Modern Real Estate Practice* (published by Real Estate Education Company®) provides a solid core of information.

HOW TO USE THE PROGRESS SCORE

After completing and correcting the diagnostic test, count the number of questions missed and enter that number in the box under "Your Score" after "Total Wrong." Then subtract the number of incorrectly answered questions from the total points. Finally, analyze your results by finding where your score of correct answers falls in the "Range" column; the rate corresponding to your score describe your progress. Your score will fall under "GOOD," "FAIR," or "NEEDS IMPROVEMENT." For example:

PROPERTY OWNERSHIP

TEST SCORE

RATING	RANGE	YOUR SCORE	
Good = 80% to 100%	28-35	Total Number	35
Fair = 70% to 79%	25-27	Total Wrong	- 6
Needs Improvement = Lower than 70%	24 or less	Total Right	29

Passing Requirement: 25 or better

If your score on a diagnostic test is rated "GOOD," this area is one of your strengths. However, we suggest that a student should strive for a 90-percent-correct score before taking the actual exam. A rating of "FAIR," or "NEEDS IMPROVEMENT" in a subject suggests this is an area you need to concentrate on.

DEVELOPING A STRATEGY FOR STUDYING

After you have pinpointed the areas that need particular study, you can begin studying the material in the concepts-to-understand outline. To increase the effectiveness of your study time, we suggest that you follow these rules.

Organize Your Study Time. Educators suggest that the regular short study periods are better than lengthy cram sessions. You should study when you are at your best mentally and physically; this may be early in the morning. The following chart will help you organize your study time in relation to the specific areas on the examination.

Scheduled Hours for Study

NATIONAL EXAM	M	T	W	Th	F	Sa	Su	TOTAL
Property Ownership								
Land Use Controls and Regulations								
Valuation and Market Analysis								
Financing								
Laws of Agency								
Mandated Disclosures								
Contracts								
Transfer of Property								
Practice of Real Estate								
Mathematics								
Specialty Areas								

STATE EXAM	M	T	W	Th	F	Sa	Su	TOTAL
Real Estate Law								
Rules and Regulations								
Special State Considerations								

Study in Depth. It is important to realize that you cannot simply read the text in preparing to complete the exam successfully. You must arrive at a thorough understanding of the subject matter. This can be easily achieved by writing a sample test question to yourself about the paragraph you have just read. It is a good practice to outline the thoughts of the paragraph in your own words or develop relationships between items. In other words, create mental images that will help you recall difficult concepts. Acronyms are useful when memorizing a series of items. For example, the five duties that an agent owes to a principal are COALD: care, obedience, accounting, loyalty, and disclosure. During this stage, you should work alone.

Regularly Review Material Studied. In many cases this can be accomplished by having a study partner assist you in reviewing your knowledge of vocabulary words, concepts and relationships. This also can be achieved by taking regular exams on the subject matter. Other tips include the following:

- Make flash cards with terms on the front and definitions on the back.
- Tape-record terms: term. . . pause . . . definition.
- Encourage group or one-on-one discussion.

A study and review checklist follows for your use in preparing for the PSI exam.

STUDY AND REVIEW CHECKLIST

National Exam

I. **Property ownership**

A. Classes of ownership

1. Real
2. Personal
3. Fixtures

B. Land characteristics

1. Physical
2. Economics
3. Legal description

C. Encumbrances

1. Liens
2. Encroachments
3. Easements

D. Types of ownerships

1. Estates
2. Tenancies
3. Leasehold

II. **Land use controls and regulations**

A. Planning and zoning

B. Property taxation

C. Flood plain, wetlands and shoreline regulation

    D. Health and safety codes

    E. Environmental concerns

    F. Deed restrictions

    G. Water rights

III.   **Valuation and market analysis**

    A. Methods of estimating value

        1. Sales comparison approach
        2. Cost approach
        3. Income approach
        4. Reconciliation process

    B. Elements of value

        1. Utility
        2. Cost approach
        3. Income approach
        4. Reconciliation process

    C. Depreciation

    D. Capitalization rate

    E. Difference between competitive market analysis and appraisal, gross-rent multiplier, and gross-income multiplier

IV.   **Financing**

    A. Mortgage insurance

    B. Secondary market

    C. Government/conventional loans

    D. Seller financing

    E. Discount points

    F. Closing statements

    G. Notes and mortgages or trust deeds

    H. Assumptions/assignments

    I. Interest on contracts

V.   **Laws of agency**

    A. Law, definition, and nature of agency relationships

    B. Creation of agency and agency agreements

    C. Responsibilities of agent to seller/buyer as principal

    D. Termination of agency

    E. Commission and fees

VI.   Mandated disclosures

   A. Agency disclosures

      1. Disclosure of latent defects
      2. Need for inspection
      3. Obtaining/verifying information
      4. Material facts

   B. Environmental hazard disclosure

   C. Federal Fair Housing Law disclosures

   D. The Americans With Disabilities Act disclosures

   E. Antitrust laws

VII.   Contracts

   A. Listing Contract

   B. Buyer/broker contracts

   C. Offers to purchase

   D. Counteroffers

   E. Multiple counteroffers

   F. Amendments

   G. Land contracts for deed

   H. Cancellation agreements

   I. Leasing agreements

   J. Options

   K. Addenda

VIII.   Transfer of property

   A. Deeds

   B. Escrow process

   C. Title insurance

   D. Tax aspects

   E. Legal vs. equitable title (broker only)

   F. Special processes

IX.   Practice of real estate

   A. Fair housing laws

   B. Truth-in-lending (Regulation Z)

   C. Agent supervision (broker only)

X. Mathematics

   A. Percentage

   B. Areas

   C. Property tax

   D. Loan-to-value ratios

   E. Points

   F. Equity

   G. Qualifying buyers

   H. Prorations

   I. Commissions

   J. Settlement

   K. Comparative market analysis (CMA)

   L. Income properties

   M. Depreciation

   N. Gross rent multipliers (GRM) (broker only)

XI. Speciality areas

   A. Property management and landlord/tenant

   B. Common interest ownership properties

      1. Condominiums
      2. Cooperatives
      3. Time-shares

   C. Subdivisions

   D. Commercial property/income property

   E. Business opportunities (broker only)

   F. Agricultural property (broker only)

XII. Brokerage management

   A. Types of ownership

   B. Sales associate relationships

   C. Risk management

   D. Trust accounts

State Exam

XIII. General topics

   A. State statutes

   B. State license laws, rules, and regulations

C. Responsibilities of broker and salesperson

D. Contractual forms

XIV.   Specific topics

A. Listing agreement

B. Sales contract

C. Closing

D. Land descriptions

E. Title and method of transfer

F. Deeds, land contract, contract for deed, trust

G. Financing, mortgages and usury

H. Interests in real estate

I. Forms of ownership

J. Leases and landlord/tenant law

K. Land use controls, such as zoning

L. Taxation

M. Consumer protection laws

N. Equal opportunity laws

O. Condominiums, cooperatives, and time-shares

P. Transfer fees

Q. Mortgage foreclosure and redemption

R. Disclosure requirements

S. Real estate education

T. Professional organizations

U. Trust accounts

Property Ownership

OUTLINE OF CONCEPTS TO UNDERSTAND

I. **Property ownership**

   A. Classes of property

      1. Real property—the land and anything permanently affixed to it; includes the interests, benefits, and rights inherent in the ownership of real estate

      2. Personal property—movable objects (chattels) that do not fit into the definition of real property; conveyed by bill of sale

      3. Fixture—an item of personal property that has been converted to real property by being permanently affixed to the land or building

      4. A fixture that is permitted to be and is detached from the land or the building would revert to personal property

      5. Trade fixture—an item installed by a commercial tenant according to the terms of a lease and removable by the tenant before the expiration of the lease—personal property

        a. If not removed, the trade fixture becomes real property of the building owner by accession.

II. **Land characteristics**

   A. Physical

      1. Immobile—the geographic location of a parcel of land is fixed—can never be changed.

      2. Indestructible—the long-term nature of improvements plus permanence of land tends to create stability in land development.

      3. Unique or nonhomogeneous—all parcels differ geographically and each parcel has its own location.

   B. Economic

      1. Scarcity—although there is a substantial amount of unused land, supply in a given location or of a specific quality can be limited.

      2. Improvements—placement of an improvement on a parcel of land affects value and use of neighboring parcels of land.

      3. Permanence of investment—improvements represent a large fixed investment; some, such as drainage and sewerage, cannot be dismantled or removed economically.

4. Area preference, or situs—this refers to people's choices and desires for a given area.

C. Legal descriptions

1. Metes and bounds
   a. Begins at a specific point and proceeds around boundaries of parcel by reference to linear measurements and directions
   b. Boundaries established on basis of actual distance between monuments (fixed objects)
   c. A boundary must return to the point of beginning so that the land described is fully enclosed.

2. Rectangular (government) survey
   a. Based on measurements from base lines and principal meridians
   b. Base lines run east and west; principal meridians run north and south.
   c. Designed to set up checkerboard pattern of identical squares over specific area
      1. Parallel lines six miles apart divide land into rows, east and west of the principal meridian, that are referred to as *ranges*.
      2. Parallel lines six miles apart divide land into rows north and south of the baseline that are referred to as *tiers*.
      3. The grid that divides the land into townships is formed by superimposing these two sets of lines.
         a. A township is six miles square (36 square miles).
         b. A township contains 36 sections; each section is a square mile and contains 640 acres (one acre = 43,560 square feet).
         c. Sections are numbered from the northeast corner; the first row of six sections runs east to west, the second row west to east, and so on, with section 36 located in the southeast corner of the township.
      d. The land description is based on references to either a section or some portion of a section, such as one quarter-section (160 acres) or one half-section (320 acres).
      e. A typical description: the NE¼ of the SW¼ of Section 4, Township 3 North, Range 2 east of the Principal Meridian

3. Subdivision plats
   a. Location of an individual parcel is indicated on a map of the subdivision, which is divided into numbered blocks and lots.
   b. Each parcel is referred to a lot, block, subdivision name, city, and state.

4. Street address: an informal reference too inaccurate for a legal description

III. Encumbrances

A. A charge, claim, or liability that attaches to and is binding on real estate

B. General classifications of encumbrances

1. Liens—affect the title
   a. A lien is a charge against property that provides security for a debt or obligation of the property owner.
   b. If the debt is not repaid, the lienholder has the right to have it paid out of the debtor's property, generally from the proceeds of a court or foreclosure sale.

    c. A specific lien relates to specific property; a general lien, such as a judgment or court decree, applies to all the debtor's property.

    d. Possible specific liens against an owner's real estate include real estate taxes, mortgages, and mechanics' liens.

    e. Real estate taxes and special assessments usually take priority over all other liens, regardless of date.

    f. In some states, mechanics' liens may be given priority over previously recorded liens because mechanics' liens revert to the date the work was started, not to when the lien was recorded.

2. Encumbrances that affect the physical condition of the property include encroachment, easements, and restrictions.

    a. Use restriction—a deed restriction or covenant is a private limitation placed in the public record that affects the use of the land. One person may place a restriction upon the property. No "agreement" is present.

    b. Easement—an easement is a right acquired by one party to use the land of another party for a specific purpose.

        1. Easement appurtenant

            a. An easement annexed to ownership for the benefit of such parcel of land

            b. Requires that there be two tracts of land, either contiguous or noncontiguous, owned by different parties

            c. The tract over which the easement runs is known as the *servient tenement;* the tract that benefits from the easement is known as the *dominant tenement.*

            d. Appurtenant easements "run with the land" and are not terminated by the sale of either the servient or dominant tenement.

        2. Easement in gross—a mere personal interest in or right to use the land of another, such as the right of way for a pipeline; there is no dominant tenement, just a servient tenement

        3. Easement by necessity—arises when there is no other access to a street or public way; must be necessary rather than convenient and the grantor of the dominant and servient estates must have been the same party

        4. Easement by prescription

            a. Acquired when the claimant has made use of another's land for the prescriptive period, generally from 5 to 20 years

            b. Claimant's use must have been continuous, without the owner's approval, visible, open, and notorious. Successive periods of use by different parties may establish a claim for an easement by prescription.

        5. License

            a. Permission to enter the land of another for a specific purpose, such as permission to park in a neighbor's driveway or to go hunting on another's property

            b. Differs from easement in that it can be canceled or terminated by licensor at any time

        6. Encroachments—illegal extension of a building or some other improvement, such as a wall or fence, beyond the boundaries of the land of its owner and onto the land of an adjoining owner

IV. Types of ownership—freehold and non-freehold

    A. Interests in real estate—feudal versus allodial rights

        1. Feudal—system of land ownership in which the king or government held title to the land; the individual was merely a tenant who held rights of use and occupancy at the sufferance of the overlord

        2. Allodial—system in which an individual can hold land free and clear of any rent or service due the government; system under which land is held in the United States

    B. Limitations on ownerships—individuals' ownership rights subject to certain rights of government:

        1. Police power—power of the state to establish legislation to protect public health and safety and promote general welfare

        2. Eminent domain—right of government to acquire private property for public use while paying just compensation to the owner through a process known as condemnation

        3. Escheat—reversion of real estate ownership to the state after a statutory time period has elapsed, as provided by state law, when an owner dies and leaves no heirs or no will disposing of the real estate or when the property is abandoned

        4. Taxation—charge on real estate to raise funds to meet the public needs of the government

    C. Estates in land

        1. Refers to degree, quantity, and nature of interest that a person has in real property for a lifetime (life estate) or forever (inheritable freehold)

        2. Freehold estates—estates of indeterminable length, such as those existing for a lifetime or forever

        3. Fee simple

            a. Highest type of interest in real estate recognized by law

            b. Holder entitled to all rights incident to property

            c. Continues for indefinite period and is inheritable by heirs of owner

        4. Defeasible fee (qualified, conditional, determinable, or base fee)

            a. Continues for an indefinite period; may be inherited

            b. Estate extinguished on the occurrence of a designated event, the time of such occurrence being uncertain

            c. May be based on either certain or uncertain event

    D. Life estate

        1. Limited in duration to life of life tenant or life or lives of some other designated person or persons

        2. Not an estate of inheritance, because estate terminates at the death of the life tenant or the designated person

        3. May be created for the life of another person (estate pur autre vie)

         4. Future interests in the property after the death of the life estate owner

            a. Remainder interest—if the deed or the will names a third party to whom title will pass on the death of the life estate owner, then such party is said to own remainder interest.

            b. Reversionary interest—if the deed does not convey remainder interest to a third party, then on the death of the life estate owner, full ownership reverts to the original fee simple owner or, if he or she is deceased, to heirs.

    5. Limited to the lifetime of the owner of the life estate (life tenant)

E. Life tenant

    1. Interest in real property is time-ownership interest.

    2. Generally not answerable to the holder of future interest (remainderman)

    3. Has limited rights, that is, can enjoy the rights of the land but cannot encroach upon the rights of the remainderman

    4. May not commit waste (permanently injure the land or property)

    5. Entitled to possession of the property and to all income and profits arising from property during the term of ownership

    6. Life interest may be sold, leased, mortgaged, or gifted but may be of little value because all interest must be forfeited at the death of the life tenant; remainder interest cannot be encumbered by the life tenant.

F. Legal life estates

    1. Curtesy—husband's life estate in all inheritable real estate of the deceased wife

    2. Dower—wife's life estate in all inheritable real estate of the deceased husband

    3. Many states have abolished curtesy and dower in favor of the laws of descent and distribution, by which the surviving spouse is frequently allowed to take a specific portion of the estate in fee rather than life estate.

    4. Inchoate—a right not yet perfected

G. Homestead

    1. Tract of land owned and occupied as the family home

    2. In states with homestead-exemption laws, a portion of the area or value of land is exempted, or protected, from judgment for unsecured debts.

V. Freehold estates—leasehold estates

A. Ownership by natural persons

    1. In severalty—one owner

    2. In co-ownership—two or more owners

        a. Tenancy in common

            1. Each owner holds an individual interest in severalty.

            2. Each owner can sell, convey, mortgage or transfer his or her interest without the consent of the other co-owners.

            3. Upon the death of a co-owner, the individual interest of the deceased passes to heirs or devisees according to the will; there is no right of survivorship.

            4. Tenants in common may partition the land.

        b. Joint tenancy

            1. Owners have the right of survivorship, which states that all title, right, and interest of a deceased joint tenant in certain property passing to the surviving joint tenants by operation of law is free from claims of heirs and creditors of the deceased.

            2. Four unities—title, time, interest, and possession—are required to create a valid joint tenancy.

            3. Termination results from the destruction of any of the four unities.

        4. Joint tenants may partition the land.
- c. Tenancy by the entirety
  1. Owners must be husband and wife.
  2. Owners have the right of survivorship.
  3. Title may be conveyed or encumbered only by the deed signed by both parties (one party cannot convey a one-half interest).
  4. Usually no right of partition
- d. Community property (marital property)
  1. Husband and wife may have sole ownership of the separate or individual property if it was owned solely by either spouse before the marriage or was acquired by gift or inheritance after marriage.
  2. Husband and wife are equal partners in the community or marital property (property acquired during the marriage).
  3. Upon the death of one spouse, the survivor automatically owns one-half of the community property, the other half being distributed according to the deceased's will.
  4. Antenuptial agreements are contracts (prior to marriage) that preserve separate property ownership.
3. In trust—by a third person for the benefit of another
4. Ownership by a business organization
5. Partnerships
   - a. Association of two or more persons to carry on business as co-owners and share in the profits and losses of that business
   - b. Types of partnerships
     1. General—all partners participate in the operation of the business and may be held personally liable for business losses and obligations.
     2. Limited
        - a. Includes general as well as limited, or silent, partners
        - b. General partner runs the business
        - c. Although limited partners do not participate, they may be held liable for business losses, but only to the extent of their investment unless they take an active role in management.
6. Corporations
   - a. Ownership in severalty—corporations are considered by law to be a single entity.
   - b. Each stockholder's liability for losses generally is limited to the amount of investment.
7. Syndicates—joining together of two or more parties to create and operate a real estate investment

VI.   Other important terms

- A. Accession—acquiring the title to additions or improvements to real property as a result of accretion of alluvium or annexation of fixtures (including accession of trade fixture not removed by the tenant prior to lease termination)
  1. Accretion —increase in land resulting from soil's being deposited by the natural force of water
  2. Alluvion—actual soil increase resulting from accretion
- B. Appurtenances—rights belonging to land
- C. Assignment—transfer of rights and/or duties under a contract

D. Attachment—procedure by which property of debtor is placed in the custody of the law and is held as security, pending the disposition of a creditor's suit.

    1. Rights can be assigned, unless the contract expressly forbids assigning them.

    2. Obligations often can be assigned, but the original party is secondarily liable for them.

E. Benchmark—permanent metal marker embedded in cement, used as a reference to measure the elevation above sea level

F. Cloud on title—any claim that may impair the title to a property

G. Cul-de-sac—street open at only one end and generally with a circular turnaround at the other end

H. Datum—horizontal plane from which elevations are measured

I. Erosion—washing away of land caused by flowing water

J. Estovers—legally allowed necessities, such as the right of a tenant to use timber on leased property to support a minimum need for fuel or repairs

K. Fixtures—personal property that has been affixed to and becomes part of the real property

L. Good consideration—love and affection with no monetary measure of value

M. Inchoate right—incomplete right, such as a wife's dower interest in her husband's property during his life

N. Laches—court doctrine that bars a legal claim because of undue delay to assert the claim

O. Lis pendens (Latin term for action pending)—recorded document that creates constructive notice that an action relating to a specific property has been filed in court

P. Novation—also a transfer of rights and/or duties under a contract

    1. Original contract canceled.

    2. New contract negotiated and drawn, with the same parties or a new second party

    3. Original party, if replaced, not liable

Q. Parol-evidence rule—law that states that no prior or contemporary oral or extraneously written agreement can change the terms of the contract

R. Quiet-title action—court action to establish the title to a specific property, for example, where there is a cloud on the title

S. Statute of frauds—law that requires that certain contracts be in writing before they can be enforced; contracts for the sale of land and leases of more than one year are generally required to be in writing and signed by all parties

T. Statute of limitations—law that refers to the length of time within which a party may sue

U. Valuable consideration—consideration with a monetary measure of value

V. Waste—tenant abuse that results in permanent injury to the land or property

W. Writ of attachment—writ filed during a lawsuit that prevents the debtor from transferring the property involved in the suit

REVIEW LIST

The student should have an understanding of the following areas of property ownership:

1. Classes of property
   a. Real
   b. Personal
   c. Fixtures

2. Land characteristics
   a. Physical
   b. Economic
   c. Legal description

3. Encumbrances
   a. Liens
   b. Easements
   c. Encroachments

4. Types of ownership—freehold and non-freehold
   a. Estates
   b. Other important terms

DIAGNOSTIC TEST

1. The term *situs* refers to
   1. uniqueness.
   3. immobility.
   2. area preference.
   4. scarcity.

2. Which of the following is a physical characteristic of land?
   1. Indestructibility
   2. Scarcity
   3. Permanence of investment
   4. Situs

3. The owner of a life estate in property
   1. does not pay real estate taxes.
   2. is entitled to possession of the property.
   3. may not receive income from the property.
   4. is not responsible for all repairs to the property.

4. Three women own a motel as tenants in common. One of the women decides to sell all of her assets. She may legally
   1. sell, because a tenant in common may sell her portion of assets if a majority of the co-owners also agree to sell.
   2. not sell, because a tenant in common's interests always remains encumbered.
   3. sell because a tenant in common has an undivided interest in real property that is transferable.
   4. not sell, because there is a right of survivorship.

5. Which of the following statements is FALSE?
   1. Fixtures that are purchased, paid for, and installed after the execution of a mortgage are subject to liens of the mortgage.
   2. When a landowner tears down a fence, with the intention that it be permanently removed, and piles the material on the land, such material is real property.
   3. Generally, trade fixtures that were installed by the tenant are personal property.
   4. A hot-water heater installed on the property becomes a fixture.

6. Specific liens would NOT include which of the following?
   1. Mortgage liens
   2. Judgments
   3. Real estate taxes
   4. Mechanic's liens

7. A farmer purchased land with no access to a street or public way. After an unsuccessful attempt to gain access through negotiation he was able to gain access through an
   1. easement appurtenant.
   2. easement in gross.
   3. easement by necessity.
   4. easement by prescription.

8. A woman built a fence that extended beyond the boundary of her property onto her neighbor's property. This is an example of
   1. laches.
   2. easement by necessity.
   3. encroachment.
   4. easement appurtenant.

9. A grandmother owned a life estate measured by her own life in residence. She leased the property for five years using a standard lease contract. Shortly thereafter, she died. The lease was
   1. valid only as long as she was alive.
   2. valid for five years.
   3. invalid because she, as an owner of a life estate, cannot lease property.
   4. valid for up to one year after her death.

10. An electrician did some rewiring in a home for which he has not yet been paid. One month after the work was completed, the electrician drove by the home to discover a For Sale sign on the property. The electrician should
    1. file a mechanic's lien.
    2. offer to purchase the house.
    3. obtain injunctive relief.
    4. sue the listing broker.

11. A tenant failed to remove her trade fixtures prior to the expiration of her lease, which resulted in the landlord's acquiring title to the trade fixtures. Acquiring property in this way is known as
    1. accession.   3. laches.
    2. novation.   4. partition.

12. Included among the features of taking title to real property as tenants in common is that
    1. ownership interest must be equal.
    2. each co-owner's interest may be conveyed separately.
    3. a co-owner cannot will his interest in a property.
    4. the last survivor owns the property in severalty.

13. A homeowner employed a contractor to build a swimming pool on his property. Upon completion of the swimming pool, the contractor filed a lien to receive payment of the contract fee. Such filing could be considered any of the following **EXCEPT**
    1. a specific lien.
    2. an encumbrance.
    3. a general lien.
    4. a mechanic's lien.

14. A family buys a 40 year old house, and the broker tells them the garage was built 30 years ago. Because the buildings are located on a "postage-stamp-sized" lot, the family hires a surveyor who tells them the garage extends six inches onto the neighbor's lot. Because the husband has taken a real estate course, he realizes that this might be a prescriptive easement and is similar to
    1. a dominant easement.
    2. a license.
    3. a servient easement.
    4. adverse possession.

15. A man has a claim affecting the title to another man's property. The owner has been trying to sell the property, and the man with the claim is concerned about the possibility of a bonafide purchaser's buying it before he obtains a judgment to protect himself during the course of the court action. To protect himself, the man with the claim should
    1. file a lis pendens or notice of intent.
    2. publish a notice in the newspaper.
    3. bring a quick summary proceeding.
    4. notify the owner that any attempt to sell the property will be considered fraud.

16. *X* and *Y* own adjoining parcels of real estate. *X* has granted *Y* an easement over his property for ingress and egress. If *Y* decided to sell his land to *Z*, which of the following would be true?
    1. The status of the dominant and servient tenements will not change.
    2. The easement will be terminated, for *Y* no longer is the owner of the property.
    3. *X* may sell the easement to the new owner.
    4. To be valid, the deed of conveyance of *Y* to *Z* must specifically mention the easement.

17. Legal seizure of property to be held for payment of money pending the outcome of a suit to enforce collection is
    1. a lis pendens.
    2. an attachment.
    3. a writ of execution.
    4. an abstract of judgment.

18. Two women bought a building and took title as joint tenants. One of the owners died testate. The remaining owner now owns the building
    1. as a joint tenant with rights of survivorship.
    2. in severalty.
    3. in absolute ownership under the law of descent.
    4. subject to the terms of the deceased owner's will.

19. A husband and wife own property as tenants in the entireties. The husband dies and his will names their son as inheritor of the property. Which of the following statements is correct?
    1. The son and his mother own the property as tenants in common.
    2. The son owns the property in severalty.
    3. The son and his mother own the property as joint tenants.
    4. The son has no interest in the property.

20. Two brothers may take title to income property in unequal shares under which of the following?
    1. Severalty
    2. Tenants by the entirety
    3. Joint tenants
    4. Tenants in common

21. A contractor builds an addition to a house for a contract price of $52,000 and records his mechanic's lien notice. Before making any payment, the owner has the house jacked up and put on a platform prior to moving it to another location. The contractor should
    1. have his attorney prepare and record a covenant.
    2. file an encroachment notice.
    3. record an attachment.
    4. have his attorney prepare and record a notice of lis pendens.

22. Legal descriptions may NOT be based on
    1. the government survey.
    2. metes and bounds.
    3. a street address.
    4. a survey.

23. A land description that begins at a specific point and proceeds around the boundaries of a parcel by reference to linear measurements and directions is based on
    1. metes and bounds.
    2. the rectangular survey.
    3. a subdivision plat.
    4. a survey.

24. In the government survey method
    1. base lines run east and west.
    2. principal meridians run east and west.
    3. base lines run north and south.
    4. a township contains 26 sections.

25. A section contains
    1. 43,560 square feet.
    2. 640 acres.
    3. 160 square rods.
    4. 320 square rods.

26. You and your sister own a house. Your sister would like to sell her interest in the house to her cousin. You and your sister own the house under which of the following?
    1. Tenancy by the entirety
    2. Tenancy at will
    3. Tenancy in common
    4. Estate for years

27. A plumber sells his home, in which he has installed washerless faucets. After the contract has been executed, he decides to replace the faucets with standard faucets. Which of the following is true?
    1. The plumber may remove the faucets at any time.
    2. Standard faucets are a good replacement.
    3. The plumber can be held liable for removing the faucets because they are fixtures that were in place before the contract was signed.
    4. This question should be decided by the broker who took the listing.

28. Which of the following forms of ownership may only be held by a wife and husband?
    1. Tenancy in common
    2. Tenancy by the entirety
    3. Tenancy at will
    4. Joint tenancy

29. R sold his house; it included a water softener, which he had bought the previous year. R's water softener would be classified as
    1. chattel.
    2. personalty.
    3. a trade fixture.
    4. a fixture.

30. You bought a property that measured ⅙ of a mile by ⅙ of a mile. How many acres did you buy?
    1. 17.78 acres   3. 92.83 acres
    2. 36 acres   4. 106.67 acres

31. You are traveling directly from Section 6 to Section 36 of the same township. You would be traveling
    1. northeast
    2. southwest
    3. northwest
    4. southeast

32. In the government survey system of land description, townships are measured and numbered from east to west along a
    1. monument.
    2. base line.
    3. principal meridian.
    4. datum.

33. A holds a life estate in a house. A's life estate is
    1. an estate of inheritance.
    2. an example of a future interest.
    3. limited to the owner of the life estate.
    4. a non-freehold estate.

34. A man and woman own their house as tenants by the entirety. Which of the following statements would NOT correctly describe the status of their ownership?
    1. Each owner has the right of survivorship.
    2. The owners must be husband and wife.
    3. Either owner may convey a one-half interest in the house to a third party.
    4. Title may be conveyed only by a deed signed by both parties.

35. The county zoo holds title to its land with the condition that if it charges admission fees, the title will revert to the original grantor of the estate. This is an example of a
   1. fee simple estate.
   2. defeasible fee estate.
   3. legal life estate.
   4. conventional life estate.

NOTE: The information in parentheses at the end of each explanation refers to the page number where this material is discussed.

ANSWER KEY WITH EXPLANATIONS

1. **(2)** Situs is used interchangeably with area preference. (28)
2. **(1)** Scarcity, permanence of investment, and situs are economic characteristics of land. (27–28)
3. **(2)** The life estate owner is responsible for paying real estate taxes and is entitled to all income and profits as well as being rezonable for all repairs on the property. (31)
4. **(3)** Tenants in common have the right to sell their interest in a property without the consent of one of the other co-owners. (31)
5. **(2)** The fence material is an example of severance. (27)
6. **(2)** Judgments are general liens while mortgage liens, real estate taxes, and mechanic's liens are specific liens. (29)
7. **(3)** An easement appurtenant and easement in gross must be acquired from the owner of servient tenement while the easement by prescription is acquired when the claimant has been using the servient tenement for a statutorily determined period of time. (29)
8. **(3)** *Laches* refers to the inability to enforce right because of undue delay in asserting it. Easements are rights to use real property. An encroachment is the unauthorized use of another's property. (29)
9. **(1)** A life estate may be leased but that interest is forfeited upon the death of the life tenant. (31)
10. **(1)** The electrician cannot prevent the property from being sold; however, he can file a mechanic's lien to protect himself from not being paid. (29)
11. **(1)** Laches was described above. Novation involves a transfer of liability from one debtor to another. Partition is a court procedure to divide co-tenants interests in real property when parties do not agree to terminate. (32)
12. **(2)** The other answers are features of joint tenancy. (31)
13. **(3)** A mechanic's lien is a specific lien and an encumbrance. A general lien would apply to all of the homeowner's property. (29)
14. **(4)** A prescriptive easement is similar to adverse possession in that if one uses another's property for a statutorily period of time, one has acquired a real property interest. The difference is that an easement gives one the right to use while adverse possession gives ownership of the land used. (29)
15. **(1)** The claimant cannot prevent the property owner from selling his property. A lis pendens will provide public notice that a lawsuit affecting title to the property has been filed in court. (33)
16. **(1)** *Y*'s personal easement in gross is a real property interest, which may not be conveyed to a third party. There is no dominant tenement in a personal easement in gross. The easement belongs to *Y* rather than running with a parcel of land. (29)
17. **(2)** Lis pendens was described above. A writ of execution is a court order directing the county sheriff to seize and sell the prop-

erty of a debtor. An abstract of judgment is a summary of judgments that have become public record. (33)

18. **(2)** The remaining owner automatically takes title to the property under the right of survivorship. The joint tenancy is effective only until one owner remains; the surviving owner then holds title is severalty. (31)

19. **(4)** Tenancy by the entirety is characterized by the right of survivorship. The husband has no right to transfer his interest by will. The wife will hold an interest in severalty. (32)

20. **(4)** Severalty refers to one owner while tenancy by the entirety requires the owners to be husband and wife. Joint tenancy requires equal shares of ownership. (31)

21. **(3)** An attachment places an encumbrance (lien) upon debtor's property held as security for a possible judgment obtained by attaching creditor. (33)

22. **(3)** A street address is too inaccurate for deeds. (28)

23. **(1)** Metes and bounds is an accepted method of legal description. (28)

24. **(1)** Principal meridians run north and south, while a township contains 36 sections. (28)

25. **(2)** An acre contains 43,560 square feet or 160 square rods. (28)

26. **(3)** Tenants by the entirety must be husband and wife. Tenancy at will and estate for years are types of leases. (31)

27. **(3)** The faucets are fixtures that would be considered to be included in the selling price unless agreed otherwise by the parties. (27)

28. **(2)** Tenants in common and joint tenants do not have to be related. A tenancy at will is not a form of ownership. (32)

29. **(4)** The water softener is a fixture or real property. The other answers are personal property. (27)

30. **(1)** $6 \times 6 = 36$
640 acres $\div 36 = 17.78$ acres (28)

31. **(4)** Section 6 is in the upper left hand corner and section 36 is in the lower right hand corner. (28)

32. **(2)** Townships are measured and numbered from north to south along a principal meridian. (28)

33. **(3)** A life estate is a freehold estate that terminates upon the death of the owner of the life estate. (30)

34. **(3)** Tenants by the entirety may not convey their property unless they both sign the deed. (32)

35. **(2)** A defeasible fee estate may be terminated upon the violation of a deed condition. (30)

PROPERTY OWNERSHIP

TEST SCORE

RATING	RANGE	YOUR SCORE	
Good = 80% to 100%	28-35	Total Number	35
Fair = 70% to 79%	25-27	Total Wrong	-
Needs Improvement = Lower than 70%	24 or less	Total Right	

Passing Requirement: 25 or better

PART 5

Land-Use Controls And Regulations

OUTLINE OF CONCEPTS TO UNDERSTAND

I. **Local, state, and federal government land rights**

A. Police power—power of the state to promulgate laws aimed at promoting the general welfare and protecting public health and safety; examples of the use of police power include zoning, building codes, environmental protection; enabling acts are created by states to grant zoning power to municipal governments.

B. Taxation—power to tax real estate to meet the public needs of the government

C. Eminent domain—power of the government to acquire private property for public use while providing just compensation for the property owner

D. Escheat—state laws that provide for ownership of real estate to revert to the state when the owner dies intestate and leaves no heirs or when the property is abandoned

E. Water rights—ownership of water and land adjacent to it as determined by state law, which is based on either the doctrines of riparian and littoral rights or on the doctrine of prior appropriation; owners generally have the right to use water so long as they do not pollute or interrupt the flow

1. Riparian rights—rights granted to owners along a non-navigable river or stream

2. Littoral rights—rights granted to owners along an ocean or large lake

3. Prior appropriation—the right to use water is controlled by the state rather than by the adjacent landowner. A person must show a beneficial use for the water, such as crop irrigation, in order to secure water rights.

II. **Control of land use**

A. Public land-use controls—under police power, each state has the authority to adjust regulations required for protecting public health, safety, and the general welfare.

1. Zoning—zoning laws are local laws that regulate and control the use of land in the community, generally pertaining to the height, bulk, and use of the buildings. Powers to zone are conferred on municipal governments by state enabling acts.

a. Nonconforming use—use in existence prior to the passage of a zoning ordinance and allowed to continue even though it does not conform

1. If property that exists as nonconforming is destroyed, it cannot be rebuilt without the approval of the zoning authority.
   b. Variance—approval by a zoning authority that allows an individual to deviate from the zoning requirement
   c. Conditional use permit—allows for a use that does not conform with existing zoning but is necessary for the common good, such as locating a medical clinic in a primarily residential neighborhood
   d. Downzoning—land zoned for residential or commercial use is rezoned for conservation only; it also applies to changes from dense to less-dense usage. The state generally is not responsible for compensating property owners for any loss of value unless the court finds that a "taking" of value has occurred such as land's being rezoned from residential to conservancy.
   e. Buffer zone—a land area that separates one land use from another; a part that separates a residential neighborhood from a shopping center
   f. Spot zoning—reclassification of a small area of land for use that does not conform to the zoning of the rest of the area
   g. Planned unit development (PUD)—planned mix of diverse land uses such as housing and recreation in one comprehensive plan
2. Building codes—ordinances that specify standards for construction, maintenance, and demolition
3. City plan specifications—a master plan to guide physical development of a community
4. Subdivision regulations—apply to the location of streets, minimum lot size, etc.
5. Environmental protection laws
   a. Federal—examples include National Environmental Policy Act, Clean Air Act
   b. State—many states, counties, and cities have passed their own environmental legislation.

A. Private land-use controls—restrictions specified by the owner in the deed when conveying the property

B. If conflict exists between a zoning ordinance and a deed restriction, the more restrictive of the two takes precedence.

C. Taxation on real estate
   1. Real estate taxes generally take priority over other liens; may be enforced by the court sale of real estate that is free of other liens
   2. Ad valorem tax (Latin for "according to the value")—includes taxes levied on real estate by various governmental units and municipalities
   3. Assessment—appraisal of value for tax purposes by an assessor representing the municipality in which the property is located
   4. Equalization factor—used in some states to correct general inequalities in statewide tax assessment
   5. Computation of tax rate
      a. The taxing district adopts a budget that identifies the amount of income to be raised from real estate taxes.
      b. To arrive at the tax rate, divide the amount of money required for the budget by the total assessed value of all properties within the taxing district. For example, if the taxing district must raise $600,000 from real

estate taxes and the total assessed value is $10,000,000, the tax rate would be $600,000 ÷ $10,000,000 = 0.06, or 6 percent.

    c. The tax rate may be expressed in mills (a mill is 1/1,000 of a dollar, or $0.001); the tax rate in (b) would be 60 mills ($6) per $100 of the assessed value or $60 per $1,000 of the assessed value.

    d. The tax bill for a property is calculated by applying the tax rate to the assessed valuation of the property; for example, a home assessed for tax purposes at $60,000 at a rate of 6 percent, or 60 mills, would have a tax bill of $3,600.

  1. Special assessments—special taxes levied on real estate; require property owners to pay for improvements that specifically benefit their real estate (installation of a curb and gutter, streets, water system, sewers, etc.)

III. Flood plain, wetlands, and shoreline regulations

A. Floodplain—portions of land located near running bodies of water, such as rivers or lakes, that are subject to flooding; government controls generally restrict building in a floodplain

B. Wetlands—areas of land where groundwater is close to or at the surface of the ground for a period of time each year that may produce swamps, flood plains or marshes; because these areas of land are prone to flooding, they are covered by various federal, state, and local controls, such as zoning for conservation

C. Shoreline regulation—zoning laws that reflect environmental as well as health and safety concerns; usually require zoning of all lands within a given distance of all navigable waters in each state; generally include tree-cutting rules, setback requirements for structures, filling and grading controls, dredging regulations, minimum standards for water supply and waste disposal, minimum lot sizes and widths, and subdivision regulations

IV. Health and safety codes

A. Building codes

  1. Specify construction standards that must be met when erecting, maintaining, or demolishing buildings

  2. Generally identify requirements for electrical wiring, sanitary equipment, and fire-prevention standards

  3. Enforced by issuing building permits that verify compliance with building codes and zoning ordinances

  4. The building inspector issues a certificate of occupancy when the completed structure has been inspected and found satisfactory.

  5. Issuing a building permit does not take precedence over the violation of a deed restriction.

V. Environmental concerns

A. Pollution and environmental risks in real estate transactions

  1. Increasing public awareness of and concern about pollution problems and their health and economic effects have had significant consequences on real estate sales and values.

  2. The actual dollar value of real property can be affected significantly by both real and perceived pollution.

3. The cost of cleaning up and removing pollution may be much greater than the dollar value of the property before pollution occurred.

4. In some areas of the United States, mortgage and title insurance approval may depend on the inspection of the property for hazardous substances and proof of their absence.

B. Role of real estate licensees regarding environmental risks in real estate transactions

1. Be alert to the possibility of pollution and hazardous substances on the property being sold.

2. Ask clients about the possibility of hazardous substances associated with the property.

3. Expect increasing numbers of questions from customers concerned about pollution.

4. Consider the consequences of the potential liability in real estate transactions where hazardous substances may be involved.

5. Contact government agencies and private consulting firms for information, guidance, and detailed study; real estate licensees often, however, do not have the technical expertise required to determine whether hazardous material is present on or near the property.

6. Be scrupulous in considering environmental issues and exercise a high degree of care in all real estate transactions.

C. Hazardous substances of concern to real estate professionals

1. Radon gas—an odorless radioactive gas produced by the decay of radioactive materials in rocks under the earth's surface

    a. Radon is released from the rocks and finds its way to the surface; usually it is released into the atmosphere. Radon comes into a house through holes in the foundation or basement or crawl space.

    b. Long-term exposure is believed to cause lung cancer.

    c. The U.S. Environmental Protection Agency (E.P.A.) has established radon levels that are thought to be unsafe.

    d. Testing techniques have been developed that allow homeowners to determine the exact quantity of radon in their homes.

    e. If a home is determined to have radon gas, the seller may, if the contract requires, be obligated to remediate the hazard, whether the danger is actual or only perceived.

    f. Most homes with elevated levels of radon can be fixed for between $500 and $2,500, with an average cost of about $1,200.

2. Asbestos—material used for many years as insulation on plumbing pipes and heat ducts and as general insulation because it is a poor heat conductor; also was used in floor tile and roofing material

    a. Relatively harmless if not disturbed; can become life-threatening during its removal because of accompanying dust

    b. Exposure to asbestos dust may exist if

        1. The asbestos ages and starts to disintegrate

        2. Remodeling projects include the removal of asbestos shingles, roof tile, or insulation that can cause the dust to form in the air and expose people in the area to the health hazard

3. Urea-formaldehyde foam insulation (UFFI)—a synthetic material generally used to insulate buildings

    a. Typically pumped between walls as a foam that later hardens and acts as an insulating material

    b. Becomes dangerous because of gases released from the material after it hardens

4. Lead poisoning—lead is a mineral that has been used extensively because of its pliability and its ability to impede water flow.

    a. Becomes a health hazard when ingested

    b. Sources of lead poisoning

        1. Peeling or flaking paint

        2. Plumbing systems

    c. Federal regulations on lead-based paint disclosure

        1. Owners of residential properties built before 1978, when the use of lead-based paint was banned, will have to disclose to buyers or renters the presence of known lead-based paint hazards, if known to owner (seller) or landlord.

        2. A lead-based paint disclosure statement must be attached as a separate item to all real estate sales and lease contracts on pre-1978 residential properties.

        3. Real estate practitioners must distribute to buyers and renters a federal lead hazard pamphlet but won't be responsible for ensuring that people read and understand the brochure.

        4. Buyers will have up to 10 days to have a lead-risk assessment performed on the property if they want one.

        5. Exemptions from the regulations are provided for housing for the elderly and disabled, provided children are not regularly present; for vacation homes and short-term rentals; for foreclosure sales; and for single-room rentals within dwellings.

5. PCBs (Polychlorinated biphenyls)—used in the manufacture of electrical products such as voltage regulators as well as in paints and caulking materials

    a. PCBs haven't been used since 1977; however, they still are dangerous because many of the products still are being used.

    b. An environmental consultant can assess the property and recommend procedures for cleanup.

6. Waste-disposal sites—landfill operations

    a. Landfill—a specific site that has been excavated and should be lined with either a clay or a synthetic liner to prevent leakage of waste material into the local water system

    b. Construction and maintenance of a landfill operation is heavily regulated by state and federal authorities

    c. Landfills at improper locations and improperly managed sites have been sources of major problems; for example, landfills constructed in the wrong type of soil will leak waste into nearby wells, causing major damage.

    d. Real estate licensees must be aware of such facilities within their areas and take appropriate steps when dealing with potential clients.

7. Underground storage tanks—used in residential and commercial settings for many years

    a. An estimated 3 million to 5 million underground storage tanks exist in the United States that hold hazardous substances such as gasoline.

    b. Risk occurs when containers become old, rust, and start to leak.

    c. Toxic material may enter the groundwater, contaminate the wells, and pollute the soil.

    d. Sources of pollution

        1. Older gas stations with steel tanks that develop leaks through oxidation (rusting)

        2. Underground containers used to hold fuel oil for older homes

    e. Recent federal legislation calls for removal of such tanks and all the polluted soil around them.

  8. Groundwater contamination

    a. Groundwater includes runoff at ground level as well as underground water systems that are sources of wells for both private and public facilities.

    b. Sources of contamination

        1. Waste-disposal sites

        2. Underground storage tanks

        3. Pesticides and herbicides typically used in farming communities

    c. The only protection for the general public against water contamination is heavy government regulation.

    d. Once contamination is identified, its source can be eliminated; the process often is time-consuming and may be very expensive.

  9. Electromagnetic fields (EMFs)—generated by movement of electrical currents.

    a. High-tension power lines reflect a major concern with regard to EMFs.

    b. The potential for EMFs being a health hazard is a source of controversy; however, they are suspected of causing cancer and related health problems.

    c. Real estate licensees should be aware of continuing research on EMFs.

D. Agencies administering federal environmental laws

  1. Environmental Protection Agency

    a. Toxic Substance Control Act

    b. Resources Conservation and Recovery Act

    c. Federal Clean Water Act

  2. U.S. Department of Transportation—administers the Hazardous Materials Transportation Act

  3. The Occupational Safety and Health Administration (OSHA) and the U.S. Department of Labor—administer standards for all employees working in the manufacturing sector

  4. Federal government encourages state and local governments to prepare legislation in their areas.

E. Statutory law

  1. Resource Conservation and Recovery Act (RCRA) of 1976—created to regulate the generation, transportation, storage, use, treatment, disposal, and cleanup of hazardous waste

  2. The Comprehensive Environmental Response Compensation and Liability Act (CERCLA) was created in 1980.

    a. Established fund of $9 billion called Superfund to clean up uncontrolled hazardous waste dumps and respond to spills

    b. Created a process for identifying liable parties and ordering them to take responsibility for the cleanup

    c. Liability under Superfund considered to be strict, joint and several, and retroactive

1. Strict liability—owner is responsible to the injured party without excuse.
2. Joint and several liability—each individual owner personally responsible for the damages in whole; if only one owner financially able to handle the total damage, that owner will have to pay all and attempt to collect the proportionate share of the rest of the owners from them.
3. Retroactive liability—liability not limited to the person who currently owns the property; also extends to people who have owned the site in the past

3. Leaking Underground Storage Tanks (LUST) regulations—established in 1984
   a. Governs the installation, maintenance, monitoring, and failure of underground storage tanks
   b. Aimed at protecting groundwater in the United States through release prevention, detection, and correction
4. Superfund Amendments and Reauthorization Act (SARA)—created in 1986
   a. Established stronger cleanup standards for contaminated sites
   b. Substantially increased the funding of the Superfund
   c. Attempted to clarify the obligation of the lenders
   d. Created the concept called innocent landowner immunity

E. Common law

1. Provides the backdrop for existing legislation to catch situations that do not specifically fall within the law
2. California case of *Easton v. Strassburger* (1986) led to state laws requiring that all real estate agents conduct a "reasonably diligent and competent inspection" of the property for sale, examining for potential problems dealing with pollution, and mandating the use of disclosure forms that must be presented to the prospective purchaser.

VI. Deed restrictions or covenants

A. Private restrictions written into deeds or leases that limit the use of property—for example, restrictions on the type or the size of the building

B. May be terminated by the affected necessary parties by a quitclaim deed or mutual release properly recorded.

C. Generally enforced by means of a court injunction

D. Adjoining lot owners in a subdivision can lose the right to the court's injunction by inaction, under the doctrine of laches (the loss of a right through undue delay or failure to assert the right).

E. Deed restrictions or covenants differ from deed conditions in that violation of a condition can give the grantor the right to take back ownership; this right does not apply where a violation of a private restriction occurs.

VII. Water rights

A. Riparian rights—rights of owners of land adjacent to a river or stream.

B. Littoral rights—rights of owners adjacent to commercially navigable lakes, seas, and oceans

C. Amount of land owned adjacent to water may be affected by

1. Accretion—land increase caused by water's action causes soil deposits, if water recedes, new land would be acquired by reliction.
2. Erosion—the slow loss of land caused by wearing away of land by wind or rain
3. Avulsion—sudden loss of land caused by act of nature such as an earthquake
4. Doctrine of prior appropriation—with exception of limited domestic use, right to use water controlled by the state instead of the owner of land adjacent to the water

REVIEW LIST

1. The student should have an understanding of the following areas of land-use controls and regulation:
   a. Planning and zoning
   b. Property taxation
   c. Flood plain, wetlands, and shoreline regulations
   d. Health and safety codes
   e. Environmental concerns
   f. Deed restrictions

DIAGNOSTIC TEST

1. When the county board acquires land for a freeway, it is exercising the power of
   1. zoning.
   2. environmental protection laws.
   3. escheat.
   4. eminent domain.

2. One example of the use of police power by a city is
   1. taxation.
   2. eminent domain.
   3. laches.
   4. environmental protection laws.

3. An insurance agency existed <u>before</u> the land was zoned residential by a new zoning ordinance. The insurance agency is an example of
   1. a variance.
   2. a nonconforming use.
   3. spot zoning.
   4. a planned unit development.

4. An investor purchased a large parcel of land zoned for commercial development, but the land was rezoned by the city to recreational right after the purchase was made. This was an example of
   1. eminent domain.
   2. down zoning.
   3. nonconforming use.
   4. a planned unit development.

5. Zoning laws that include tree-cutting rules, dredging regulations, and waste disposal exemplify
   1. subdivision regulations.
   2. city plan specifications.
   3. shoreline regulations.
   4. deed restrictions.

6. Radon enters a house through the
   1. roof.   3. chimney.
   2. foundation.   4. windows.

7. A mineral used for many years as insulation on heat ducts is
   1. asbestos.
   2. lead.
   3. urea-formaldehyde foam.
   4. radon.

8. Which of the following is typically pumped between the walls of a house to act as an insulating material?
   1. Asbestos
   2. Radon
   3. Urea-formaldehyde foam
   4. Lead

9. A material that has been used extensively because of its ability to impede water flow is
   1. lead.
   2. asbestos.
   3. urea-formaldehyde foam.
   4. radon.

10. Which of the following statements most correctly describes a waste-disposal site?
    1. Construction is relatively unregulated by state authorities.
    2. Landfills at appropriate locations have been sources of major problems.
    3. Real estate licensees need not be concerned about such facilities within their areas.
    4. Landfills constructed on the wrong type of soil may leak water into nearby wells, causing major damage.

11. All of the following may be sources of groundwater contamination **EXCEPT**
    1. underground storage tanks.
    2. waste-disposal sites.
    3. use of pesticides on farms.
    4. cement.

12. All of the following requirements generally are covered by building codes **EXCEPT**
    1. fire-prevention standards.
    2. electrical wiring.
    3. sanitary equipment.
    4. minimum number of square feet of land area per apartment unit.

13. Strict liability means that
    1. an owner is responsible to an injured party without excuse.
    2. each owner is personally responsible for damages as a whole.
    3. liability extends to people who have owned the site in the past.
    4. an owner is not responsible to an injured party.

14. State laws that require real estate agents to conduct a reasonably diligent and competent inspection of the property for sale, examining for potential problems dealing with pollution, are a result of
    1. *Jones v. Mayer.*
    2. *Easton v. Strassburger.*
    3. the Superfund Amendments and Reauthorization Act.
    4. the Resource Conservation and Recovery Act.

15. Which of the following statements concerning deed restrictions is NOT true?
    1. Violation of a restrictive condition may result in the forfeiture of title to real property.
    2. Encumbrances in the form of restrictive conditions generally run with restricted land into the indefinite future.
    3. The penalty for violation or breach of a restrictive covenant is more severe than that for breach of a restrictive condition.
    4. The general goal of deed restrictions is to protect the value of all properties in a development.

16. Which of the following best describes a buffer zone?
    1. An industrial park located between a shopping center and a residential neighborhood
    2. A high-rise apartment complex located between a commercial development and a town-house subdivision
    3. A recreational area located between a residential area and an office park
    4. A sound barrier located alongside a major highway

17. Police-power controls include all of the following **EXCEPT**
    1. city plan specifications.
    2. building codes.
    3. zoning.
    4. deed restrictions.

18. A tire company has a manufacturing plant located in an area that recently has been zoned residential. The company is allowed to operate under the new zoning ordinance. If the plant is destroyed by fire, the company may
    1. appeal for an exculpatory provision.
    2. not construct another tire plant in the neighborhood without being granted a zoning variance.
    3. not construct another tire plant in the neighborhood under any conditions.
    4. reconstruct the tire company in the same neighborhood.

19. Which of the following provides for monetary compensation to an owner in the event of a loss of property value?
    1. Taxation
    2. Eminent domain
    3. Escheat
    4. Police power

20. A recorded restriction is best described as
    1. a limitation on use.
    2. a condition.
    3. a lien.
    4. a lien and an encumbrance.

ANSWER KEY WITH EXPLANATIONS

1. **(4)** Zoning and environmental protection laws do not provide monetary compensation in the event that a property owner suffers a loss in value. Escheat is a law that provides for title to real estate to pass to the state when an owner dies intestate and leaves no heirs or abandons the property. Eminent domain is the right of the government to take land for public good. (41)

2. **(4)** Taxation and eminent domain are not exercised under the police power. Laches refers to the equitable doctrine that bars a legal claim because of undue delay in asserting the claim. (42)

3. **(2)** A variance allows one to deviate from the zoning ordinance while spot zoning allows for reclassification of land for nonconforming use. A planned unit development (PUD). (42)

4. **(2)** Downzoning involves an economic taking whereas eminent domain results in a complete taking. A planned unit development is an example of contract zoning in that a developer has his or her plan approved by the municipality, thereby establishing a special planning district based on the developer's own plans. A nonconforming use is allowed to continue after a zoning ordinance prohibiting it has been established for the area. (42)

5. **(3)** Subdivision regulations deal with location of streets, etc., while city plan specifications or master plans guide the physical development of a community. Deed restrictions are private land use controls. (43)

6. **(2)** Radon may also enter the house through the basement or crawl space. (44)

7. **(1)** Lead was used in paint and plumbing systems. UFFI was used to insulate buildings. Radon was discussed above. (44)

8. **(3)** Asbestos was used as insulation on heating pipes and ducts as well as in floor tile and roofing material. Radon is an odorless radioactive gas that generally enters through the basement of a house. Lead was used in water pipes and paint. (45)

9. **(1)** Lead impedes water flow. Asbestos and UFFI are used for insulation; radon is an odorless gas. (45)

10. **(4)** Agents should be aware of landfills and make appropriate disclosures. (45)

11. **(4)** Leaking underground storage tanks are a major source of groundwater contamination. Pesticide use and waste disposal also may contaminate groundwater. Cement is neutral. (46)

12. **(4)** The minimum number of square feet of land area per apartment unit would be regulated by the local zoning ordinance. (43)

13. **(1)** For example, an individual who knowingly buys contaminated land can also be liable for damages even though she had no involvement in the events leading up to the contamination. (46)

14. **(2)** *Jones vs. Mayer* was a landmark case in Fair Housing Law. It made clear that there is no exception for racial discrimination in housing. RCRA and SARA were created to regulate the disposal and cleanup of hazardous waste. (47)

15. **(3)** Restrictive covenants are statements in a deed that limit the use of ownership of real estate. The breach of a covenant would

result in damages. The breach of a condition may result in the loss of title. (47)

16. **(3)** A buffer zone is a land area that separates one land use from another such as residential from commercial, as when a recreational area is located between a residential area and an office park. (42)

17. **(4)** Police-power controls are public land use controls. Only deed restrictions are private land use controls, and therefore incorrect. (41–42)

18. **(2)** If a nonconforming use is destroyed, as in the case of the tire manufacturing plant, it cannot be rebuilt without the approval of the zoning authority. (42)

19. **(2)** Escheat is a state law that provides that if a decedent dies intestate and has no heirs, the decedent's property will revert to the state. Taxation is a process by which the government raises funds necessary for it to operate. The police power is the right of the government to protect the public welfare through such measures as zoning and building codes. (41)

20. **(1)** A restriction would be classified as an encumbrance. The violation of a restriction would not generally result in loss of title as it would in the case of a violation of a condition. (47)

LAND USE CONTROLS AND REGULATIONS

TEST SCORE

RATING	RANGE	YOUR SCORE	
Good = 80% to 100%	16-20	Total Number	20
Fair = 70% to 79%	14-15	Total Wrong	- _____
Needs Improvement = Lower than 70%	13 or less	Total Right	

Passing Requirement: 14 or better

Valuation and Market Analysis

OUTLINE OF CONCEPTS TO UNDERSTAND

I. **Financial Institutions Reform, Recovery, and Enforcement Act (FIRREA) and the appraisal industry**

   A. The collapse of many savings and loan associations as a result of the surge into unsound investments was at least partly the consequence of questionable property appraisals.

   B. Congress introduced appraisal regulation by passing FIRREA in 1989.

   C. Appraisals performed as part of a federally related transaction must comply with state standards and must be performed by a state-certified or state-licensed appraiser.

   D. State appraiser licensing requirements and appraisal standards must meet minimum levels set by the Appraisal Standards Board and Appraisal Qualifications Board of the Appraisal Foundation, a national group of representatives of major appraisal and related organizations.

II. **Appraisal and value**

   A. Appraisal—an estimate or opinion of value; a detailed estimate of a property's value by a professional appraiser

   B. Competitive market analysis (CMA)—used by the broker or the salesperson to help the seller determine a listing price for the property; basically, a comparison of prices of recently sold and currently for sale properties that are similar in location, style, and amenities to the property of the listing seller. CMA will generally estimate market value as likely to fall within a range of figures

   C. Value
   1. Definition—the present worth of future benefits arising from the ownership of real property
   2. Characteristics a property must have to have value in the real estate market include
      a. Utility—capacity to satisfy human wants and needs
      b. Scarcity—finite supply
      c. Effective demand—need supported by purchasing power
      d. Transferability—transfer of ownership rights with relative ease

    D. Market value

       1. Most probable price a property will bring in a competitive market, allowing for reasonable time to find a knowledgeable purchaser
          a. The buyer and seller are not under pressure to act.
          b. Payment is made in cash or equivalent.
       2. Typical goal of an appraiser, although a property may have different values at the same time
       3. Estimated price (compare to market price, which is the actual selling price)

III. Principles of valuation

    A. Highest and best use—most profitable use to which a property may be adapted, given legal constraints

    B. Substitution—the value of a property tends to be set by the cost of purchasing an equally desirable and similar property.

    C. Supply and demand—the price of a property will increase if the supply decreases and will decrease if the supply increases.

    D. Conformity—maximum value is realized if the land use conforms to existing neighborhood standards.

    E. Increasing and decreasing return—improvements to land and structures produce a proportionate increase in value until some point beyond which the impact of improvements begins to decrease, until improvements cause virtually no change in the property value.

    F. Competition—high levels of profits attract competitors into an industry; increase in competition results in decreased profits throughout the industry.

    G. Change—no economic or physical condition remains constant.

    H. Contribution—the value of any component of property consists of what its addition contributes to the value of the whole property.

    I. Anticipation—value can increase or decrease in anticipation of some future benefit or detriment that will affect the property.

    J. Assemblage plottage—the act of combining two or more adjacent parcels of land, with a resulting increase in value

    K. Balance is achieved when adding improvements to land and structures will increase the property value.

    L. Regression—the principle between dissimilar properties: the worth of the better property is affected adversely by the presence of the lesser-quality property

    M. Progression—the worth of a lesser property tends to increase if it is located among better properties.

IV. Approaches to value

    A. Cost approach

       1. Based on the principle of substitution
       2. Steps of cost approach
          a. Estimate the land value.
          b. Estimate the replacement cost of the improvements.
          c. Estimate the depreciation.

        d. Deduct the depreciation from the replacement cost.

        e. Add the land value to the depreciated cost of improvements—do not depreciate land.

   3. Depreciation—generally applies to a wasting asset, such as a building.

        a. Physical deterioration (wear, tear, poor maintenance)—may be curable or incurable

        b. Functional obsolescence—may be curable or incurable (outdated items, poor design)

        c. External (economic, environmental or locational) obsolescence—loss of value due to factors outside the property: is incurable only

        d. Most reliable approach for special-purpose buildings such as churches, schools, etc.

B. Market/data approach (sales comparison or direct sales)

   1. A value estimate is obtained by comparing the subject property with recent sales of comparable properties through adjustment of sales prices of comparables.

   2. Four areas of adjustment

        a. Date of sale

        b. Location

        c. Physical characteristics

        d. Terms of the sale

   3. The adjustment process involves three basic steps:

        a. Adjust the price of the comparable for any difference between the comparable and the subject property (the property being appraised).

        b. C.B.S.—*Comparable better subtract* the difference between the comparable and the subject property.

        c. S.B.A.—*Subject better add* the difference between the comparable and the subject property.

   4. Considered the most reliable of the three approaches in appraising residential property

A. Income capitalization approach

   1. Based on the present value of the rights to future income

   2. Steps in the income approach

        a. Estimate the annual potential gross income.

        b. Deduct the vacancy and rent loss to arrive at the effective gross income.

        c. Deduct the annual operating expenses to arrive at the annual net operating income.

        d. Estimate the capitalization rate.

        e. Apply the capitalization rate to the annual net income.

   3. Formula for capitalization rate: net income ÷ capitalization rate = value

   4. As risk increases, the rate of return increase and the value decreases, and vice versa

   5. Gross rent multiplier (GRM)

        a. Used as a substitute for the income approach in appraising a single-family home

        b. Formula for GRM: sales price ÷ monthly rental income = GRM

        c. Monthly rental income × GRM = estimated market value

   6. Gross income multiplier (GIM)

        a. Used as a quick way to appraise commercial and industrial properties

      b. Formula for GIM: sales price ÷ annual rental income = GIM

   7. Most reliable approach for income-producing property

V.   Steps in the appraisal process

A. State the problem.

B. List the types of data needed and the sources.

C. Gather, record and verify the *general data.*

D. Gather, record and verify the *specific data.*

E. Gather, record and verify the data for the valuation approach needed.

F. Analyze and interpret the data.

G. Reconcile the data for the final value estimate.

H. Prepare the appraisal report.

VI.   Neighborhood analysis

A. Neighborhood—homogeneous grouping of individuals or businesses within, or as part of, a larger community

B. Residential neighborhoods generally pass through four stages: growth, stability, decline, and revitalization.

C. Factors to consider in analysis

   1. Physical—street pattern, relation to the rest of the community
   2. Economic—rent levels, new construction
   3. Social—population density, frequency of crime
   4. Governmental—zoning, special assessments

VII.   Ethics of appraising

A. The appraiser should have no present or planned interest in the property being appraised.

B. The appraiser should have no personal interest in the property being appraised or the parties involved.

C. The appraiser should not improperly disclose the confidential parts of an appraisal report.

VIII.   Other important terms

A. Amenities—intangible benefits of ownership in addition to the property's legal description

B. Capitalization—a mathematical process for estimating a property's value using a proper rate of return on investment and anticipated annual net income

C. Capitalization rate—the rate of return a property will produce on the owner's investment

D. Comparables—properties listed in the appraisal report generally equivalent to the subject property

E. Reconciliation—final step in the appraisal process, in which the appraiser reconciles the estimates of value received from the market data, cost and income approaches to arrive at a final estimate of the market value for the property being appraised

F. Replacement cost—construction cost at current prices of property not necessarily an exact duplicate of the subject property but serving the same purpose or function as the original

G. Reproduction cost—construction cost at current prices of exact duplicate of the subject property

H. Subject property—property being appraised

I. URAR—Uniform Residential Appraisal Report

REVIEW LIST

The student should have an understanding of the following areas of valuation and economics.

1. Concept and purpose of appraisal

2. Difference between comparative market analysis and appraisal

3. The appraisal process

4. Depreciation

5. Neighborhood analysis

6. Ethics of appraising

7. Economic and urban development

DIAGNOSTIC TEST

1. The characteristics required for a property to have value include all of the following **EXCEPT**
   1. effective demand.
   2. scarcity.
   3. depreciation.
   4. transferability.

2. Which of the following laws require that appraisals performed as part of a federally related transaction must comply with federal standards and be performed by a state-certified or state-licensed appraiser?
   1. Financial Institutions Reform, Recovery, and Enforcement Act (FIRREA)
   2. Regulation Z
   3. RESPA
   4. Statute of Frauds

3. You own land worth $40,000 and your building has a replacement cost of $160,000. What would be the value if the appraiser used a depreciation rate of 30 percent?
   1. $148,000
   2. $152,000
   3. $188,000
   4. None of the above

4. Which of the following does NOT apply to the definition of market value?
   1. Both buyer and seller must be well informed.
   2. Market value is the average price that a property will bring.
   3. Both buyer and seller must act without undue pressure.
   4. Payment must be made in cash or its equivalent.

5. The annual net income for an office building is $20,000. If an owner realized a 9 percent return on her investment, the value of the building would be
   1. $1,800.   3. $222,222.
   2. $22,222.   4. $285,714.

6. You look at four similar houses for sale in the same area and choose the house with the lowest asking price. You probably are basing your decision on the principle of
   1. highest and best use.
   2. substitution.
   3. contribution.
   4. conformity.

7. A builder developed a subdivision in which the demand for homes was great. He sold the last lot in his subdivision for a much higher price than that for which he had sold the first lot in the area. This example illustrates the principle of
   1. highest and best use.
   2. substitution.
   3. conformity.
   4. supply and demand.

8. In appraising a special-purpose building such as a post office, the most reliable approach to an indication of its value would generally be the
   1. cost approach.
   2. market/data approach.
   3. income approach.
   4. sales comparison approach.

9. Which of the following is an example of locational obsolescence?
   1. Termite damage
   2. Negligent care of property
   3. A zoning ordinance allowing a decrease in the minimum lot size
   4. Poor architectural design

10. Economic obsolescence does NOT result from
    1. adverse zoning changes.
    2. a city's leading industries moving out.
    3. an inharmonious land use in a neighborhood.
    4. outdated kitchens.

11. Depreciation generally applies to
    1. the building only.
    2. the land only.
    3. both the land and the building.
    4. the net income of the building.

12. A principal factor for which adjustments must be made in using the market/data approach is
    1. depreciation.
    2. the date of sale.
    3. the amount of real estate taxes.
    4. the cost of replacement.

13. An appraiser is estimating the value of a building that has a net income of $5,000 per quarter and a capitalization rate of 8 percent. What is the value of this property?
    1. $25,000   3. $250,000
    2. $62,500   4. $312,500

14. An appraiser is using the gross-rent-multiplier (GRM) method to estimate the market value of a single-family home. The home has an annual gross income of $7,200, with quarterly expenses of $900. The recognized GRM for the neighborhood is 110. The appraiser's estimate of value is likely to be
    1. $22,000.
    2. $33,000.
    3. $66,000.
    4. none of the above.

15. The GRM is used in the
    1. market/data approach.
    2. income approach for office buildings.
    3. cost approach.
    4. income approach for single-family homes.

16. An office building recently sold for $600,000, with a monthly rental income of $5,000. The GIM for the property was
    1. 120.
    2. 100.
    3. 10.
    4. none of the above.

17. In determining the value of a 20-unit apartment building, the appraiser has established the gross income from rents. After deducting the loss for vacancies and collection losses from this gross income, the appraiser would have established the
    1. net income.
    2. spendable income.
    3. gross income.
    4. effective gross income.

18. What is the first step an appraiser would take to arrive at an estimated value using the income approach?
    1. Determine annual potential gross income.
    2. Determine operating expenses.
    3. Determine effective gross income.
    4. Determine the vacancy rate.

19. An airport routing was changed, with the result that airplanes flew over a residential area. The subsequent loss in value caused by the airplane noise would be best described as
    1. physical depreciation.
    2. functional obsolescence.
    3. economic obsolescence.
    4. eminent domain.

20. Which of the following factors would be considered in the market/data approach to value?
    1. Conditions under which property was sold
    2. Annual gross income
    3. Replacement cost
    4. Original cost

21. Outmoded plumbing fixtures are an example of
    1. curable physical deterioration.
    2. curable functional obsolescence.
    3. incurable physical deterioration.
    4. curable economic obsolescence.

22. In the income approach to appraisal, if the net income was $42,000 and the capitalization rate was 12 percent, to find the value of the property the appraiser would
    1. multiply the income by the capitalization rate.
    2. multiply the capitalization rate by the net income.
    3. divide the net income by the capitalization rate.
    4. divide the capitalization rate by the net income.

23. *D* lived in a house with a well. The groundwater became contaminated and lessened the value of *D's* home. The loss in value would be an example of
    1. physical deterioration.
    2. environmental obsolescence.
    3. functional obsolescence.
    4. regression.

24. The appraiser profession is regulated at the national level by
    1. Congress.
    2. the FDIC.
    3. the national real estate commission.
    4. the Appraisal Foundation.

25. Which of the following reflects the stages through which a neighborhood passes?
    1. Growth, decline, stability, and revitalization
    2. Growth, stability, decline, and revitalization
    3. Decline, growth, stability, and revitalization
    4. Decline, growth, revitalization, and stability.

26. Gross rent multipliers are generally used in appraising
    1. forms.
    2. shopping centers.
    3. single-family homes.
    4. hotels.

27. You purchased an apartment building for $600,000 nearly 6 years ago. The building accounts for 80 percent of the property value. The building's economic life is estimated to be 60 years. The total depreciation of the property would be
    1. $36,000.   3. $60,000.
    2. $48,000.   4. $72,000.

28. *R* purchased an office building with an effective gross income of $208,000 and expenses of $74,000. What capitalization rate was used by R to arrive at a value of $1,576,470?
    1. 7.5 percent   3. 9.5 percent
    2. 8.5 percent   4. 10.5 percent

29. *M* was appraising a three-bedroom house. *M* had a comparable with four bedrooms that sold for $160,000. *M* makes an adjustment of $5,000 to the comparable for the difference in the number of bedrooms. The adjusted sales price of the comparable will be
    1. $155,000.
    2. $165,000
    3. $170,000
    4. None of the above

30. If the house you are appraising has central air conditioning valued at $2,500 and your comparable does not, you will adjust the sales price of the comparable by
   1. – $2,500.
   2. + $2,500.
   3. – $1,250.
   4. none of the above.

ANSWER KEY WITH EXPLANATIONS

1. **(3)** Depreciation is used in the cost approach to value. (53)
2. **(1)** FIRREA became effective in 1989. (53)
3. **(2)** Replacement cost
   of building $160,000
   Depreciation of 30% × .30
   Depreciation $ 48,000

   $160,000 Replacement Cost
   – Depreciation of $48,000 = $112,000
   Added land value = $ 40,000
   Value = $152,000
   (54–55)

4. **(2)** Appraisers do not average to determine market value. Appraisers work from comparable transactions to arrive at an estimate of market value for the subject property. (53)
5. **(3)** Income ÷ Rate = Value
   $20,000 ÷ .09 = $222,222 (55)
6. **(2)** The principle of highest and best use deals with the most profitable use while contribution refers to cost and benefits of a particular improvement. Conformity is a factor in the stability of property values; zoning is an example of conformity. (54)
7. **(4)** A limited supply combined with a great demand will result in a higher price for lots. (54)
8. **(1)** The cost approach is most applicable to the appraisal of a special purpose building. (55)

9. **(3)** Decreasing lot size is locational obsolescence; termite damage and negligent care are physical deterioration, while poor architectural design represents functional obsolescence. (55)
10. **(4)** Economic obsolescence is a loss in value due to factors outside the property. Functional obsolescence is a loss in value due to a deficiency in the floor plan or design of a building. (55)
11. **(1)** Land is not depreciated; it is assumed that the land value will be recovered at the end of the economic life of the building. (55)
12. **(2)** Time, location, physical characteristics, and terms of sale are factors considered in the market or sales comparison approach. (55)
13. **(3)** $5,000 per quarter × 4 = $20,000 annual net income
    $20,000 ÷ 08 capitalization rate = $250,000 value (55)
14. **(3)** $7,200 gross ÷ 12 = $600 × 110 = $66,000 value (55)
15. **(4)** The GRM is used as a substitute for the income approach is appraising a single-family home. (55)
16. **(3)** $5,000 monthly rental income × 12 months = $60,000 annual gross income
    Selling price of $600,000 ÷ Gross annual rental income =
    $600,000 ÷ $60,000 = 10 - GIM (56)
17. **(4)** The gross income would be reflected in the first step of the operating statement. Annual net income is the bottom line in the operating statement and serves as the basis for capitalization of the income stream. (55)
18. **(1)** Annual potential gross income is based on 100% of economic or market rent plus other income such as income from vending machines. Effective gross income is annual potential gross income minus vacancy and rent loss. Operating expenses include fixed

expenses such as real estate taxes and variable expenses such as management expenses. The vacancy rate is used to calculate effective gross income.(55)

19. **(3)** Economic obsolescence is a loss in value from factors external to the property. (55)

20. **(1)** Conditions under which the property was sold would be used in the market/data approach. Cost would be used in the cost approach; annual gross income would be used in the income approach. (55)

21. **(2)** Functional obsolescence is a loss in the value due to deficiency in the floor plan or design of a building. The obsolescence would be curable if it were economically feasible to update the plumbing fixtures. Economic obsolescence is assumed to be incurable only because it is caused by factors outside the property. (55)

22. **(3)** The capitalization approach was discussed above. (55)

23. **(2)** This is an example of external obsolescence, which would generally be incurable depending on the cost to cure. (55)

24. **(4)** Congress delegated the regulatory responsibility to the Appraisal Foundation. (53)

25. **(2)** There are numerous examples in cities like Chicago and New York where neighborhoods have gone through the entire process resulting in higher than ever property values. (56)

26. **(3)** The gross rent multiplier is used as a substitute for the income approach in the appraisal of a single-family home. (55)

27. **(2)** $600,000 × .80 = $480,000 value of building
$480,000 ÷ 60 years = $8,000 annual depreciation charge
$8,000 × 6 years = $48,000 current total depreciation. (54–55)

28. **(2)** $208,000 effective gross income - $74,000 expenses = $134,000; $134,000 ÷ $1,576,470 = .085 = 8.5 (55)

29. **(1)** C.B.A.—Comparable Better Subtract $160,000 price of comparable – $5,000 adjustment for one bedroom = $155,000 adjusted sales price of comparable (55)

30. **(2)** S.B.A.—Subject Better Add. The subject property is better than the comparable; thus you add the value of the air conditioning to the sale price of the comparable. (55)

VALUATION AND MARKET ANALYSIS

TEST SCORE

RATING	RANGE	YOUR SCORE	
Good = 80% to 100%	24-30	Total Number	30
Fair = 70% to 79%	21-23	Total Wrong	-
Needs Improvement = Lower than 70%	20 or less	Total Right	

Passing Requirement: 21 or better

Financing

OUTLINE OF CONCEPTS TO UNDERSTAND

I. Theories of mortgage law

A. Lien theory—the mortgage is viewed as a lien on real property in many states.

B. Title theory—the lender is viewed as the conditional owner of mortgaged land in some states.

C. Intermediate theory—a number of states allow the lender to take possession of the mortgaged real estate on default.

II. Mortgage loan

A. Mortgage—the mortgagor (borrower) places a lien on the property in favor of the mortgagee (lender) as security for debt.

B. Note—promise to repay debt; a negotiable instrument

III. Trust deed—three-party instrument used in place of a mortgage in some areas of the country

A. Conveys real estate as security for loan to a third party, the trustee

B. Trustee holds the title on behalf of the lender, known as the beneficiary; the trustee is the legal owner, and the beneficiary is the holder of the note; the borrower retains the equitable title to the property, and the deed of the trust becomes the lien against it

C. The trustee may commence a foreclosure action if the borrower (trustor) defaults; reconveyance deed returns title to trustor when trust deed has been paid in full.

IV. Payment plans

A. Constant amount—payment credited first to interest due, then applied to the loan balance (amortized loan payment plan)

B. Differing installments—each payment consists of the fixed amount credited toward the principal, as well as the additional amount for the interest due on the loan balance.

C. Flexible payment—allows for smaller payments in early years, larger payments in later years (graduated payment mortgage)

D. Straight note or term payment—allows for periodic payments of interest only with lump-sum payment at the maturity of all principal

E. Balloon payment—payments of principal and interest are paid to the lender over a relatively short period; the outstanding principal balance is due in a lump sum at a predetermined future date (partially amortized loan payment plan).

   F. Amortization—loan payment process

      1. Mortgage loans are repaid in equal monthly payments.

      2. The monthly payment is a fixed amount that both reduces the principal and pays interest on the unpaid balance.

V. Mortgage provisions

   A. Acceleration clause—if the borrower defaults, the lender has the right to declare the entire debt due and payable.

   B. Assignment—the mortgagee becomes the assignor and executes assignment to the assignee, who becomes the new owner of the mortgage and debt.

   C. Defeasance clause—the mortgagee is required to execute the release or satisfaction of the mortgage when the note is fully paid.

   D. Alienation (due-on-sale) clause—if the borrower sells the property, the lender has the choice of either declaring the entire debt due and payable or allowing the buyer to assume the loan.

   E. Buying "subject to" versus assuming—if the property is sold "subject to" the mortgage, the buyer is not personally liable to pay the entire debt (the seller remains liable); if the buyer assumes the mortgage, he or she becomes personally liable for payment of the entire debt. The seller is secondarily liable.

VI. Mortgage foreclosure and redemption

   A. Judicial foreclosure

      1. Lender sues the borrower in court; obtains judgment and court order to sell

      2. Property sold at public sale to the highest bidder

   B. Nonjudicial foreclosure

      1. The mortgage generally must include a power-of-sale clause.

      2. A notice of default must be recorded and a public sale advertised in the newspaper.

      3. Property sold at a public sale to highest bidder

   C. Strict foreclosure—the court may award title to the lender.

   D. Deed in lien of foreclosure - mortgagor gives deed to mortgagee when mortgagor is in default under terms of mortgage; this allows mortgagor to avoid foreclosure.

   E. Redemption—process by which the borrower regains interest in the property

      1. Equitable redemption

         a. Occurs prior to public sale

         b. If the borrower pays the amount due plus the costs prior to the public sale, the mortgage is reinstated.

         c. If not redeemed, the property is sold at a public sale to the highest bidder.

      2. Statutory redemption

         a. Occurs after public sales in some states and continues for a period of time specified by law

b. The borrower may pay the sale price in full plus costs.

F. Deficiency judgment—if the property is sold and the proceeds are insufficient to pay the mortgage and foreclosure costs, the difference is a deficiency; the lender usually can sue the original borrower for the difference (process of deficiency judgment).

VII. Types of mortgages

A. Conventional
   1. Payment of the debt based solely on the borrower's ability to pay, with security provided by the mortgage; neither insured nor guaranteed by government agency
   2. Lender sets the terms subject to the law and policy
   3. Ratio of the loan to value lower than with insured and guaranteed loans
   4. If the loan-to-value ratio exceeds a given level, the lender may require private mortgage insurance (PMI).

B. Federal Housing Administration (FHA) insured

   1. FHA insures lenders against loss on loans made on real property.
   2. Interest rates are set by the lender.
   3. The borrower pays the FHA insurance premium (up to 2.25 percent of the mortgage amount) either at the time of closing or financed into the loan amount; the borrower also pays the monthly insurance premium of up to ½ of 1 percent of the mortgage amount over the first few years of the loan, depending on the amount of the down payment and length of loan.
   4. Mortgaged property must be appraised by an FHA-approved appraiser.
   5. Generally, the loan-to-value ratio cannot exceed 97 percent on the first $25,000 of the appraised value, 95 percent on the next $100,000, and 90 percent on amounts more than $125,000, up to the allowable maximum in the area. The only exceptions are loans on a property with an appraisal value of $50,000 or less where the loan value cannot exceed 98.75 percent. There is a limitation that the loan amount for any loan more than $50,000 cannot exceed 97.75 percent of the purchase price or appraised value, whichever is less.
   6. FHA does not allow a prepayment penalty.
   7. FHA mortgages are assumable with qualification.
   8. Discount points generally used to reduce the interest rate (1 point = 1 percent of the loan balance); generally negotiated between the seller and the buyer.

C. Department of Veterans Affairs guaranteed (DVA loans)

   1. DVA does not allow a prepayment penalty.
   2. A DVA loan may be assumed by a non-veteran.
   3. DVA guarantees home loans for eligible veterans or eligible dependents with little or no down payment.
   4. The interest rate is set by the lender.
   5. DVA does not charge the borrower for the guarantee; however, the borrower must pay up to 3 percent in funding fees on the loan amount to the DVA, in addition to any other fees.
   6. Mortgaged property must be appraised by a DVA-approved appraiser.
   7. DVA sets a limitation on the loan amount of up to four times the amount of the veteran's entitlement.

8. DVA guarantees the lender up to $50,750 of the loan balance.
   a. 50 percent of the loan balance, up to $45,000
   b. 45 percent guarantee applied to loan balance from $45,000 to $56,250
   c. 40 percent of the loan balance, up to $144,000
   d. 25 percent of the loan balance, up to $203,000
9. Discount points generally are negotiated between the seller and the buyer.
10. In some cases, the DVA will make direct loans to eligible veterans or their dependents.
11. DVA requires appraisers to complete a Certificate of Reasonable Value (CRV); the DVA guarantee is based on either the amount of the CRV or the selling price, whichever is less.
12. National Guard members and reservists with at least six years of service now are eligible for DVA-guaranteed loans.

D. Rural Development and Farm Agency (formerly Farmers Home Administration)

   1. Rural Development makes and guarantees housing loans to people with low-incomes in rural areas in communities of 10,000 population or less.
   2. Farm Service Agency makes and guarantees loans to farmers and ranchers.

E. Rural Economic and Community Development services makes and guarantees loans to homeowners in rural areas.

F. Privately insured

   1. The buyer may obtain a conventional mortgage for up to 95 percent of the appraised value with PMI insurance.
   2. The buyer is charged the market rate of interest plus reasonable insurance premium costs.
   3. The borrower's insurance protects the lender against loss on the upper 20 to 25 percent portion of the loan.
   4. PMI premiums vary among the insurers. The general rule is
      a. The first-year premium is approximately 1 percent of the loan amount.
      b. Subsequent years are ¼ of 1 percent (.0025) of the loan amount.
      c. Many insurers now charge monthly premiums with no premium deposits up front.
   5. As property values rise and the loan-to-value ratio is 80 percent or less, the PMI insurance may be dropped.
      a. Requires lender approval and new appraisal
      b. Insurance must be held for two years, and the mortgagor must have a 25 percent equity position to drop the insurance.

G. Purchase-money mortgage—given by the buyer to the seller as part of the purchase price (owner financing); legal title passes to the buyer

H. Blanket mortgage—covers more than one property or lot; generally includes a partial release clause

I. Package mortgage—includes real estate and (expressly) all fixtures and appliances located on the property

J. Open-end mortgage

   1. Secures the note executed by the borrower to the lender and any future advances of funds by the lender to the borrower

    2. Terms usually restrict an increase in debt to a limit of either the original debt or a specified amount in the mortgage.

    3. Additional loan amounts are figured at prevailing interest rates.

K. Construction loans

    1. Generally short-term or interim loan to finance construction of an improvement

    2. Periodic payments or draws made by the lender to the owner for work completed since the previous payment

L. Wraparound mortgage (all-inclusive deed of trust)

    1. Allows the borrower who is paying an existing mortgage to obtain additional financing from a second lender

    2. New lender assumes payment of the existing loan; gives the borrower a new, increased loan at a higher interest rate

    3. The new lender makes payments on the original loan; the borrower makes payments to the new lender on the larger loan on the increased amount.

M. Graduated payment mortgage

    1. Initial payments are low but increase over the life of the loan.

    2. Allows the buyer to purchase a home with monthly payments lower than those on a level payment

    3. Aimed at helping first-time buyers who have increasing income potential

N. Adjustable-rate mortgage

    1. Contains interest-rate provision related to the selected index

    2. The interest rate may be adjusted periodically (either up or down). A margin is added to the index to determine the interest rate.

O. Reverse annuity mortgage

    1. Allows the borrower to receive periodic payments from the lender on the equity in the home

    2. The note becomes due on a specific date, at the sale of the property, or at the death of the borrower.

P. Participation mortgage—lender receives interest and an equity position in project known as equity kicker or a percentage of the income of the property.

VIII. The money market

A. General characteristics

    1. Money may be viewed as a means of payment, storehouse of purchasing power, standard value

    2. Money market is regulated by the federal government through the Federal Reserve System and the U.S. Treasury.

B. Federal Reserve System (FED)

    1. Regulates the flow of money through member banks by controlling their reserve requirements and discount rates

    2. Tempers the economy through open-market operations

C. U.S. Treasury

    1. In effect, our nation's banker and fiscal manager

       2. Responsible for supervising the daily fiscal operations of the federal government

IX. Sources of real estate financing

  A. Savings and loan associations

    1. Principal function: to promote thrift and home ownership
    2. Regulated on the national level by the Office of Thrift Supervision
    3. Deposits are insured by the Savings Association Insurance Fund (SAIF) for up to $100,000 per account; SAIF is part of the FDIC.
    4. Local in nature

  B. Commercial banks

    1. Prefer short-term loans but have been significant participants in residential mortgage lending
    2. Deposits are insured by the Bank Insurance Fund (BIF) for up to $100,000 per account; BIF is part of the FDIC.

  C. Mutual savings banks

    1. Primarily savings institutions in the northeastern United States
    2. Active in mortgage market
    3. Prefer FHA and DVA loans

  D. Life insurance companies

    1. Prefer long-term commercial, industrial loans
    2. Seek equity position in projects financed
    3. Regulated by state law

  E. Mortgage banking companies

    1. Originate loans with their own money and money belonging to other institutions and from other sources (pension funds, private individuals)
    2. Service loans they originate

  F. Mortgage brokers—originate loans for other lenders but do not service loans

  G. Sale of state mortgage bonds

    1. Authorized by federal government
    2. Lower interest rates are usually charged to low-income and moderate-income buyers.
    3. Usually for first-time buyers only

  H. Owner assisted

    1. Contract for deed, land contract
    2. Take back second mortgage

X. Secondary mortgage market

  A. Market in which loans are bought and sold after they have been originated and funded

  B. Warehousing agencies play a major role in the secondary market by purchasing a number of mortgage loans and assembling them into packages for resale to investors.

  C. Major warehousing agencies

1. Federal National Mortgage Association (FNMA)—Fannie Mae.
    a. Privately owned corporation authorized to purchase conventional as well as FHA and DVA loans
    b. Raises funds to purchase loans by selling government-guaranteed FNMA bonds at market interest rates
2. Government National Mortgage Association (GNMA)— Ginnie Mae
    a. Federal agency designed to administer a special assistance program and to work with the FNMA in secondary market activities
    b. Can join forces with the FNMA in times of tight money and high interest rates; through a tandem plan, the FNMA can purchase high-risk, low-yield loans at full market rates, while the GNMA guarantees payment and absorbs the difference between low-yield and current market prices
3. Federal Home Loan Mortgage Corporation (FHLMC)—Freddie Mac.
    a. Government chartered corporation created to provide secondary mortgage market for conventional loans
    b. Has the authority to purchase conventional, FHA, and DVA mortgages; pool them; and sell bonds in the open market with mortgages as security

XI.   Closing statements (settlement statement or adjustment sheet)

A. Related to the completion of the real estate transaction, when the seller delivers title to the buyer in exchange for payment of the purchase price by the buyer

B. Detailed accounting of real estate transaction; shows all cash received, all charges and credits made, all cash paid out

C. Prepared by the broker, escrow office, attorney, or any other person designated to process the details of the sale

D. Indicates how all closing costs plus prepaid and unpaid expenses are allocated between the buyer and the seller

E. Closing statement procedures generally reflect local custom as well as state and federal laws (for example, RESPA).

XII.   Other important terms

A. Amortized mortgage (direct-reduction loans)—regular monthly payments, applied first to the interest with the balance to the principal, over the term of the loan

B. Balloon payment—final payment of the loan, larger than previous payments and repays the debt in full

C. Equity—value of the owner's interest in the property; the difference between the value of the property and all the liens on the property

D. Subordination agreement—changes the order of priority of the liens between two creditors

E. Usury—rate of interest in excess of the maximum rate allowed by state law

F. Seller financing—the seller of the real estate provides financing for the sale by taking back a secured note in the form of a purchase-money mortgage, land contract, or deed of trust.

G. Disintermediation— process by which investors place funds directly rather than in financial institutions for investment; reduces the availability of mortgage money

H. Arbitrage—difference between interest rates in financing arrangements such as wraparound mortgages.

I. Hypothecation—pledging property as security for the loan without losing possession of it, such as in lien theory states

J. Impound account—trust account created to set aside funds for the future needs of a property; for example, to provide funds for the payment of real estate taxes and renewal premiums for insurance

REVIEW LIST

The student should have an understanding of the following areas of finance:

1. Policies and procedures used by mortgage lending agencies
2. Government mortgage institutions
3. Mathematics of financial practice

DIAGNOSTIC TEST

1. All of the following statements concerning real estate financing are correct **EXCEPT**
    1. the mortgage generally is considered a lien.
    2. the mortgagee is the lender.
    3. an owner of property by whom the mortgage is executed is called a *mortgagor.*
    4. a promissory note is security for a mortgage.

2. A promissory note is NOT
    1. a negotiable instrument.
    2. evidence of debt.
    3. a document in which the debtor agrees to repay the stated loan.
    4. evidence of title.

3. Which of the following payment plans allows for periodic payments of interest *only,* with the principal due as a lump sum payment at maturity?
    1. Amortized   3. Straight
    2. Flexible   4. Balloon

4. All of the following are participants in the secondary mortgage market **EXCEPT**
    1. FHLMC.   3. FDIC.
    2. FNMA.   4. GNMA.

5. Which of the following is NOT characteristic of a conventional loan?
    1. It is neither insured nor guaranteed by public agency.
    2. Security rests on the borrower's ability to pay and the collateral pledged.
    3. It is never insured by a private agency.
    4. The ratio of the loan to the value of the property usually does not exceed 80 percent without private mortgage insurance.

6. Department of Veterans Affairs (DVA) guarantees a lender from 25 to 50 percent of the loan balance on a Veterans Administration (VA) loan, up to
    1. $25,000.   3. $46,000.
    2. $36,000.   4. $50,750.

7. Which of the following is NOT characteristic of a Federal Housing Administration (FHA) loan **EXCEPT**
    1. A mortgage insurance premium is charged.
    2. The lender is insured against loss.
    3. The maximum mortgage debt is determined by a formula.
    4. The FHA provides the money for the loan.

8. Which of the following is NOT characteristic of a DVA loan?
    1. The loan is guaranteed.
    2. Only an eligible veteran or eligible dependents of veterans, as well as reservists and National Guard members who have served for six years, may qualify for the loan.
    3. The loan is insured.
    4. Little or no down payment is required.

9. A mortgage that covers more than one piece of real property is
    1. a junior mortgage.
    2. a blanket mortgage.
    3. a package mortgage.
    4. an open-end mortgage.

10. Granting a conventional loan requires that the borrower provide the lender with which of the following?
    1. Sales contract and hypothecation instrument
    2. Mortgage and promissory note
    3. Deed of trust and sales contract
    4. Mortgage and letter of intent

11. A graduated-payment mortgage
    1. contains an interest-rate provision related to a selected index.
    2. is granted for a term of 3 to 5 years and is secured by a long-term mortgage of up to 30 years.
    3. allows a buyer to purchase a home with initial monthly payments lower than the level payment, amortized mortgage.
    4. allows the mortgagor to borrow additional money during the term of the loan, up to the original amount of the mortgage.

12. Under judicial foreclosure, the
    1. mortgage generally must include a power-of-sale clause.
    2. court may award title to the lender.
    3. lender sues the borrower in court and obtains a judgment and court order to sell.
    4. lender may sell the property without obtaining a judgment.

13. The process by which a mortgagor regains his or her interest in a property is called
    1. foreclosure.
    2. redemption.
    3. a deficiency judgment.
    4. laches.

14. You financed the purchase of a home by means of a trust deed. Until you pay off the trust deed, title will be held by the
    1. trustee.   3. seller.
    2. trustor.   4. beneficiary.

15. The tandem plan involves
    1. the VA and FHA.
    2. Fannie Mae and Freddie Mac.
    3. Fannie Mae and Ginnie Mae.
    4. Ginnie Mae and Freddie Mac.

16. Which of the following statements about FHA mortgages is FALSE?
    1. FHA mortgages require a larger down payment than VA mortgages.
    2. There is no prepayment penalty.
    3. FHA mortgages are assumable with qualification.
    4. FHA mortgages are not assumable.

17. The difference between interest rates in financing arrangements such as a wraparound mortgage is called
    1. equity.
    2. usury.
    3. disintermediation.
    4. arbitrage.

18. On the FHA loan, the buyer would NOT be required to
    1. provide mortgage insurance to protect the lender.
    2. meet FHA credit standards.
    3. find an approved lender willing to make the loan.
    4. make a 20 percent down payment on the loan.

19. A mortgage on four lots with a partial release clause would be
    1. a wraparound mortgage.
    2. a blanket mortgage.
    3. a package mortgage.
    4. an open-end mortgage.

20. Funds for DVA loans usually are provided by
    1. HUD.
    2. the secondary mortgage market.
    3. Freddie Mac.
    4. approved lenders.

21. Charging a rate of interest in excess of the maximum rate allowed by law is
    1. laches.
    2. hypothecation.
    3. subordination.
    4. usury.

22. Pledging property as security for a loan without losing possession of it is
    1. a subordination agreement.
    2. hypothecation.
    3. an impound account.
    4. seller financing.

23. A veteran buys a home with a DVA-guaranteed loan. Two years later, the veteran sells the home to a buyer who, with the lender's approval, assumes the veteran's loan. In this situation, the veteran is
    1. responsible for paying an insurance fee charged by the DVA.
    2. responsible for paying the loan origination fee.
    3. no longer financially responsible if the buyer defaults six months later.
    4. financially responsible if the buyer defaults six months later.

24. If a lender charges a borrower two points on a $60,000 loan, what will be the service charge for points?
    1. $120
    2. $1,200
    3. $2,400
    4. None of the above

25. Reserve requirements for banks are controlled by which of the following federal agencies?
    1. FNMA
    2. GNMA
    3. Federal Deposit Insurance Corporation (FDIC)
    4. The "Fed"

ANSWER KEY WITH EXPLANATIONS

1. **(4)** The mortgage creates a lien on the property while the note is the promise to repay the debt. (63)
2. **(4)** Title insurance would insure title. (63)
3. **(3)** The amortized, flexible, and balloon all provide for payment of principal. (63)
4. **(3)** The FDIC insures checking accounts of banks and savings and loan associations up to $100,000 per account. (68–69)
5. **(3)** Conventional loans may be insured by a private agency. (65)
6. **(4)** The veteran is entitled to a loan up to four times the amount of the entitlement. (65)
7. **(4)** The FHA will not provide money for a loan. However, the VA will provide the money for a loan where the supply of money is scarce. (65)
8. **(3)** A FHA loan provides public mortgage insurance for which the buyer pays an insurance premium. The VA does not charge the veteran for the guarantee of the loan. (65)
9. **(2)** A blanket mortgage would be used to finance the development of a subdivision. (66)
10. **(2)** A deed of trust is used in place of a mortgage in states such as California. A mortgage and a note are required for a conventional loan. The mortgagee creates a lien on the property as security for the debt while the note is a promise to repay the debt. (63)
11. **(3)** An adjustable rate mortgage uses an index note. An open end mortgage allows for borrowing additional money up to the original loan amount. (67)
12. **(3)** Judicial foreclosure is one of the three alternative procedures available to the lender for mortgage foreclosure. Nonjudicial foreclosure does not require the lender to sue the borrower in court. Under strict foreclosure, the court may award title to the lender. Strict foreclosure is frequently used for foreclosing on land contracts. (64)
13. **(2)** Foreclosure is related to the redemption period, which may end with the foreclosure sale (equitable redemption) or after

the foreclosure sale (statutory redemption). If the lender does not recover what is owned by the borrower, it may sue for a deficiency judgment. Laches was discussed above. (64)

14. **(1)** The trustor is the borrower and the beneficiary is the lender. (63)

15. **(3)** Freddie Mac is the third warehousing agency in the secondary mortgage market. VA and FHA are not involved in the secondary mortgage market purchase of mortgages. (69)

16. **(4)** FHA and VA mortgages are assumable with qualification. (65)

17. **(4)** Equity is the difference between what an asset is worth and what is owed on it. Usury laws limit the interest rate that can be charged to borrowers by lenders. Disintermediation refers to an outflow of funds from a lender which limits the lender's lending capacity. (70)

18. **(4)** The down payment on a FHA loan varies from 3 percent to 5 percent. (65)

19. **(2)** A wraparound mortgage is a second mortgage wrapped around a first mortgage. A package mortgage is used on an individual property. An open-end mortgage allows for future advances of funds by the lender to the borrower. (66)

20. **(4)** Freddie Mac functions in the secondary mortgage market while HUD is a regulatory agency. (66)

21. **(4)** Subordination allows a lender to agree to consent to a subsequent mortgage having legal priority thus placing the original lender on a lesser position. Laches refers to the inability to assert a legal right because of undue delay in asserting it. Hypothecation is pledging property as security for a loan without giving up possession of the property. Usury is charging an interest rate higher than that allowed by state law. (69)

22. **(2)** An impound account is a trust account established for funds to meet the customary requirements of a property, e.g. taxes and insurance. Subordination and hypothecation were discussed above in answer 21. A land contract would be an example of seller financing. (70)

23. **(4)** The veteran remains liable for the assumed mortgage unless released by the lender. (65)

24. **(2)** One point is one percent of the loan amount. $60,000 × 0.02 = $1,200. (65)

25. **(4)** FNMA and GNMA functions in the secondary mortgage market. The FDIC insures lenders' checking accounts. (79)

FINANCING

TEST SCORE

RATING	RANGE	YOUR SCORE	
Good = 80% to 100%	20-25	Total Number	25
Fair = 70% to 79%	18-19	Total Wrong	-
Needs Improvement = Lower than 70%	17 or less	Total Right	

Passing Requirement: 18 or better

Laws of Agency

OUTLINE OF CONCEPTS TO UNDERSTAND

I. **Laws of Agency**

   A. The brokerage business is one of agency; the broker is hired by the principal to become her or his agent.

   1. The agent is a broker who consents to represent the interest of another person and is authorized to act accordingly.
   2. The principal is the buyer or seller who employs and delegates to the agent the responsibility of representing the principal's interests.
   3. *Agency* refers to the fiduciary relationship between the agent and the principal.
   4. *Fiduciary* means the relationship of trust and confidence that the agent has with the principal.
   5. The client is the principal to whom the agent gives counsel and advice.
   6. The customer is the third party for whom a service is provided.
   7. The principal is obligated to compensate the agent unless otherwise agreed as well as cooperate with and not hinder the agent's ability to fulfill the fiduciary obligations.
   8. Simple agency involves a broker representing either the seller or buyer in a transaction; limitation avoids conflicts and results in loyalty and client-based service to just one client.
   9. Subagency is brought about when one broker, generally the seller's agent, appoints other brokers (with written authorization of the seller) to assist in carrying out client-based functions on behalf of the principal; cooperating brokers have the same fiduciary responsibilities to the seller as the listing broker.

   B. The broker owes a fiduciary duty to the principal, who may be the seller, buyer, lessor, or lessee of property; the broker must perform duties of care, obedience, accounting, loyalty, and disclosure for the principal (COALD).

   C. The broker owes a fiduciary duty to the principal, but the broker is obligated to disclose to the customer material facts relating to a property; in addition, the seller usually is responsible for revealing any latent defects to the buyer.

   D. General agent versus special agent

   1. A general agent is one authorized by another to negotiate contracts for that person in a given range of matters.

2. A general agent, for example, a property manager, is authorized to represent the principal in all matters concerning one area of the principal's interest.
3. A special agent is authorized to represent the principal in one specific transaction; a real estate broker is a special agent.
4. A broker is a special agent employed by a seller to find a buyer for the seller's property or employed by a buyer to assist in the buying process.
5. As a special agent, the real estate broker is not authorized to sell property or to bind the principal to any contract.

E. To be entitled to a brokerage commission, a broker must

1. Be a licensed broker
2. Be the procuring cause of the sale/purchase
3. Be employed by the principal
4. Act according to the laws of agency

F. When a broker is employed by a seller and finds a buyer who is "ready, willing, and able" to purchase on the terms and conditions of the listing or on any terms acceptable to the seller, the broker then is entitled to the commission even if

1. The sale is not completed because of the principal's default.
2. The buyer cancels because of the seller's fraud, of which the broker had no knowledge.

G. Real estate brokers may share a commission only with their own salespeople or with other licensed brokers.

H. Real estate brokers may not offer legal advice; only a licensed attorney may do so.

I. Dual agency—the broker is prohibited from representing both the seller and the buyer in the transaction without their prior written, mutual knowledge and consent.

J. The broker must exercise reasonable care when representing the principal.

K. The broker is obligated to act in good faith and conform with the principal's legal instructions and authority.

L. The broker may not act as both the agent and the party to a transaction without prior knowledge and consent of all the parties.

M. All offers must be presented by the broker to the principal promptly when received.

N. A fixed place of business must be maintained by the broker.

O. The broker may be required to deposit all the funds entrusted to her or him in a trust account or do what all parties agree should be done with the funds and may not commingle such funds with operating funds.

P. The broker generally is prohibited from placing blind ads—those that do not identify the broker as the advertiser.

Q. The broker's commission is negotiable between the seller and the broker, is specified in the listing agreement, and is computed as a percentage of the total amount of money involved, but may be expressed as a flat fee; net listings generally are not allowed in most states.

R. Buyer agency—the broker may be hired by a potential buyer; the broker and the buyer usually draw up a buyer agency agreement. The buyer/broker must

1. Be fair and honest to the seller, but owes greater responsibility to the buyer, including duties of skill and care to promote and safeguard the buyer's best interest

2. Disclose to the buyer pertinent facts (which he or she might not be able to disclose if a subagent of the seller) such as the seller is near bankruptcy or the property is overpriced

3. Use negotiating strategy and bargaining talents in the buyer's best interest

S. The transactional broker (nonagent or facilitator) is not an agent of either party. The transactional broker

1. Assists the buyer and seller with formalities and necessary paperwork required for transferring ownership of real property

2. Is expected to treat all parties honestly and competently and is equally responsible to both

3. May not disclose confidential information to either party and may not negotiate for either the seller or buyer

T. Broker Protection Clause—states that the property owner will pay the listing broker a commission if, within a specified number of days after the listing expires, the owner transfers the property to someone the broker originally introduced to the owner

U. Cooperative brokers, generally selling brokers, who work with the listing broker to bring the seller and buyer together

II. Salespersons

A. Salespersons are responsible only to the brokers under whom they are licensed and can carry out only those responsibilities assigned by their brokers.

B. Salespersons have no authority to make contracts or receive compensation directly from the principals.

C. All salespersons' activities must be carried out in the name of their supervising brokers.

D. Salespersons may work under brokers either as independent contractors or as employees.

E. Salespersons are compensated on the basis of agreements between themselves and their brokers.

F. Salespersons may not place ads without identifying their associated brokers unless allowed under state law.

G. Salespersons are agents of their brokers and subagents of the party represented, which may be a buyer or a seller.

III. Broker's ethics

A. Fraud

1. Fraud versus puffing
   a. Fraud is a misrepresentation of facts known to be false, made with the intent to deceive and relied on by the injured party to his or her detri-

ment; it also includes intentional or negligent nondisclosure of pertinent facts by silence.

    b. Puffing is an opinion not made as a representation of fact.

  2. Fraudulent acts not only are unethical but can result in the revocation or suspension of a broker's license.

B. Code of Ethics—standards of ethical conduct subscribed to by members of the National Association of REALTORS® or other real estate trade organizations. Sections of the REALTORS® code have been made a part of the rules and regulations governing the conduct of real estate licensees in many states.

IV. Antitrust Law

A. Antitrust law prohibitions

  1. Allocation of customers or markets—agreement among brokers to divide their markets and refrain from competing for each other's business; division may take place on a geographic basis or on a certain price range of homes.

  2. Price fixing—conspiracy among brokers to set prices for their services, rather than negotiate such fees.

  3. Boycotting—two or more businesses conspire against other businesses to reduce competition

  4. Tie-in agreements—agreements to sell one product only if the buyer purchases another product as well.

  5. People violating the Sherman Antitrust Act may be found guilty of a felony punishable by a maximum of $100,000 fine and three years in prison

  6. In a civil suit a broker found guilty of a violation of the Sherman Antitrust Act will be liable for three times the actual damages plus attorney's fees and costs.

REVIEW LIST

The student should have an understanding of the following areas of the laws of agency:

1. Representation and disclosure

2. Agent for seller

3. Agent for buyer

4. Dual agent

DIAGNOSTIC TEST

1. *A* agrees to buy *B*'s real estate for $123,000. *A* signs a sales contract and deposits $12,300 earnest money with *B*'s broker, *C*. *B* is unable to show good title, and *A* demands the return of his earnest money from *C*, as provided in the contract. What should *C* do?
   1. Deduct the commission and return the balance to A
   2. Deduct the commission and pay the balance to B
   3. Return the entire amount of earnest money to A
   4. Pay the entire amount to B to dispose of as B sees fit

2. A broker employs several salespeople at her office. Early one day one member of the sales staff submits a written offer with an earnest money deposit on a house listed with the broker. Later the same day another salesperson submits a higher written offer on the same property, also including an earnest money deposit. The broker, in accordance with the policy of her office, does not submit a second offer unless the first has been presented and *rejected* by the seller. In this case the seller accepts the first offer, so the seller is not informed of the second offer. In this situation, the broker's actions are
   1. permissible, provided the commission is split between the two salespeople.
   2. permissible, if such arrangement is written into the salespeople's employment contracts.
   3. not permissible, because the broker must submit all offers to the seller.
   4. not permissible, because the broker must notify the second buyer of the existence of the first offer.

3. An owner listed her home for $98,000, and the broker told the prospective buyer to submit a low offer because the seller was desperate. The buyer offered $96,000 and the seller accepted. In this situation
   1. the broker was unethical, but because no one was hurt, the broker's conduct is not improper.
   2. the broker violated the agency relationship.
   3. the broker's action was proper in obtaining a quick offer.
   4. any broker is authorized to encourage bidders.

4. A salesperson can advertise a property for sale without including her broker's name if she
   1. is advertising her own listing.
   2. includes her name in the ad.
   3. pays for the ad.
   4. is allowed to run a blind ad under state law.

5. A doctor listed his home with a broker under an exclusive-right-to-sell agreement. The listing salesperson and her broker signed the listing contract. Which of the following statements does NOT correctly describe the relationship among the parties?
   1. The broker has a fiduciary relationship with the seller.
   2. The salesperson has a fiduciary relationship with the broker.
   3. If the salesperson dies, the listing contract will be terminated.
   4. If the broker dies, the listing contract will be terminated.

6. A real estate broker is usually
   1. a special agent.
   2. a universal agent.
   3. a general agent.
   4. an ostensible agent.

7. Which of the following is FALSE concerning a real estate broker?
   1. All offers must be presented by the broker to the principal.
   2. Brokers may place blind ads.
   3. A fixed place of business must be maintained by the broker.
   4. The broker's commission usually is specified in the listing agreement.

8. Which of the following is FALSE concerning a real estate salesperson?
   1. The salesperson is responsible to the broker under whom she or he is licensed.
   2. All of a salesperson's activities must be carried out in the name of his or her principal broker.
   3. The salesperson must work under the broker as an independent contractor.
   4. A salesperson is compensated on the basis of an agreement between herself or himself and the broker.

9. You are a broker who has listed a home for a neighbor. Which of the following terms describe your relationship with the seller?
   1. You are a subagent of the seller.
   2. The seller is your client.
   3. The seller is your customer.
   4. The seller is your agent.

10. A man who owned a single-family house had his unlicensed son-in-law do the electrical work in preparing his home for sale. The man did not disclose this to the broker at the time of executing the listing. After completion of the sale, the new owner suffered a financial loss because of the faulty electrical wiring done by the owner's son-in-law. The broker
    1. could be reprimanded for not forewarning the purchaser.
    2. is innocent of any wrongful act.
    3. will be held liable for monetary damages suffered by the purchaser.
    4. should have arranged for a proper electrical inspection prior to the sale.

11. A home is listed for $100,000 and sells for $90,000. The broker's commission is 7 percent of the selling price. The commission is
    1. $630.
    2. $700.
    3. $6,300.
    4. $7,000.

12. You are a broker acting as a facilitator in the sale of a house without being an agent of either party. You are a(n)
    1. buyer's broker.
    2. cooperative broker.
    3. listing broker.
    4. transactional broker.

13. The responsibilities of a broker in an agency relationship include
    1. managing the property.
    2. providing financing.
    3. accountability for funds received.
    4. accepting an offer for the seller.

14. The listing broker owes fiduciary duty to the
    1. buyer.
    2. lender.
    3. seller.
    4. buyer's attorney.

15. A broker lists an accountant's property. The broker may
    1. reject an offer for the seller's property.
    2. bind the seller to a contract.
    3. advertise the seller's property.
    4. offer legal advice to the seller.

16. A broker has received several offers for a property he has listed. The broker must present each offer to the seller
    1. promptly on receipt.
    2. individually.
    3. as soon as the seller has decided on any previous offer.
    4. prior to the seller's deciding on any previous offer.

17. A salesperson sells a property listed by her broker. The salesperson may accept her share of the commission from
    1. the seller.
    2. her broker.
    3. the buyer.
    4. the buyer's attorney.

18. Which of the following is a violation of the broker's fiduciary relationship with a seller?
    1. The broker charges no commission.
    2. The broker charges a 40 percent commission.
    3. The broker tells a prospective buyer the lowest price the seller will accept.
    4. The broker tells a prospective buyer the highest price the seller will accept.

19. Which of the following statements does NOT correctly describe a fiduciary?
    1. A fiduciary owes loyalty to the principal.
    2. A fiduciary must conform to the principal's legal instructions.
    3. A fiduciary is an agent.
    4. A fiduciary is a neutral third party.

20. A salesperson is working under a broker. The salesperson may
    1. work under the broker as an independent contractor.
    2. place an ad without identifying the broker.
    3. receive a commission directly from a seller.
    4. receive a commission directly from another broker.

21. A special agent is best described as someone who
    1. has power of attorney.
    2. has authority to sell a property.
    3. has authority to represent a principal in a specific transaction.
    4. has authority to represent a principal in all matters concerning an area of the principal's interest.

22. A broker presents a seller with a written offer to purchase. The broker is responsible for
    1. explaining the advantages or disadvantages of the offer to the seller.
    2. explaining the legal implications of accepting the offer.
    3. binding the seller to the offer.
    4. preparing the title search once the offer is accepted.

23. A broker is listing her neighbor's home. The commission should be determined by
    1. the size of the broker's firm.
    2. rates approved by the Real Estate Commission.
    3. rates approved by the local Board of REALTORS®.
    4. negotiation with her neighbor.

24. A broker recently has listed a home under an exclusive-right-to-sell listing contract. The broker generally will earn his commission when
    1. he submits an offer to purchase to the seller.
    2. the seller signs an offer to purchase.
    3. he finds a buyer "ready, willing, and able" to buy on the terms of the listing.
    4. the closing has taken place.

25. A broker has earned a commission on the sale of her listing by another broker. The listing broker may pay part of her commission to
    1. the selling broker.
    2. the selling salesperson.
    3. the out-of-state salesperson who referred the seller to her.
    4. the buyer's attorney.

26. A broker has just received an earnest money payment on an offer to purchase. The broker must place the earnest money in his
    1. trust account.
    2. business account.
    3. personal checking account.
    4. savings account.

27. A salesperson working for a broker has just written an offer to purchase on her broker's listing in which the buyer has written a check for earnest money and stated that the broker hold the funds. Which of the following statements describes how the earnest money payment should be handled?
    1. The salesperson should place the earnest money in her checking account and await the closing of the transaction.
    2. The salesperson should give the earnest money check to the seller's attorney.
    3. The salesperson should place the earnest money check in a safe deposit box until the transaction is concluded.
    4. The salesperson should give the earnest money check to her broker for deposit in the broker's trust account.

28. A licensed real estate broker who engages the services of a licensed salesperson on the basis that the broker can direct what the salesperson can do but not how it is done has
    1. engaged an independent contractor.
    2. discriminated illegally.
    3. practiced steering.
    4. established an employer-employee relationship.

29. A broker's license can be revoked if he or she
    1. advertises property for sale without including the salesperson's name in the ad.
    2. negotiates a commission based on what the broker says is the rate set by the local board of REALTORS®.
    3. pays a commission that exceeds the customary rate.
    4. advertises free market analysis as a means of obtaining listings.

30. What is the listing broker's legal responsibility to a prospective purchaser?
    1. The broker must not use fraud or deceit.
    2. The broker must help the buyer get the lowest price possible.
    3. The broker is only a middleman. Neither the buyer nor the seller can charge her or him with avoiding a legal duty.
    4. There is none at all.

ANSWER KEY WITH EXPLANATIONS

1. **(3)** *B* is not entitled to any compensation as she was responsible for breaching the contract. *C* cannot deduct commission because the sale did not close. (76)

2. **(3)** Brokers are responsible for submitting all offers to clients. (76)

3. **(2)** The broker owes loyalty to the client as part of the fiduciary responsibilities. The broker should encourage the buyer to make his

or her highest and best offer, which would be the list price of the property. (75)

4. **(4)** A broker is generally prohibited by state law from advertising with blind ads; the broker's name must be included in the ad. (77)

5. **(3)** The salesperson works on behalf of the broker but is not a party to the contracts prepared by him. The listing contract is between the doctor and the broker. (77)

6. **(1)** A special agent has a specific responsibility as compared to a general agent who has greater responsibilities such as a property manager. A universal agent has newly unlimited authority. (76)

7. **(2)** The blind ad was discussed in Question 4. (77)

8. **(3)** A salesperson may work under a broker as either an employee or an independent contractor. (77)

9. **(2)** The listing broker is the agent of the seller. (75)

10. **(2)** The broker would not be responsible for disclosing something which he would have no way of knowing. (75)

11. **(3)** Commission is based on the selling. $90,000 \times 7\%$ (0.07) = $6,300. (76)

12. **(4)** A transactional broker is also referred to as a nonagent whose job is to help the parties with the paperwork and procedure required to complete the transaction. (77)

13. **(3)** Accountability is part of the fiduciary relationship. (75)

14. **(3)** The listing contract creates an agency relationship and thus a fiduciary duty to the seller. (75)

15. **(3)** The listing broker is responsible for marketing the property. The broker would not have the authority to respond to an offer for the client or to offer legal advice. (75)

16. **(1)** The broker must present all offers simultaneously. The broker does not have the right to withhold offers from the seller. (76)

17. **(2)** A salesperson is an agent of the broker and may not accept real estate related compensation from anyone. (76)

18. **(3)** The commission is negotiable. A buyer broker could suggest that the client offer the lowest price a seller might accept. (75)

19. **(4)** The broker has a fiduciary duty to work in the best interest of his or her client. (75)

20. **(1)** Blind ads are prohibited. A salesperson may receive a commission only from the broker for whom she is working. (77)

21. **(3)** The incorrect answers reflect the authority of a universal agent. (76)

22. **(1)** A broker may not give legal advice nor bid a seller to an offer. A title company licensed by the state insurance commission or an attorney or a title abstractor insurance would do the title search. (75)

23. **(4)** Commissions are negotiable. A rate approved by more than one broker would be a violation of antitrust law. (76)

24. **(3)** The commission is earned when a full price offer consistent with the terms in the listing is presented to the seller. The commission is received at the closing. (76)

25. **(1)** Commissions must be shared on a broker-to-broker basis. (76)

26. **(1)** Brokers are required to set up a trust account for earnest money payments unless otherwise agreed to by the buyer and seller. (76)

27. **(4)** The salesperson is required to give all earnest money to her broker. The listing broker is responsible for holding the earnest money in his trust account. (77)

28. **(1)** A broker cannot control sales-people's working conditions as in an employer-employee relationship. An agent is not required to follow illegal instructions such as discrimination. (77)

29. **(2)** Negotiating commissions on the basis of the board rate would be an example of violating antitrust law. The broker's name must be included in an ad but it is not necessary to include the name of the salesperson. It is perfectly legal for the broker to advertise a free market analysis as a means of soliciting listings. (76)

30. **(1)** The listing broker must treat the customer fairly, but is required to get the seller the highest price possible. (75)

LAWS OF AGENCY

TEST SCORE

RATING	RANGE	YOUR SCORE	
Good = 80% to 100%	24-30	Total Number	30
Fair = 70% to 79%	21-23	Total Wrong	-
Needs Improvement = Lower than 70%	20 or less	Total Right	

Passing Requirement: 21 or better

Mandated Disclosures

OUTLINE OF CONCEPTS TO UNDERSTAND

I. Agency disclosure

A. Disclosure of the agency relationship is required in every state; it is generally required at the first meaningful contact with a buyer or seller.

B. Dual agency is not allowed unless all parties agree to it, however, dual agency is illegal in some states. The disclosure should be made before the individual discloses any confidential information to the broker.

II. Property disclosure

A. Latent defects - a hidden structural defect that would not be discovered by ordinary inspection, such as a part of the property being built partly on an adjoining property or a zoning violation.

1. Seller has duty to discover and disclose any known latent defects that threaten personal safety or structural soundness.
2. Buyers have been able to receive damages or terminate the offer to purchase in case where a seller did not reveal known latent defects.
3. Some states require a seller of residential property to provide a property condition report for all prospective buyers.
4. Some states also require the licensee to discover and disclose an prospective buyers any material facts that may affect the property's desirability or value in spite of the seller's lack of knowledge or failure to disclose.

B. Environmental disclosures

1. A real estate broker should be able to notice potential environmental hazards in a property that would be readily apparent to a real estate broker and urge that the buyer or seller have the potential hazard evaluated by a qualified third party.
2. Broker should be aware of the Comprehensive Environmental Response Compensation and Liability Act (CERCLA) of 1980 which was amended as the Superfund Amendment and Preauthorization Act of 1986.
   a. Established fund of $9 billion called Superfund to clean up uncontrolled hazardous waste dumps and respond to spills.
   b. Created a process of identifying liable parties and ordering them to take responsibility for the cleanup.

      c. Liability under Superfund considered to be strict, joint and several, and retroactive.

        1. Strict liability—owner is responsible to the injured party without excuse.

        2. Joint and several liability—each individual owner is personally responsible for the damages in whole; if only one owner is financially able to handle the total damage, then that owner will have to pay all and attempt to collect the proportionate share of the rest of the owners from them.

        3. Retroactive liability—liability not limited to the person who currently owns the property; also extends to people who have owned the site in the past.

C. Brokers should be familiar with environmental hazards known to be common to their market area.

D. The listing broker and selling broker, if a subagent, must inform the seller or lessor of their obligations for environmental disclosures under the Residential Lead-Based Paint Hazard Reduction Act of 1992 for dwellings built prior to 1978:

    1. Homebuyers must be alerted to any lead-based paint or related hazards.

    2. Homebuyers must be given an agreed upon time period for the opportunity to conduct a lead-based paint inspection or risk assessment at their expense.

    3. A Certification and Acknowledgment of Disclosures must be attached to the offer to purchase.

    4. A copy of the Certification and Acknowledgment must be kept by the seller and both agents for three years after closing on the beginning of the lease.

 E. Material facts for seller's agent include

    1. disclosure of all offers

    2. buyer's ability to offer a higher price (in most states)

    3. disclosing names of prospective buyers as well as any relationship, such as buyer is related to licensee

    4. disclosure of known material defects in property

 F. Material facts for buyer's agent include

    1. disclosing property deficiencies.

    2. disclosing provisions of offer to purchase that are not favorable to the buyer

    3. recommending the lowest price the buyer should offer regardless of the list price

    4. disclosing how long the property has been listed.

REVIEW LIST

The student should have an understanding of the following areas of mandated disclosures.

1. Agency disclosure

2. Need for inspection and obtaining/verifying information

3. Material facts

DIAGNOSTIC TEST

1. Broker *M* is going to contact customer *P* who would like to see one of *M*'s listings. *M* should make his agency disclosure
   1. prior to meeting with *P*.
   2. prior to discussing *P*'s financial qualification and type of house desired.
   3. prior to actually showing the listed property.
   4. prior to writing an offer to purchase.

2. Which of the following would not be classified as a latent defect?
   1. An unknown underground oil tank
   2. Hidden structural damage
   3. A large crack in the living room ceiling.
   4. A cracked heat exchange in the furnace.

3. Which of the following statements does NOT correctly describe the status of dual agency?
   1. Dual agency is legal in all states.
   2. Dual agency is not allowed unless all parties agree to it.
   3. Disclosure of dual agency should be made when preparing an offer to purchase.
   4. Disclosure of dual agency should be made prior to the closing of a real estate transaction.

4. The Comprehensive Environmental Response Compensation and Liability Act was amended in
   1. 1978.   3. 1986.
   2. 1980.   4. 1990.

5. The residential Lead-Based Paint Hazard Reduction Act of 1992 does not require that
   1. the seller disclose any lead-based paint or related hazards.
   2. homebuyers be given an agreed upon time period for the opportunity to conduct a lead-based paint inspection or risk assessment at their own expense.
   3. a Certification and Acknowledgment of Disclosure be attached to the offer to purchase.
   4. a copy of the Certification and Acknowledgment be kept by only the listing broker.

6. The Residential Lead-based Paint Hazard Reduction Act of 1992 requires that copies of the Certification and Acknowledgment be kept for
   1. one year after closing.
   2. two years after closing.
   3. three years after closing.
   4. five years after closing.

7. Which of the following statements would NOT be a material fact to be disclosed by a seller's agent?
   1. The buyer's ability to make a higher offer
   2. Disclosure of the property's deficiencies
   3. Discussion of advantages of offer to purchase
   4. Presentation of all offers

8. Which of the following statements would NOT be a material fact to be disclosed by a buyer's agent?
   1. Disclosure of how long the property has been located
   2. Buyer's ability to make a higher offer
   3. Recommend the lowest price the buyer should offer regardless of the list price
   4. Disclosure of provisions of offer to purchase which are not favorable to buyer

9. Which of the following does NOT correctly describe the status of agency disclosure?
   1. Disclosure is required in some states.
   2. Disclosure is required at the first meaningful contact with a buyer.
   3. Disclosure is required at the first meaningful contact with the seller.
   4. Disclosure is required in every state.

10. CERCLA became law in
    1. 1978.   3. 1986.
    2. 1980.   4. 1992.

ANSWER KEY WITH EXPLANATIONS

1. **(2)** While this is generally correct, you should check with your state licensing board on the disclosure timing. (85)

2. **(3)** A latent defect would not be discovered by an ordinary inspection. (85)

3. **(1)** Dual agency is not legal in some states. Moreover, dual agency is not allowed in any state unless all parties agree to it. (85)

4. **(3)** CERCLA became law in 1980 and was amended as the Superfund Amendment and Preauthorization Act of 1986. (85)

5. **(4)** A copy of the Certification and Acknowledgment must be kept by the seller and both agents. (86)

6. **(3)** Copies must also be kept for three years after the beginning of a lease. (86)

7. **(2)** A buyer's agent would be required to disclose the property's deficiencies. (85)

8. **(2)** A seller's agent would be required to disclose the buyer's ability to make a higher offer unless prohibited by state law. (86)

9. **(1)** The disclosure is generally required at the first meaningful contact with a client or customer. (85)

10. **(2)** CERCLA makes owners of real estate responsible for cleaning up hazardous material found on their property. (85)

MANDATED DISCLOSURES

TEST SCORE

RATING	RANGE	YOUR SCORE	
Good = 80% to 100%	8-10	Total Number	10
Fair = 70% to 79%	7	Total Wrong	___
Needs Improvement = Lower than 70%	6 or less	Total Right	

Passing Requirement: 7 or better

PART 10

Contracts

OUTLINE OF CONCEPTS TO UNDERSTAND

I. **Voluntary agreement between legally competent parties to do or refrain from doing some legal act, supported by legal consideration**

II. **Essential elements of a valid contract**

   A. Competent parties—must be of legal age and mentally competent

   B. Offer and acceptance (mutual assent)—must be a "meeting of the minds"

      1. Any offer or counteroffer may be withdrawn at any time prior to acceptance by the offeree.

   C. Legality of object—purpose must be legal

   D. Consideration—an act of forbearance, or the promise thereof, given by one party in exchange for something from the other. Forbearance is a promise not to do something which party is legally entitled to do.

   E. Description of real estate—must be accurate

   F. Written and signed—generally required by the statute of frauds for most real estate contracts.

III. **Contract classifications**

   A. Expressed—parties state terms and show intentions in words; may be either oral or written.

   B. Implied—agreement demonstrated by acts and conduct.

   C. Bilateral—both parties promise to do something; one promise is given in exchange for another.

   D. Unilateral—only one party makes a promise; if the second party complies, the first party is obligated to keep the promise, such as an option or open listing.

   E. Executed—both parties have fulfilled their promises and thus performed the contract.

   F. Executory—something remains to be done by one or both parties.

IV. **Legal effect of a contract**

   A. Valid—complies with all essentials of a contract; binding and enforceable on both parties

   B. Void—lacks an essential element of a valid contract; has no legal effect

C. Voidable—appears to be valid on its surface but may be disaffirmed because one of the parties signed when a minor, when under duress or as a result of fraud or misrepresentation

D. Unenforceable—appears to be valid, but neither party may sue the other to force performance; for example, an oral agreement to pay a commission

V.   Discharge of contract

A. Performance—all terms carried out

B. Substantial performance—party remains liable because the contract was not completed exactly as required

C. Mutual agreement—parties agree to cancel

D. Operation of law—voided by minor or because of fraud or the expiration of the statute of limitations

VI.   Default/breach of contract

A. Buyer recourse if seller defaults

1. Rescind, or terminate, the contract and recover the earnest money.
2. Sue for specific performance.
3. Sue the seller for damages.

B. Seller recourse if buyer defaults

1. Declare the contract forfeited.
2. Rescind the contract and keep all or part of the deposit as liquidated damages.
3. Sue for specific performance.
4. Sue for damages.

VII.   Types of listing agreements

A. Open listing

1. The seller may employ any number of brokers.
2. The seller is obligated to pay a commission only to the broker who produces a buyer (procuring cause).
3. If the seller personally sells the property without the aid of any broker, the seller is not obligated to pay the commission.

B. Exclusive-agency listing

1. Only one broker is authorized to act as the exclusive agent of the principal.
2. The seller retains the right to sell the property without obligation to the broker.

C. Exclusive-right-to-sell listing

1. One broker is given the exclusive right to sell the property.
2. The seller gives up the right to sell the property without paying the broker's commission.
3. The broker receives the commission regardless of who sells the property.

D. Net listing

1. The list price is based on the amount of money the seller will receive if the property is sold, plus the commission.
2. If the property is sold, the seller receives only the net amount for which the property was listed, and the broker retains the remainder.
3. Prohibited or discouraged in many states.

E. All listings are agreements between the broker and the seller, not the salesperson.

F. Types of buyer agency agreements
   1. Exclusive right agreements—the buyer must compensate his or her agent whenever purchasing a property of the type described within the period described.
   2. Exclusive agreement—the buyer's agent is assured of buyer loyalty relative to any other agents. The buyer may, however, purchase property on his or her own without the assistance of an agent and thus without any compensation being due to the buyer's agent.
   3. Open agreement—the buyer can work with more than one buyer's agent at the same time but owes compensation only if the buyer uses the services of a buyer's broker.
   4. Situations where it is appropriate for a buyer to enter into a relationship with buyer broker.
      a. A family business relationship or friendship exists, which makes it difficult for broker to be completely loyal to the seller.
      b. Working with former seller clients as buyer customers.
      c. A buyer prefers to have the agent as her advocate.
      d. A broker is buying for himself; he must disclose he is a licensed agent and representing himself and not a seller.

G. Ways in which buyer's broker can be compensated
   1. Retainer fee.
   2. Gives buyer incentive to perform contract.
   3. Fee may be refundable or nonrefundable.

H. Flat or fixed fee
   1. Can calculate a straight fixed fee
   2. The fee can be paid by the buyer or as a co-op fee by the seller.
   3. The hourly fee should reflect the market as well as what other professionals are receiving.
   4. Percentage fee
      a. It can be a percentage of the sales price or MLS (mulitple listing service) co-op fee.
      b. Creates a disincentive for buyer's broker to get a lower price for buyer.

VII. Termination of listings or buyer agency agreements

A. Operation of law
   1. Contracting with an individual while she or he is in a state of diminished capacity
   2. Death or incapacity of either party
   3. Destruction of the property or change in the property use because of an outside force
   4. Bankruptcy of either party, at option of trustee

    B. Acts of the parties

      1. Mutual consent

      2. Completion of the objective

      3. Expiration

      4. Revocation by the principal

      5. Renunciation by the agent

        a. Subject to liability for damages caused by revoking or renouncing the agreement

VIII. Contract for the sale of real estate

    A. Required by the statute of frauds to be in writing to be enforceable.

    B. Sets forth all details of the agreement between the buyer and the seller for the purchase and sale of real estate

    C. When the contract has been prepared and signed by the purchaser, it is an offer to purchase the subject real estate.

    D. An offer becomes accepted when the sellers sign the offer communicated to the buyer and binding acceptance occurs.

    E. More detailed than the deed itself because the contract in effect dictates the contents of the deed and all other terms and conditions of the transaction.

    F. After both the buyer and the seller have executed the sales contract, the buyer acquires the interest in the land, known as *equitable title*.

    G. A "time is of the essence" contract must be performed in the time specified; any party who does not perform on time is guilty of breach of contract.

IX. Earnest money deposits—not required for a legal contract

    A. Generally give evidence of intention to carry out the terms of contract

      1. Usually must be held by the broker in a special trust, or escrow, account

      2. Cannot be commingled, mixed with a broker's operating funds, or converted to a broker's own use

      3. The amount is generally determined by negotiation between the buyer and seller.

      4. A deposit is not legally required to create a valid contract.

X. Options

    A. Contract by which the optionor (owner) gives the optionee (prospective buyer) the right to buy at a fixed price within a stated period of time.

    B. The optionee pays the fee for the option right and assumes no obligation to make any other payment until the optionee decides, within a specified time, to either exercise the option right or allow the option to expire.

XI. Installment contract/contract for deed/land contract

    A. Means of financing a purchase: the buyer gives the seller a nominal down payment and regular periodic payments over a number of years, including interest.

    B. Legal title to real estate remains in the vendor's (seller's) name during the term of contract.

C. The vendee (purchaser) takes possession when the contract is executed.

D. The vendee will not receive the deed to the property until the entire purchase price has been paid.

E. The vendee has the equitable title during the life of the contract.

XII. **Other real estate contracts**

A. Counteroffer—new offer made in response to an offer received; the original offer is, in effect, rejected and cannot be accepted thereafter unless it is revived by the offeror

B. Amendments—licensees in many states are required to fill out amendment forms to change the language in either the listing contract or the offer to purchase.

C. Cancellation agreements—forms used to terminate a transaction; used in some states by a broker to get a written release from both the buyer and the seller to authorize the refund of earnest money

D. Leasing agreement—written or oral contracts between the tenant (lessee) and the landlord (lessor); transfers the right to exclusive possession and the use of the landlord's real property to the lessee for a stated consideration (rent) and for a specified period of time; the statute of frauds requires that the lease for more than one year be in writing to be enforceable

E. Addendum—adds additional terms and conditions to the approved forms, thus incorporating them into the legal document; may or may not require preparation by an attorney

REVIEW LIST

The student should have an understanding of the following types of contracts:

1. Listing contracts
2. Buyer/broker contracts
3. Offers to purchase
4. Counteroffers
5. Amendments
6. Cancellation agreements
7. Leasing agreements
8. Options
9. Addenda

DIAGNOSTIC TEST

1. A contract in which the intentions of the parties are shown by their actions is
   1. an expressed contract.
   2. an implied contract.
   3. an executory contract.
   4. a bilateral contract.

2. Which of the following is NOT an essential element of a contract?
   1. Intent of parties
   2. Legality of object
   3. Offer and acceptance (mutual assent)
   4. Competent parties

3. The lessee in a leasing agreement is the
   1. tenant.
   2. property manager.
   3. landlord.
   4. rental agent.

4. A lease that is signed by a person who is 17 years of age (still a minor) is
   1. unilateral.   3. illegal.
   2. void.   4. voidable.

5. Contracts for sale of real estate must be in writing to be enforceable, according to the
   1. statute of limitations.
   2. parol evidence rule.
   3. statute of frauds.
   4. real estate commission.

6. A broker lists a home for $80,000. The broker brings an offer to the seller for $78,000, which is rejected by the seller. The broker obtains another offer, for $80,000, for the seller. Before he can deliver the offer, however, the offeror withdraws it by calling the broker at the seller's home. There is
   1. an implied contract.
   2. a unilateral contract.
   3. an executory contract.
   4. no contract.

7. You have entered into an option contract with an optionee who has 30 days to exercise his option. Your option could be called a (an)
   1. voidable contract.
   2. unilateral contract.
   3. unenforceable contract.
   4. bilateral contract.

8. Which of the following contracts generally is prohibited or discouraged in many states?
   1. Option
   2. Land contract
   3. Open listing
   4. Net listing

9. You order dinner in a restaurant. You are required to pay for the dinner through what kind of contract?
   1. Bilateral   3. Voidable
   2. Express   4. Implied

10. A broker and a seller have signed an open listing contract. This agreement is an example of
    1. a unilateral contract.
    2. an executed contract.
    3. a bilateral contract.
    4. an unenforceable contract.

11. Which of the following correctly describes an open listing?
    1. The seller may employ any number of brokers.
    2. Only one broker is authorized to act as agent for the seller.
    3. The broker is entitled to a commission regardless of who sells the property.
    4. The broker's commission is based on the excess over the sales price stated in the listing.

12. A salesperson obtains a written offer to purchase a home that she has listed for sale. The seller accepts the offer, and the salesperson promptly telephones the purchaser to notify him of the acceptance. Because the purchaser lives in a nearby town, the salesperson informs him that she will deliver a copy of the contract in three days. The salesperson has an enforceable contract when
    1. the seller signs the acceptance.
    2. the offer to purchase is presented to the seller.
    3. the acceptance is telephoned to the salesperson representing the purchaser.
    4. a copy of the contract is delivered to the purchaser in three days.

13. A contract that has no legal effect because it does not contain all essential requirements of a contract is
    1. voidable.
    2. unenforceable.
    3. void.
    4. canceled.

14. Which of the following might NOT legally terminate a listing with a broker?
    1. Bankruptcy of the client
    2. Insanity of the broker
    3. Inability of the broker to find a buyer within a reasonable amount of time
    4. An economic depression

15. A gave an option on her property for 90 days to B and received a cash consideration of $100. B later assigned the option to C for a valuable consideration. Before expiration of the option, A stated that she no longer wanted to sell the property. Which of the following is correct?
    1. The option is void, for an option cannot be assigned.
    2. The option is not binding on A, for $100 is not sufficient consideration.
    3. C would have a good chance in court to compel A to sell to him, if he exercises the option before its expiration date.
    4. A can refuse to sell, for the consideration paid by C was not in cash.

16. Both the buyer and the seller agree to wait until the broker's exclusive-right-to-sell listing has expired. They then have a third party buy the home. After a short while, the third party conveys ownership to the interested buyer, who was introduced to the owner by the listing broker. In this case,
    1. the broker is not entitled to a commission because the listing expired.
    2. if the listing broker can prove collusion, he can collect full commission.
    3. the broker may sue both the buyer and the seller for the commission.
    4. the broker is entitled to his commission because he performed the task for which he was hired.

17. Procuring cause would not be required for a broker to receive a commission in a(n)
    1. open listing.
    2. exclusive-right-to-sell listing.
    3. net listing.
    4. exclusive agency listing.

18. When a broker sold a property, the sales contract contained the following statement: "Buyer to accept property in an 'as is' condition." Both the seller and the broker knew the plumbing was in a major state of disrepair but did not tell the buyer. Would an action for damages against the broker, based on fraud, be successful?
    1. No. The "as is" provision in the contract is evidence of a meeting of the minds.
    2. No. The contract specifically stated that the property was being sold "as is."
    3. Yes. The duty to disclose a material fact cannot be avoided by an "as is" provision.
    4. Yes. "As is" refers only to exterior defects.

19. A broker brings a seller an offer-to-purchase contract for the listed price of $114,500, with the stipulation that the seller must furnish a title insurance policy to prove marketable title. The seller refuses the offer. The broker
    1. can collect full commission because sellers must always provide title insurance.
    2. can collect one-half of the commission.
    3. can collect nothing.
    4. can collect one-half of the first month's mortgage payment.

20. A seller listed her home with a broker. Shortly thereafter, the seller telephoned the broker and withdrew the exclusive-right-to-sell listing. A week later, she sold the home to her neighbor for a higher price than the price on the listing. In this situation, which of the following is true?
    1. The owner has the right to terminate the listing at any time without being liable for damages.
    2. Under an exclusive right-to-sell listing, the broker is not entitled to damages.
    3. The broker is not entitled to a commission because the seller obtained a better price than she would have received through the broker's efforts.
    4. If the owner withdrew the listing after the broker spent money on it, the owner might be liable to the broker for damages.

21. A salesperson for a broker listed an owner's home under an exclusive-right-to-sell listing contract. Which of the following statements correctly describes this situation?
    1. The listing belongs to the salesperson.
    2. If the principal sells his own house, he will not have to pay a commission.
    3. The listing belongs to the broker.
    4. The listing belongs to both the salesperson and the broker.

22. An owner gives an exclusive-right-to-sell listing to a broker for a six-month period. During the exclusive period, the owner also gives an open listing to another broker who produces a buyer. What is the owner's liability for payment of a commission?
    1. Only one commission must be paid, which both brokers share on a 50/50 basis.
    2. The owner is liable only to the first broker for the payment of a commission.
    3. The owner is liable for payment of a commission to both brokers.
    4. The owner is liable only to the second broker for the payment of a commission.

23. A buyer has contracted with a seller to purchase property. The contract was ratified on January 10. The closing was on March 31. What is the status of the contract on April 1?
    1. Void
    2. Anticipatory
    3. Executed
    4. Executory

24. A listing contract
    1. is a conveyance.
    2. is a contract of employment.
    3. is a unilateral contract.
    4. is terminated on the death of the listing salesperson.

25. A salesperson
    1. may receive a commission directly from a principal.
    2. can carry out activities in his or her own name.
    3. is responsible primarily to the broker under whom she or he is licensed.
    4. may place a blind ad.

ANSWER KEY WITH EXPLANATIONS

1. **(2)** An expressed contract would be oral or written. An executory contract such as an offer to purchase would have to be in writing to be enforceable. An offer to purchase would also be an example of a bilateral contract. (89)

2. **(1)** The intent of the parties is not required for a contract to be valid. (89)

3. **(1)** The landlord is the lessor while the property manager is a general agent. (93)

4. **(4)** A minor may enter into a contract; however, upon reaching majority age the minor may either ratify (accept) or disaffirm (reject) the contract. (90)

5. **(3)** The statute of limitations is the period of time within which one may judicially challenge a contract. The real estate commission is a regulatory body which is responsible for enforcing rather than making the laws of a state. The parol evidence rule provides that oral agreements modifying a written contract will not be admitted to modify or contradict a written contract in a court of law. (92)

6. **(4)** An offer can be withdrawn at any time prior to binding acceptance's occurring. (92)

7. **(2)** An option is a unilateral contract until the optionee chooses to exercise the option right to buy at which time it becomes a bilateral contract. The optionor may not void the contract, which is enforceable by the optionee. (92)

8. **(4)** Options and land contracts are commonly used while the open listing is generally allowed but used rather infrequently. (91)

9. **(4)** There is no formal agreement as there would be in a bilateral contract (offer to purchase) or express contract (listing contract). The ordering of a dinner negates the opportunity to void the contract. (89)

10. **(1)** A bilateral contract would require two promises. An open listing would be enforceable but clearly is not an executed contract as the parties must perform. (89)

11. **(1)** Answer number 4 would be a net listing while number 2 would be an exclusive agency or exclusive right-to-sell listing. The seller in an open listing has the right to sell the property herself without paying the listing broker a commission. (90)

12. **(4)** The contract is not enforceable until binding acceptance occurs, which generally involves the delivery of the signed and accepted contract to the seller. (92)

13. **(3)** A voidable contract is valid but may be disaffirmed depending on the parties involved. An enforceable contract also is valid. (89)

14. **(4)** A listing contract may be terminated by acts of the parties or by operation of law. (91–92)

15. **(3)** The optionor promises to sell and has no right to cancel; the optionee has the choice of exercising the option right. (92)

16. **(2)** The broker's rights would be based on the broker protection clause. (90)

17. **(2)** The open and exclusive agency listings allow the sellers to sell the property personally on their own without owing the broker a commission. (90)

18. **(3)** The broker is required to disclose any known fact that might affect the decision of the buyer. (86)

19. **(3)** The contingency is not consistent with the terms of the listing thus relieving the seller of the obligation to pay a commission to the broker. (92)

20. **(4)** The sellers have the power to terminate but not necessarily the right, which could result in the seller's being liable for damages. (92)

21. **(3)** The salesperson is not a party to the contract. The exclusive right-to-sell provision prevents the seller from being able to avoid paying a commission. (90)

22. **(3)** The first broker is protected under the exclusive right-to-sell provision while the second broker is entitled under procuring cause. (90)

23. **(3)** The closing means that the contract is no longer anticipatory or executory. (89)

24. **(2)** The listing salesperson is not a party to the contract which is enforceable. (90)

25. **(3)** The salesperson works for the broker and may not receive commission from anyone other than the broker for whom he works. Blind ads are prohibited. (77)

CONTRACTS

TEST SCORE

RATING	RANGE	YOUR SCORE	
Good = 80% to 100%	20-25	Total Number	25
Fair = 70% to 79%	18-19	Total Wrong	-
Needs Improvement = Lower than 70%	17 or less	Total Right	

Passing Requirement: 18 or better

Transfer of
Property

OUTLINE OF CONCEPTS TO UNDERSTAND

I.   **Deeds - transfers of title**

A. By descent

1. Every state has a law known as the statue of descent and distribution.
2. When a person dies intestate, the decedent's real estate and personal property pass to her or his heirs according to statute.

B. By will

1. A will takes effect only after the death of the testator; until that time any property can be conveyed by the owner.
2. State laws usually require that on the death of a testator, his or her will must be filed with the court and probated to pass title to the devisees. Although title automatically, upon death, vests in such devisees (will) or distributees (intestate). Title to property may not be in abeyance.

C. By involuntary alienation—transferred without owner's consent

1. Escheat—when a person dies intestate and leaves no heirs or abandons the property, title to her or his real estate passes to the state.
2. Eminent domain—the federal, state, or local government may take the private property for public use through a suit for condemnation; the owner must be given just compensation.
3. To satisfy debts—debt is foreclosed, the property sold, and the proceeds of the sale applied to pay off the debt.
4. Natural forces
    a. Accretion—slow accumulation of soil, rock and so on deposited by the movement of water on the owner's property.
    b. Erosion—gradual tearing away of the land by the action of natural forces.
    c. Avulsion—sudden tearing away of the land by the action of water or earthquake.
    d. Reliction—new land is acquired as water recedes.
5. Adverse possession—actual, visible, hostile, notorious, exclusive, and continuous possession of another's land under a claim of title; periods of time may be tacked on by successive owner/tenants.

D. Voluntary alienation—either gift or sale; to transfer title during his or her lifetime, an owner must use some form of deed or conveyance.

   1. Deeds—written instruments of conveyance from owners (grantors) to the recipients (grantees).
      a. General warranty deed—contains promises and covenants
         1. Provides the greatest protection of any deed.
         2. Covenant of seisin - the grantor has the title and possession and has the right to convey.
         3. Covenant against encumbrances - the grantor warrants that the property is free from any liens or encumbrances except those specifically stated in the deed.
         4. Covenant of quiet enjoyment—the grantor guarantees that the title is good against a third party.
         5. Covenant of further assurance—the grantor promises to obtain and deliver any instrument required to make the title good against third parties.
         6. Covenant of warranty forever—the grantor guarantees that if the title fails, the grantee will be compensated for the loss sustained.
      b. Special warranty deeds—the grantor warrants only that the property was not encumbered during the time that the title was held, except as noted in the deed.
      c. Bargain and sale deed—contains only an implied warranty that the grantor holds the title was held and possession of the property. The grantor may choose to add warranties to the deed making it similar to a special warranty deed.
      d. Quitclaim deed—contains warranties and conveys only such interest, if any, that the grantor may have when the deed is delivered but conveys that interest completely; often used to cure a defect in title.

E. Types of proof of title

   1. Abstract of title and lawyer's opinion.
      a. Abstract of title—condensed history of all instruments on record affecting the title to the property.
      b. Attorney's opinion of title to the property—the buyer's attorney examines the abstract for flaws and prepares a written opinion of the condition of ownership.
   2. Torrens system
      a. A certificate of title accompanied by the owner's signature is filed with the registrar's office and used to verify future transfers.
      b. Title to Torrens—registered property never can be acquired through adverse possession.
   3. Certificate of title—prepared by an attorney without preparation of an abstract; attorney provides an opinion on the ownership of title; is not a title insurance policy.

F. Title insurance

   1. Protects insured against loss resulting from certain defects in the title, such as a forgery or defect in the public record, other than those exceptions listed in the policy.

    2. Most standard coverage policies will not cover situations arising from questions of survey, defects of which the policyholder has knowledge, or unrecorded documents.

    3. Extended coverage policies will cover additional risks that may be discovered only by inspection of the property, including unrecorded rights of persons in possession, or by examination of an accurate survey.

    4. It is an indemnify contract.

II. Escrow process

A. Means by which the parties to a contract carry out the terms of their agreement, in some states.

B. Parties appoint a third party to act as an escrowee, or escrow agent.

C. In the sale of real estate, the seller's deed and the buyer's money are deposited with an escrow agent under an escrow agreement that sets forth conditions to be met before the sale will be consummated.

D. The escrow agent holds the deed and when the title conditions and other requirements of the escrow agreement have been met, records the deed, the title passes, and the sale is complete.

III. Title insurance/abstracts

A. Requirements for a valid conveyance

    1. Grantor—must have legal existence, be of legal age, and be legally competent to convey the title.

    2. Grantee—must be named in the deed in such a way that he or she can be identified.

    3. Consideration—must be acknowledged by the grantor; in most states, consideration must be stated in dollars.

    4. Granting clause—must contain words that state the grantor's intention to convey the property.

    5. Habendum clause—follows granting clause when necessary to define the terms of ownership to be enjoyed by grantee.

    6. Description of real estate—must use a legal description that is understood by all parties.

    7. Signature of grantor—must be signed by all the grantors named in the deed; a seal sometimes is required.

    8. Acknowledgment—provides evidence that the signature is voluntary and genuine; not essential to the validity of the deed unless required by state statutes.

    9. Delivery and acceptance—actual delivery of the deed by the grantor and either actual or implied acceptance by the grantee.

    10. Exceptions and reservations ("subject-to" clauses)—should specifically note encumbrances, reservations, or limitations that affect the title being conveyed, such as liens, easements, and restrictions.

B. Recording of deeds and conveyance of title

    1. The title generally passes to the grantee when the executed deed is delivered and accepted.

    2. Exceptions:
       a. Torrens property—the title transfer when deed has been examined and accepted for registration.
       b. Closing in escrow—the date of delivery is generally the date that it was deposited with the escrow agent; if the escrow does not close, no title passes.
    3. Recording a deed or taking possession of a property gives constructive notice to the world that one has rights in the property.
    4. An unrecorded deed is valid between the parties to a transaction.

IV. **Legal versus equitable title (broker only)**

  A. Equitable conversion

    1. A doctrine of law that gives title to property to a buyer under an executory contract in certain situations before legal title has been transferred to the buyer.
    2. Upon creation of binding offer to purchase, the seller holds legal title for the buyer, who has equitable title.
    3. The seller holds legal title as security for the purchase price.
    4. Risk of loss also becomes buyer's responsibility; this applies in some states.
    5. Many states have adopted the Uniform Vendor and Purchaser Risk Act, which states that the risk of loss shifts to the buyer only if possession or legal title has been transferred to the buyer. The contract may and usually does specify who assumes the risk of loss.

  B. Equitable title

    1. Buyer's ownership interest in real property, which occurs when an offer to purchase becomes binding upon the parties
    2. Interest may be conveyed by deed, will, etc.
    3. Interest converts to legal title upon delivery and acceptance of deed.

V. **Real Estate Settlement Procedures Act (RESPA)**

  A. Created to ensure that the buyer and seller have knowledge of all the settlement costs before closing.

  B. Requirements

    1. Lenders must give a copy of the special information booklet, *Settlement Costs and You*, to each loan applicant.
    2. The borrowers must be provided with a good-faith estimate of the settlement costs by the lenders no later than three business days after the receipt of the loan application.
    3. The loan closing expenses must be prepared on a Uniform Settlement Statement (HUD Form 1).
    4. RESPA explicitly prohibits the payment of kickbacks and prohibits referral fees when no services are actually rendered.

  C. RESPA regulations apply only to transactions involving new first-mortgage referral loans for one-family to four-family dwellings generally financed by the federally related mortgage loan.

VI. **Tax benefits**

  A. Capital gains

1. As of 1997, a married couple may exclude $500,000 from capital gains tax for profits on the sale of a principal residence if they file jointly.
2. Homeowners who file as individuals are entitled to a $250,000 exclusion.
3. There is no limit on the number of times homeowners may take advantage of this benefit, as long as the homeowners have occupied the property as their residence for at least two of the past five years.
4. A 1998 law lowers the required holding period for a non-corporate taxpayer from 18 to 12 months for long term capital gain.

B. Penalty-free withdrawals from IRAs

1. People buying homes for the first time may make withdrawals from their tax-deferred individual retirement funds (IRAs) for down payments on their homes without paying a penalty.
2. The withdrawals are limited to $10,000.

C. Home-related expenses that are tax deductible for the owners

1. Some loan origination fees
2. Interest paid on mortgages on first and second homes
3. Real estate taxes but not penalties for late payment
4. Discount points on loans
5. Prepayment penalties on loans

VII. Foreign Investment and Real Property Tax Act (IRC Section 1445)

A. A federal law aimed at ensuring that nonresident aliens and foreign corporations pay U.S. income tax based on gains from the disposition of U.S. real property interest

1. On real property located in the United States
2. In any domestic corporation that was a U.S. real property holding corporation during the period that the taxpayer held the interest after June 8, 1980, or at any time during the five-year period ending on the date of the disposition of the property, if earlier

B. Generally, transferee in any U.S. real property interest must withhold a tax equal to 10 percent of the amount realized by the foreign transferor on the disposition of the property, if actual calculation of tax is not previously approved by I.R.S.

C. If a transferor's or transferee's agent fails to furnish the notice required, the agent—for example, a broker—must withhold in the same manner as would be required of the transferee, except that the agent's liability is limited to the amount of compensation that he or she derives from the transaction.

D. A buyer or other transferee of a U.S. real property interest and any corporation, partnership, or fiduciary required to withhold tax must file an IRS Form 8288 to report and transmit the amount withheld.

E. Buyers or other transferees of a U.S. real property interest also must file an IRS Form 8288-A to show the amount withheld.

F. Generally, the amount required to be withheld with respect to any disposition of a U.S. real property interest cannot exceed the amount of the transferor's maximum tax liability.

G. Brokers involved in listing or selling U.S. real property interest for nonresident aliens or foreign corporations should contact the IRS to establish the appropriate procedures.

VIII.   IRS regulations

A. Independent Contractor and Employee—under the "qualified real estate agent" category in the Internal Revenue Code, meeting three requirements can establish independent-contractor status.

1. The individual must have a current real estate license.
2. The individual must have a written contract with the broker that contains the following clause: "The salesperson will not be treated as an employee with respect to the services performed by such salesperson as a real estate agent for federal tax purposes."
3. Ninety percent or more of the individual's income as a licensee must be based on sales production, not on the number of hours worked.
4. The broker should have a standardized agreement drafted or reviewed by an attorney.

B. 1099 Forms

1. IRS rules require closing agents to report details of closing to the IRS using IRS Form 1099 S.
2. Reports must be submitted for sales or exchanges of residences with four or fewer units.
3. Commissions paid to salespeople by brokers also must be reported on IRS Form 1099 MISC.

C. Declarations of value

1. Documents of statements of value that accompany every deed or contract to be recorded in the registrar of deeds office
2. Statements of value are used by local and state tax officials for assessment purposes and for determining conveyance tax owed to state or municipality.

D. Imputed interest

1. The IRS will impute, or assign interest at a prescribed rate, computed monthly, on an installment contract that fails to include an interest rate or states an unreasonably low rate.
2. Although no interest is paid, buyers may deduct for tax purposes imputed interest per annum on unpaid balances.
3. Rate for determining whether interest should be imputed and the amount of interest that should be imputed is based on the applicable federal rate (AFR).
4. AFR is one of three rates, depending on whether the debt instrument is:
   a. Short term—not more that three years
   b. Midterm—more than three years but not more than nine years
   c. Long term—more than nine years
5. IRS issues alternative AFRs on a monthly basis.
6. Installment sales of less than $3,000 are not covered by the imputed-interest law.

E. 1031 tax-deferred exchange
   1. Under section 1031 of the IRC real estate investors can defer taxation of capital gains by making a property exchange.
   2. A property owner may exchange his or her property for another property and have tax liability on the sale only if additional capital or property is received.
   3. Tax on an exchange is deferred rather than eliminated.
   4. Properties involved in exchange must be of like kind.
      a. Like kind refers to any real property to be held for income purposes or investment; excludes dealer property or residences.
   5. Additional capital or personal property included in a transaction to even out the exchange is considered boot; the party receiving boot is taxed at the time of the exchange.

REVIEW LIST

Students should have an understanding of the following areas of transfer of property:

1. Deeds

2. Escrow process

3. Title insurance

4. Tax aspects

5. Legal vs. equitable title (Broker only)

6. Special processes

DIAGNOSTIC TEST

1. The deed that provides the buyer the greatest protection is the
   1. bargain and sale deed.
   2. warranty deed.
   3. quitclaim deed.
   4. specialty warranty deed.

2. A warranty deed generally will transfer title to the grantee when it is
   1. acknowledged.
   2. signed by the grantee.
   3. signed by the grantor.
   4. delivered and accepted.

3. Which of the following would be an example of voluntary alienation?
   1. Sale
   2. Eminent domain
   3. Escheat
   4. Adverse possession

4. A grantee has received an executed, notarized deed. The grantee takes possession of the property but does not record the deed. The conveyance is
   1. invalid between the parties and valid as to third parties with constructive notice.
   2. valid as between the parties and valid as to the subsequent recorded interests.
   3. valid as between the parties and invalid as to subsequent recorded interests without notice.
   4. invalid as between the parties.

5. Which of the following statements does NOT correctly describe a properly executed will?
   1. It takes effect only after the death of the devisee.
   2. It specifies who will inherit the owner's property.
   3. It must conform to the state statute.
   4. It cannot supersede state laws of dower and curtesy.

6. Generally, title insurance coverage extends to
   1. defects known to the buyer.
   2. liens listed in the policy.
   3. defects listed in the policy.
   4. defect not found in public record.

7. A deed must be signed by the
   1. grantor.   3. grantee.
   2. vendee.   4. vendor.

8. What do the following situations have in common?
   I. A man's property is taken by the city and used for a new highway.
   II. A woman's land gradually is wearing away because of wind.
   III. A developer's property is sold at a foreclosure sale.
   1. They will require the use of a warranty deed to transfer title.
   2. They are all examples of voluntary alienation of title.
   3. They are all examples of eminent domain.
   4. They are all examples of involuntary alienation.

9. *A* and *B* have entered into a binding offer to purchase. *B* will buy *A*'s house. Which of the following statements correctly describes the status of the transaction?
   1. *A* will have equitable title until closing.
   2. *B* will have legal title when the offer to purchase becomes binding on both parties.
   3. *A* will have legal title until the offer becomes binding, at which time *A* will hold equitable title.
   4. *A* will hold legal title until closing and *B* will hold equitable title until closing.

10. Which of the following statements does NOT correctly describe equitable title?
    1. Upon creation of a binding offer to purchase, buyer holds equitable title.
    2. Equitable title converts to legal title upon delivery and acceptance of the deed.
    3. It may be conveyed by deed.
    4. It may not be conveyed by will.

11. The need for a loan closing to be prepared on a Uniform Settlement Statement is a requirement of
    1. Regulation Z.
    2. the federal fair housing laws.
    3. Government National Mortgage Association (Ginnie Mae) — (GNMA).
    4. RESPA.

12. The requirement that a lender give each loan applicant a copy of *Settlement Costs and You* is created under
    1. Federal Home Loan Mortgage Corporation (Freddie Mac) (FMLMC).
    2. Federal Housing Administration (FHA).
    3. RESPA.
    4. Regulation Z.

13. Which of the following is NOT a requirement for establishing independent-contractor status for a salesperson?
    1. The individual must have a current real estate license.
    2. Ninety percent or more of the individual's income as a licensee must be based on sales production.
    3. The individual's income must be based on the number of hours worked.
    4. The individual must not be included in company hospitalization and retirement program.

14. The person conducting the closing must report details on closing to the IRS on
    1. IRS form 1099.
    2. IRS form 1099 S,
    3. IRS form 1099 MISC.
    4. IRS form 1099 R.

15. Section 1031 of the Internal Revenue Code allows real estate investors to do which of the following when making a property exchange?
    1. Avoid the capital-gains tax only if the exchange is of like kind.
    2. Phase out the capital-gains tax.
    3. Defer the capital-gains tax.
    4. Avoid the capital-gains tax even if the exchange is not of like kind.

ANSWER KEY WITH EXPLANATIONS

1. **(2)** The quitclaim deed provides the least protection. (100)
2. **(4)** The grantee does not sign the deed; nevertheless, the grantee must be named in the deed. (101)
3. **(1)** Eminent domain is the right of the government to take private property for public use provided just compensation is paid to the land owner. Escheat applies when a person dies without a will and without heirs capable of inheriting. Adverse possession is the open and notorious use of another's land under a claim of title. (100)
4. **(3)** The grantee must give constructive notice that he has an interest in the property. Constructive notice is given by recording the deed in the registrar of deeds office or occupying the property. (102)
5. **(1)** Devise is a gift of real property by will. Deviser is the donor of the will and the devisee is the recipient of the will. (99)

6. **(4)** Title insurance does not cover liens or defects listed in the policy. (100)

7. **(1)** The vendor is the seller in a land contract while the vendee is the buyer. The grantee must be identified in the deed but does not have to sign it. (101)

8. **(4)** Selling or gifting property are examples of voluntary alienation. (99–100)

9. **(4)** *B* will have equitable title until closing, after which *B* will have legal title. (102)

10. **(4)** The seller will have legal title and the buyer will have equitable title until the closing. (102)

11. **(4)** Regulation Z requires disclosure of cost in credit transactions. The Federal Fair Housing laws prohibit discrimination against groups of people identified as protected classes. GNMA functions in the secondary mortgage market. (102)

12. **(3)** Freddie Mac buys and sells mortgages in the secondary mortgage market. The FHA provides public mortgage insurance for home loans. Regulation Z requires credit cost disclosure and provides for right of recession in certain types of credit transactions under certain conditions. (102)

13. **(3)** One of the three IRS requirements for independent contractor status is that 90 percent or more of the individual's income as a licensee must be based on sales production, not on the number of hours worked. (104)

14. **(2)** IRS rules also require brokers to report commissions paid to salespeople on IRS Form 1099 MISC. (104)

15. **(3)** Section 1031 of the IRC does not allow real estate investors to either avoid or phase out the capital gains tax; it only allows for the deferring of the tax. (105)

TRANSFER OF PROPERTY

TEST SCORE

RATING	RANGE	YOUR SCORE	
Good = 80% to 100%	12-15	Total Number	15
Fair = 70% to 79%	10-11	Total Wrong	-
Needs Improvement = Lower than 70%	9 or less	Total Right	

Passing Requirement: 10 or better

PART 12

Practice of Real Estate

OUTLINE OF CONCEPTS TO UNDERSTAND

I. **Federal Fair Housing Laws**

A. Civil Rights Act of 1866—prohibits racial discrimination in the buying, renting, selling, holding, or conveying of real and personal property

B. Federal Fair Housing Act of 1968—provides that it is unlawful to discriminate on the basis of race, color, religion, or national origin when selling or leasing residential property

1. In 1974, the Housing and Community Development Act added sex.

C. An amendment to the federal fair housing law went into effect in March 1989 adding handicap and familial status to the list of protected classes and giving the U.S. Department of Housing and Urban Development (HUD) more enforcement authority.

1. The new amendment defines familial status as one or more individuals who have not reached the age of 18 being domiciled with a parent or another person who has or is seeking legal custody.
   a. A person who is pregnant also is included in the definition of *familial status.*
   b. All properties must be made available under the same terms and conditions as available to all other persons unless a property meets the standards for exemption as "housing for older persons."

2. The new amendment defines disability as a physical or mental impairment that substantially limits one or more of a person's major life activities.
   a. A definition of *disability* does not include the current illegal use of or addiction to a controlled substance.
   b. Persons who have AIDS also are protected under the handicap classification as are persons in an addiction recovery program.
   c. Persons renting a dwelling are required to permit handicapped persons to make modifications of existing premises at their own expense, if these modifications are necessary to afford full enjoyment of the premises.
   d. In a rental-property situation, a landlord may condition the agreement to allow modifications upon an agreement to restore the interior of the premises to the pre-modification condition.

    e. There are a number of accessibility and usability requirements covering certain types of newly constructed residential buildings that must be met under federal law; access is required for common-use and public areas of the building as well as adaptive and accessible design for the interior of the dwelling units.

    f. A licensee may not disclose to a seller or landlord that a prospective buyer or tenant is a member of a protected class.

    g. Alcoholics and drug addicts who have been diagnosed, treated, and are not currently addicted are protected under the Federal Fair Housing Law; they are considered to have a disability. However, convicted drug dealers are not covered under any condition.

    h. People diagnosed as mentally ill are also protected under the federal laws.

        1. Mentally ill people do not have to be currently receiving treatment to be protected under the law.

        2. If a mentally ill tenant is behaving inappropriately and reasonable action such as counseling has not solved the problem, the tenant may be evicted. In other words, a landlord does not have to tolerate such behavior by a mentally ill tenant.

3. Types of illegal activity under familial status include

    a. Charging higher security deposits

    b. Segregating families within buildings

    c. Segregating families in certain buildings

    d. Maintaining "adults-only" complexes that do not constitute housing for older adults, which will be hereinafter defined shortly

4. Types of illegal activity under handicapped include

    a. Refusal to permit reasonable modifications that are necessary for the full enjoyment at the renter's expense

    b. Refusal to make reasonable accommodations in rules, policies, practices, or services

    c. Failure to design and construct for first occupancy, as of March 1991, an accessible route into and through a dwelling

5. The 1988 amendments also provide that certain properties may be restricted for occupancy by the elderly.

    a. The amendments provide an exemption from the familial-status protection for housing intended for or occupied solely by persons 62 years of age or older or housing intended for or occupied by at least one person 55 years of age or older per unit.

    b. Properties complying with the "55-or-older" exemption must provide significant facilities and services to meet the physical and social needs of older persons, and at least 80 percent of the units must be occupied by individuals who are 55 years of age or older.

    c. Exemption properties also must publish policies and procedures that demonstrate the intent to provide housing for these individuals.

6. The 1988 amendments do not require that housing be made available to

    a. Individuals whose tenancy would constitute a direct threat to the health or safety of other individuals or that would result in substantial physical damage to the property of others

    b. Individuals who have been convicted of the illegal manufacture or distribution of controlled substances

7. The 1988 amendments also made significant changes to the enforcement mechanisms under the Fair Housing Act of 1968, including
   a. Authorizing administrative law judges to award both economic and non-economic damages, injunctive relief, and reasonable attorney fees and to impose civil penalties against violators of the act
   b. Expanding the statute of limitations for initiating administrative proceedings from 180 days to one year after the alleged discriminatory housing practice
   c. Authorizing administrative law judges within HUD to hold contested case hearings
   d. Requiring HUD to proceed with cases on behalf of any person alleging that she or he has been the victim of housing discrimination, regardless of whether the alleged victim provides his or her own legal counsel
8. Remedies under the new amendments include
   a. A civil penalty against the respondent, not exceeding $10,000 for the first offense
   b. A penalty not exceeding $25,000, if another offense was committed within the past five years
   c. A penalty not exceeding $50,000, if two or more discriminatory practices have been found in the past seven years
   d. An order for "appropriate" relief that may include actual damages, injunctive relief, and "other equitable relief"
   e. A recommendation for disciplinary action against a named respondent whose licensure by a governmental agency is related to the complaint (including license suspension or revocation)
9. Other prohibited discriminatory acts include
   a. Refusing to sell, rent, or negotiate with any person as a means of discrimination
   b. Changing terms for different individuals as a means of discrimination
   c. Making discriminatory advertising statements
   d. Representing that a property is unavailable as a means of discrimination
   e. Blockbusting—making a profit by inducing owners to sell because of the prospective entry of minorities into the neighborhood
   f. Redlining—discriminatory denial of loans or insurance to people in selected areas, regardless of their qualifications
   g. Steering—leading prospective home buyers to specific areas or avoiding specific areas either to maintain or to change the character of an area
   h. Denying membership in a multiple-listing service (MLS) or related groups as a means of discrimination
10. Exemptions from the law
    a. Sale or rental of a single-family home if the home is owned by a person who does not own more than three such homes at one time and if certain conditions exist
       1. A broker is not used.
       2. Discriminatory advertising is not used.
       3. If the owner is not currently living in the home or was not the most recent occupant, only one such exempt sale has been made within any two-year period.
    b. Rental, if rooms or units are in an owner-occupied one-family to four-family dwelling

      c. Dwelling units owned by religious organizations may be restricted to persons of the same religion if membership is not restricted on the basis of race, color, sex (or gender), national origin, disability. or familial status.

      d. Lodgings of a private club may be restricted to members as long as the lodgings are not operated commercially.

D. Equal Housing Poster—the 1974 amendment to the 1968 Federal Fair Housing Act requires that the Equal Housing Opportunity logo (poster) be posted with the agent's license.

E. Federal Equal Credit Opportunity Act—prohibits discrimination against credit applicants on the basis of race, color, religion, national origin, sex, marital status, age (if the applicant is of legal age), or dependency on public assistance; it requires that all rejected credit applicants be informed, in writing, of the reasons for credit denial within 30 days.

II. Americans with Disabilities Act (ADA)

A. This 1990 law affects real estate licensees because it addresses the rights of individuals with disabilities in employment and public accommodations.

B. The ADA provides for the employment of qualified job applicants regardless of their disabilities.

C. Any employer with 15 or more employees as of July 26, 1994, must adopt non-discriminatory employment procedures and make reasonable accommodations to enable an individual with a disability to perform in her or his employment.

D. The ADA (Title III) states that individuals with disabilities have the right to full and equal access to businesses and public services; thus, building owners and managers must be sure that obstacles restricting those rights are eliminated.

E. The ADA also provides comprehensive guidance for making public facilities accessible.

F. The law seeks to protect property owners from incurring burdensome expense to extensively retrofit an existing building by recommending reasonable achievable accommodations that will accomplish the purpose of providing access to the facility and services.

G. Because it costs less to incorporate accessible features in the design than to retrofit, new construction, including remodeling, must meet higher standards, being readily accessible and usable.

H. Types of alterations that might be made to public facilities and services include

    1. Attaching grab bars to a restroom stall
    2. Providing automatic-entry doors
    3. Adjusting the height of a pay telephone to make it accessible to a person in a wheelchair
    4. Converting information on real estate listings to large print or audio format

I. The ADA provides for enforcement by allowing several remedies for a person who is discriminated against, including

    1. A temporary or permanent injunction
    2. The court may grant any equitable relief that the court considers appropriate.

3. A civil penalty of up to $50,000 may be assessed for a first violation of the law, and a penalty of up to $100,000 may be assessed for any subsequent violation.

III. Truth-in-Lending Law

A. Regulation Z

1. Disclosure requirements
   a. Requires disclosure of cost in credit transactions
   b. Customer has the right to rescind in some types of credit transactions under certain conditions, for example, a second mortgage
2. Coverage of Regulation Z
   a. Loans to individuals covered for all real estate credit transactions for personal, family and household purposes, regardless of the amount involved
   b. Loans to individuals covered for non-real estate credit transactions for personal, family, and household purposes up to $25,000
3. Agreements not covered
   a. Personal property credit transactions for amounts of more than $25,000
   b. Real estate purchase agreements
   c. Business or commercial loans
   d. Loans with four or fewer installments
   e. Loans made without interest charges
   f. Loans to government agencies
   g. Assumptions with no change in terms
   h. Agricultural loans for amounts of more than $25,000
4. Requirements of Regulation Z regarding finance charges
   a. All finance charges as well as the true annual interest rate must be disclosed to the customer before the transaction is completed.
   b. Finance charges must include interest, loan fees, points, service charges, finder's fees, credit fees, and property and credit insurance.
   c. The finance charge must be stated as the Annual Percentage Rate (APR).
5. Requirements of Regulation Z regarding liens on residences
   a. A "cooling off" period is required when liens will be placed on a principal residence; the borrower has the right to rescind the transaction up to midnight of the third business day following the transaction or until delivery of the disclosure statement, whichever is later.
   b. The right to rescind does not apply to loans to finance the purchase or initial construction of a house.
6. Advertising
   a. Regulation Z does not require brokers to advertise credit terms; if lenders advertise some credit details; however, they must fully disclose the terms.
   b. Specific credit terms (trigger terms) may not be advertised unless the ad includes all of the information below in C.
   c. Full disclosure of terms
      1. Amount of down payment
      2. Amount of loan or cash price
      3. Finance charges as annual percentage rate
      4. Number, amount, and due dates of payments

5. Total of all payments except where advertisement relates to first mortgage

7. Regulation Z is administered by the Federal Trade Commission (FTC) and promulgated by the Federal Reserve System (FRS).

8. Penalties for noncompliance

   a. Violation of an administration order enforcing Regulation Z is $10,000 for each day the violation continues.

   b. Engaging in an unfair or deceptive practice may result in the imposition of a fine of up to $10,000.

   c. A creditor may be liable to a consumer for twice the amount of the finance charge, from a minimum of $100 to a maximum of $1,000, plus court costs, attorney's fees, and any actual damages.

   d. Willful violation constitutes a misdemeanor and is punishable by a fine of up to $5,000 or one year's imprisonment or both.

B. Agent Supervision (See Part 15 on Brokerage Management)

REVIEW LIST

The student should have an understanding of the following areas of federal laws and regulations:

1. Compliance with federal fair-housing laws

2. Americans with Disabilities Act

3. Truth-in-Lending Law (Regulation Z)

DIAGNOSTIC TEST

1. You are receiving a mortgage from your local bank. Regulation Z requires your bank to disclose
   1. your right to rescind within three business days.
   2. the amount of your closing costs.
   3. the annual percentage rate.
   4. penalties to the bank if they do not comply with the laws.

2. The federal fair housing laws prohibit discrimination on the basis of
   1. sexual orientation.
   2. political beliefs.
   3. marital status.
   4. sex.

3. Persuading someone to sell by telling her or him that minorities are moving into the neighborhood is illegal and is called
   1. redlining.
   2. blockbusting.
   3. testing.
   4. steering.

4. Which of the following is exempted from the federal fair housing laws?
   1. Rental of rooms in an owner-occupied, five-family dwelling
   2. Rental of an owner-occupied, five-family dwelling
   3. Rental of a single-family home when a broker is used
   4. Lodgings of a private club when the lodgings are not operated commercially

5. The practice of channeling potential buyers of one race into one area and potential buyers of another race into another area is known as
   1. canvassing.
   2. blockbusting.
   3. redlining.
   4. steering.

6. A real estate broker may
   1. refuse to rent to a qualified minority person.
   2. solicit listings in a minority neighborhood.
   3. refuse to negotiate with a minority person.
   4. change the terms of sale for a minority person.

7. The federal fair housing laws prohibit which of the following types of private housing?
   1. A Lutheran organization giving preference to its members in renting
   2. A Norwegian advertising his house for "Norwegians only"
   3. The Elks Club operating a rooming house on a nonprofit basis
   4. A Masonic Lodge operating a rooming house when the lodgings are not operated commercially

8. Which of the following categories is NOT protected against discrimination under the federal fair housing laws?
   1. Religion
   2. Parental status
   3. Disabled status
   4. Lawful source of income

9. The denial of a loan by a lender would NOT be a violation of federal fair housing laws if it were based on
   1. lack of income.   3. age.
   2. sex.   4. marital status.

10. Which of the following laws provides comprehensive guidance for making public facilities accessible?
    1. RESPA
    2. Regulation Z
    3. Federal fair housing laws
    4. Americans with Disabilities Act (ADA)

11. Which of the following activities would be legal under the familial status category of the federal fair housing laws?
    1. Charging higher rents for people with pets
    2. Charging higher security deposits for families with children
    3. Segregating families within buildings
    4. Segregating families in certain buildings

12. Which of the following agreements would be covered by Regulation Z?
    1. A personal property credit transaction for $30,000
    2. A commercial loan
    3. An agricultural loan for $15,000
    4. A loan to an individual for a personal property credit transaction for $20,000

13. Which of the following finance charges would NOT be used by a bank to calculate the annual percentage rate for disclosure to the borrower?
    1. Loan fees
    2. Credit fees
    3. Home inspection fees
    4. Service charges

14. "Trigger terms" relates to
    1. ADA
    2. the Federal Fair Housing Law
    3. RESPA
    4. Regulation Z

15. The right of recession provided by Regulation Z is for a time period of
    1. two business days following the transaction or until delivery of the disclosure statement, whichever is later.
    2. three business days following the transaction or until delivery of the disclosure statement, whichever is later.
    3. four business days following the transaction or until delivery of the disclosure statement, whichever is later.
    4. five business days following the transaction or until delivery of the disclosure statement, whichever is later.

16. The Americans with Disabilities Act became law in
    1. 1968.   3. 1990.
    2. 1989.   4. 1994.

17. Converting information on a real estate listing to large print or audio format would be a response to the
    1. Federal Fair Housing law.
    2. Americans with Disabilities Act.
    3. Regulation Z.
    4. RESPA.

18. The Americans with Disabilities Act (ADA) would NOT require which of the following alterations to be made to public facilities and services?
    1. Attaching grab bars to a rest-room stall
    2. Providing automatic entry doors
    3. Providing an automatic sprinkler system
    4. Converting real estate listing information to large print or audio format.

19. Which of the following rental practices would be legal under the Federal Fair Housing Law?
    1. A property manager discloses to the landlord that a prospective tenant is a minority
    2. A property manager charges a mother and her six-year-old son a higher security deposit than another woman with no children
    3. A rental agent refuses to rent an apartment to a person who is a convicted drug dealer
    4. A property manager refuses to rent to a blind man because he has a life support animal.

20. The Civil Rights Act of 1866 prohibits racial discrimination in housing on the basis of
    1. religion.   3. sex.
    2. race.   4. handicap.

21. Which of the following would not be a protected class with the Federal Equal Credit Opportunity Act?
    1. Marital status
    2. Age
    3. Sexual orientation
    4. Dependency on public assistance

22. Disclosure of cost in a credit transaction is required by
    1. RESPA.
    2. Regulation Z.
    3. the Federal Equal Credit Opportunity Act.
    4. the Federal Fair Housing Law.

23. According to the Federal Equal Credit Opportunity Act, a rejected credit application must be informed, in writing, of the reason for credit denial within
    1. 3 days.   3. 30 days.
    2. 10 days.   4. 90 days.

24. A second violation of the Americans with Disabilities act can result in a civil penalty of up to
    1. $10,000.   3. $50,000.
    2. $25,000.   4. $100,000.

25. Regulation Z is administered by the
    1. Federal Trade Commission.
    2. Department of Housing and Urban Development.
    3. Federal Reserve System.
    4. Federal Housing Administration.

ANSWER KEY WITH EXPLANATIONS

1. **(3)** Kickbacks or referral fees are prohibited when no services are actually performed. (113)
2. **(4)** Some states and local governments prohibit discrimination on the basis of sexual orientation, political beliefs, and marital status. (109)
3. **(2)** Redlining is denying loans or insurance to people in selected neighborhoods regardless of their qualifications. Testing is done to enforce the law, and steering restricts freedom of choice. (111)
4. **(4)** The exemption applies to up to four units of owner-occupied rental housing. (111–112)
5. **(4)** Canvassing involves personal solicitation of opinions or sentiments which is generally legal. Blockbusting and redlining were discussed above. (111)
6. **(2)** Discrimination is treating people differently when they are members of a protected class. (109)
7. **(2)** Religious organizations and private clubs may discriminate under certain circumstances. An individual homeowner must comply with certain conditions to be exempt from the Federal Fair Housing Law. (112)
8. **(4)** Nevertheless, lawful source of income is a protected class in some states. The Federal Equal Credit Opportunity Act also protects borrowers in a similar manner. (109)
9. **(1).** Lack of income is an acceptable reason for denying a loan provided all lawful sources of income are considered as discussed above. (109)

10. **(4)** Regulation Z is the Truth-In-Lending Law while Ginnie Mae functions in the secondary mortgage market. Federal Fair Housing Law does not deal with accessibility to public facilities. (112)

11. **(1)** Since pets are not a protected class, landlords may charge higher rents for renters with pets. (109)

12. **(4)** A loan to an individual for a personal property credit transaction for more than $25,000 would be covered by Regulation Z. (113)

13. **(3)** Home inspection fees are not related to the finance charges. (113)

14. **(4)** Brokers advertising credit terms must fully disclose terms of credit if they use "trigger terms." (113)

15. **(2)** It is important to emphasize that the right of recession does not apply to loans to finance the purchase or initial construction of a house. (113)

16. **(3)** Moreover, an amendment to the Federal Fair Housing law to add handicapped and familial status as protected classes became effective in 1989. (112)

17. **(2)** The Federal Fair Housing law includes handicapped as a protected class, but the specific measures are identified in the ADA. Regulation Z requires disclosure of cost in a credit transaction. RESPA is aimed at protecting consumers from abusive lending practices. (112)

18. **(3)** The fire codes would require the providing of an automatic sprinkler system. (112)

19. **(3)** Convicted drug dealers are never protected under the Federal Fair Housing Law. (110)

20. **(2)** The Civil Rights Act of 1866 makes clear that there is no situation in which racial discrimination may be practiced. For example, the Federal Fair Housing law provides for certain exceptions. However, there are no exceptions involving race and no exceptions apply when a real estate licensee is involved in a transaction. (109)

21. **(3)** Sexual orientation is a protected class in nine states; however, it is not protected under federal housing or lending laws. (109)

22. **(2)** RESPA provides consumer protection with regard to closing procedures and costs. The Federal Equal Credit Opportunity Act prohibits credit providers from discriminating against members of selected, protected classes. The Federal Fair Housing law prohibits discrimination in the sale or rental of housing. (113)

23. **(3)** The Federal Equal Credit Opportunity Act also states that a borrower is entitled to a copy of the appraisal report, paid by the borrowers. (112)

24. **(4)** A penalty of up to $100,000 may be assessed for any subsequent violation of the Americans With Disabilities Act. (112)

25. **(1)** Regulation Z is promulgated by the Federal Reserve System. (114)

PRACTICE OF REAL ESTATE

TEST SCORE

RATING	RANGE	YOUR SCORE	
Good = 80% to 100%	20-25	Total Number	25
Fair = 70% to 79%	18-19	Total Wrong	- _____
Needs Improvement = Lower than 70%	17 or less	Total Right	

Passing Requirement: 18 or better

PART 13

Real Estate Mathematics Review

This review is designed to familiarize you with some basic mathematical formulas that are used most frequently in the computations required on state licensing examinations. These same computations also are important in day-to-day real estate transactions. If you think you need additional help in working these problems, you may want to order a copy of *Mastering Real Estate Mathematics,* 6th edition, by Ventolo, Tamper, and Allaway (Chicago: Real Estate Education Company, 1995).

PERCENTAGES

Many real estate computations are based on the calculations of percentages. A percentage expresses a portion of a whole (or total) that is expressed as 100. For example, 50 percent means 50 parts of the 100 parts constituting the whole. Percentages greater than 100 percent contain more than one whole unit. Thus, 163 percent is one whole plus 63 parts of another whole. Remember that a whole is always thought of as equaling 100 percent.

$$60\% = 0.6 \quad 7\% = 0.07 \quad 175\% = 1.75$$

To express a percentage as a fraction, place the percentage over 100. For example:

$$50\% = \frac{50}{100}$$

These fractions then may be reduced to make working the problem easier. To reduce a fraction, determine the highest number that will divide both the numerator and denominator evenly—that is, with no remainder—then divide each of them by that number. For example:

$$25/100 = \frac{1}{4} \text{ (both numbers are divided by 25)}$$

$$49/63 = \frac{7}{9} \text{ (both numbers are divided by 7)}$$

- A broker is to receive a 7 percent commission on the sale of a $50,000 house. What will the broker's commission be?

$$0.07 \times \$50,000 = \$3,500 \text{ broker's commission.}$$

119

Percentage problems contain three elements: *percentage, total,* and *part.* To *determine a specific percentage of a total,* multiply the percentage by the whole. This is illustrated by the following formula:

$$percent \times total = part$$

$$5\% \times 200 = 10$$

This formula is used in calculating mortgage loan interest, brokers' commissions, loan origination fees, discount points, the amount of earnest money deposits, and income on capital investment.

A variation or inversion on the percentage formula is used to find the total amount when the part and percentage are known. Therefore:

$$total = \frac{part}{percentage}$$

- A broker received a $3,600 commission for the sale of a house. The broker's commission was 6 percent of the total sales price. What was the total sales price of this house?

$$total\ sales\ price = \frac{\$3,600}{0.06} = \$60,000$$

This formula is used in computing the total mortgage loan principal still due if the monthly payment and interest rate are known. It also is used to calculate (1) the total sales price when the amount and percentage of commission or earnest money deposit is known, (2) the interest due if the monthly payment and interest rate are known, and (3) the market value of property if the assessed value and the ratio (percentage) of assessed value to market value are known.

To determine the percent when the amounts of the part and the total are known:

$$percent = \frac{part}{total}$$

This formula may be used to determine the tax rate when the taxes and assessed value are known or the commission rate if the sales price and commission amount are known.

An easy way to remember the *formula,* or part, percent and total, is with the diagram in Figure 13.1. First draw the circle and divide it in half; then divide the bottom half in half. Put the term *part* in the top half of the circle and the other two terms in the two bottom portions.

Next, substitute the known amounts for the words that represent those amounts. The word that remains represents the element you are solving for. If the terms for which you have figures are below the line that divides the entire circle in half, multiply them to find the third element; if one figure is above the other, divide the top term by the bottom one.

Figure 13.1

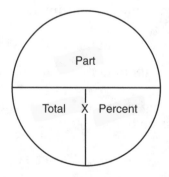

RATES

Property taxes, transfer taxes, and insurance premiums usually are expressed as rates. A rate is expressed as cost per unit; for example, in a certain county tax is computed at the rate of $5 per $100 of assessed value. The formula *for computing rates* follows:

$$\frac{\text{value}}{\text{unit}} \times \text{rate per unit} = \text{total}$$

- A house assessed at $50,000 is taxed at an annual rate of $2.50 per $100 assessed valuation. What is the yearly tax?

$$\frac{\$50,000}{100} \times \$2.50 = \text{total annual tax}$$

$$\$50,000 + \$100 = 500 \text{ (increments of } \$100\text{)}$$

$$500 \times \$2.50 = \$1,250, \text{ total annual tax}$$

AREA AND VOLUME

Area

People in the real estate profession must know how to compute the area of a parcel of land or to figure the amount of living area in a house. *To compute the area of a square or rectangular parcel,* use this formula:

$$\text{area} = \text{length} \times \text{width} \ (A = l \times w)$$

- What is the area of a rectangular lot 200 feet long by 100 feet wide?

$$200' \times 100' = 20,000 \text{ square feet}$$

Area is always expressed in square units.
To compute the width of a rectangular parcel, use

$$\text{width} = \frac{\text{area}}{\text{length}}$$

- What is the width of a rectangular lot that measures 40 feet long and has an area of 3,600 square feet?

$$\frac{\$3,600 \text{ sq. ft.}}{40 \text{ ft.}} = 90 \text{ feet}$$

To compute the amount of surface in a triangular-shaped area, use the formula

$$\text{area} = \frac{1}{2} \ (\text{base} \times \text{height}) \ [A = \frac{1}{2} \ (b \times h)]$$

The part of an equation enclosed in parentheses is always computed before any other part of the equation. The base of a triangle is the bottom, the side on which the triangle rests. The height is an imaginary line extending from the point (or vertex) of the uppermost angle straight down (perpendicular) to the base (see Figure 13.2).

Figure 13.2

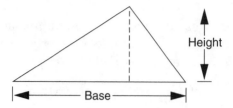

- A triangle has a base of 50 feet and a height of 30 feet. What is the area?

$$\tfrac{1}{2} (50' \times 30') = \text{area in square feet}$$

$$\tfrac{1}{2} (1{,}500) = 750 \text{ square feet}$$

To compute the area of an irregular room or parcel of land, divide the shape into regular rectangles, squares or triangles. Next, compute the area of each regular figure and add the areas together to obtain the total area.

- Compute the area in the hallway in Figure 13.3:

Figure 13.3

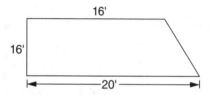

First, make a rectangle and a triangle by drawing a single line through the figure as shown in Figure 13.4.

Figure 13.4

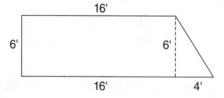

Compute the area of the rectangle:

$$\text{area} = \text{length} \times \text{width} \quad 16' \times 6' = 96 \text{ square feet}$$

Compute the area of the triangle:

$$\text{area} = \tfrac{1}{2} (\text{base} \times \text{height}) = \tfrac{1}{2} (4' \times 6') = \tfrac{1}{2} (24) = 12 \text{ square feet}$$

Add the two areas:

$$96 + 12 = 108 \text{ square feet total area}$$

Volume

The cubic capacity of an enclosed space is expressed as volume. Volume is used to describe the amount of space in any three-dimensional area. For example, it would be used in measuring the interior airspace of a room to determine what capacity heating unit is required. *The formula for computing cubic or rectangular volume is*

$$\text{volume} = \text{length} \times \text{width} \times \text{height} \ (V = lwh)$$

- The bedroom of a house is 12 feet long and 8 feet wide and has a ceiling height of 8 feet (Figure 13.5). How many cubic feet does the room contain?

$$8' \times 12' \times 8' = 768 \text{ cubic feet}$$

Figure 13.5

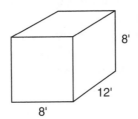

Volume is always expressed in cubic units.

To compute the volume of a triangular space, such as the airspace in a house with a peaked roof, use the following two formulas:

$$V = lwh \text{ and}$$

$$\text{volume} = \tfrac{1}{2} (\text{base} \times \text{height} \times \text{width}) \ [V = \tfrac{1}{2} (bhw)]$$

What is the volume of airspace in the house shown in Figure 13.6?

Figure 13.6

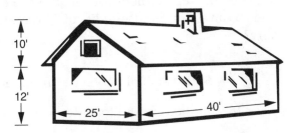

First, divide the house into two shapes, rectangular and triangular, as shown in Figure 13.7:

Figure 13.7

Second, find the volume of T.

$$\text{volume} = \tfrac{1}{2}(\text{base} \times \text{height} \times \text{width})$$

$$\tfrac{1}{2}(25' \times 10' \times 40') = \tfrac{1}{2}(10,000) = 5,000 \text{ cubic feet}$$

Third, find the volume of R.

$$25' \times 10' \times 40' = 12,000 \text{ cubic feet}$$

Finally, total volumes *T* and *R*.

$$5,000 + 12,000 = 17,000 \text{ cubic feet of airspace in the house}$$

Cubic measurements of volume are used to compute the construction costs per cubic foot of a building, the amount of airspace being sold in a condominium unit, or the heating and cooling requirements for a building.

Be sure that when you compute either area or volume, all dimensions are in the same units of measure. For example, you cannot multiply two feet by six inches; you have to multiply two feet by ½ foot or 24 inches by 6 inches.

DEPRECIATION

Depreciation is used in appraisal to calculate the loss of value in a building due to all causes. It is the difference in value between a new building and the existing building being appraised. It is not related to the IRS method of depreciation.

You should be familiar with the straight-line method of depreciation, which allocates the total depreciation over the useful life of a building in equal annual amounts.

To calculate the amount of straight-line depreciation use the formula:

$$\frac{\text{Replacement cost}}{\text{Years of useful life}} = \text{annual charge for depreciation}$$

An appraiser has estimated the replacement cost of an office building at $200,000. The building is 16 years old and has an estimated useful life of 50 years. What is the current total depreciation of the property?

$$\frac{\$200,000}{50} = \$4,000 \text{ annual depreciation charge}$$

$$\$4,000 \times 16 = \$64,000 \text{ current total depreciation}$$

CAPITALIZATION

Capitalization is the process of converting the net operating income expected from a property into an estimated value. The capitalization rate is the rate of return on the investment.

You may use the following formula to solve a capitalization problem:

$$\frac{I}{R \quad V} \qquad
\begin{array}{l}
I = \text{Part or net operating income} \\
R = \text{capitalization rate} \\
V = \text{value of investment}
\end{array}$$

To solve a capitalization problem use one of the following:

$$\frac{I = V}{R} \quad I = RV$$

What is the value of an office building expected to produce a net annual income of $30,000, if the owner estimates that he should receive a return of 12% on his investment?

$$I \text{ divided by } R = V$$

$30,000 divided by 12% = $250,000 estimated value

PRORATIONS

When closing a real estate transaction, it generally is necessary to divide the financial responsibility between the buyer and seller for items such as taxes, loan interest, fuel bills, and rents. Prorations provide for an equitable distribution of income and expenses between the seller and the buyer. Accrued items such as real estate taxes are owed by the seller but will be paid at a later date by the buyer. The seller pays for accrued items by giving the buyer a credit at closing. A prepaid item—such as fuel oil that has not been used—requires a credit to the seller at closing.

Proration may be done through the day prior to closing or through the day of closing. The sales contract or custom of the area (offer to purchase) will generally determine whether the buyer or seller will pay for the actual day of closing. For example, if real estate taxes are prorated through the day of closing, the seller will pay the taxes for the day of closing.

Prorations may be calculated on either a 360-day year (12 months of 30 days each) or a 365-day year. The 365-day year requires determination of the daily charge multiplied by the actual number of days in the proration period. All prorations should be computed by carrying the division to four decimal places. The third and fourth decimal places should not be rounded off to cents until the final proration figure has been determined.

The first step in the proration process is to determine the time period involved in the proration process (the number of days charged to or through the closing date).

The second step is to calculate the dollar amount per day.

The third step is to determine the proration by multiplying the time period by the dollar amount per day.

I. **General guidelines for prorations**

   A. Because property taxes are paid in arrears, the taxes are prorated through either the day prior to closing or the day of closing. The prorated tax will be credited to the buyer and debited (charged) to the seller.

   B. If a buyer assumes a seller's existing loan, the balance of the loan will be credited to the buyer and debited to the seller. Because interest on the loan is paid in arrears, the amount of interest owed from the day of the last payment through the day of closing will be debited to the seller.

   C. Because a water bill is prepaid, the prepaid time must be computed. The amount of this prepaid item will be debited to the buyer and credited to the seller.

D. If the buyer assumes the seller's existing fire and hazard insurance policy, the seller is credited for the unused portion of the premium, which is usually paid for in advance.

E. The broker's commission is debited to the seller.

F. Items credited to the seller and debited to the buyer generally include

1. The sales price
2. Any tax and insurance reserve in the case of a buyer's assuming the seller's loan
3. Prepaid real estate taxes. Homeowner association dues and condominium common charges
4. Any fuel oil remaining in the storage tank on the day of closing

G. Items credited to the buyer and debited to the seller include

1. Unpaid utility bills
2. The buyer's earnest money
3. Tenants' security deposits and any statutory interest due thereon
4. The unearned portion of rent collected in advance

Example
Using a 365-day year, prorate the taxes for a December 14 closing, if the annual tax bill is $1,224 and is prorated through the day of closing.
Solution
First, determine the time period during which taxes have accrued.

Jan	— 31 days	July	— 31 days
Feb	— 28 days	Aug	— 31 days
Mar	— 31 days	Sept	— 30 days
Apr	— 30 days	Oct	— 31 days
May	— 31 days	Nov	— 30 days
June	— 30 days	Dec	— 14 days Total = 348 days

Second, divide the annual tax by the days in the year to determine the amount per day.
$$\$1,224 \div 365 \text{ days} = \$3.3534 \text{ per day}$$
Finally, multiply the time period by the amount per day.
$$\$3.3534 \times 348 = \$1,166.99 \text{ debit to the seller and credit to the buyer (rounded)}$$

AMORTIZATION

The majority of mortgage and deed of trust loans are amortized loans. Regular payments are made for up to 30 years with each payment being applied first to interest owed and the balance deducted from the principal. The amount of interest due on a specific payment date is determined by calculating the total yearly interest based on the unpaid loan balance and dividing that figure by the number of payments each year. For example, if the current outstanding loan balance is $100,000 with interest at the rate of 8 percent per year and constant payments of $769, the interest and principal due on the next payment would be calculated as shown below.

$$\$100,000 \times .08 = \$8,000$$

$$\$8,000 \div 12 = \$666.666 \text{ (round to } \$666.67)$$

$769.00	monthly payment
666.67	month's interest
$102.33	month's principal

All interest due and the full amount of principal due will be paid at the end of the term.

Lenders generally use the fully amortized loan plan in which the borrower pays a constant amount that usually is monthly. Each payment is credited first to the interest due with the balance of the payment being applied to the principal amount of the loan. A prepared mortgage payment book or a mortgage factor chart is used to determine the amount of the constant payment. The mortgage factor chart indicates the amount of monthly payment per $1,000 of loan depending on the term and interest rate.

The factor is multiplied by the number of thousands (and fractions thereof) of the amount being borrowed. The monthly payment chart is shown below.

Monthly Payment Factors

(Per $1,000)

Rate	15 Years	30 Years
7.00%	$8.99	$6.65
7.25	9.13	6.82
7.50	9.27	6.70
7.75	9.41	7.16
8.00	9.56	7.34
8.25	9.70	7.51
8.50	9.85	7.69
8.75	10.00	7.87
9.00	10.15	8.05
9.25	10.30	8.23
9.50	10.45	8.41
9.75	10.60	9.60
10.00	10.75	8.78
10.25	10.90	8.97
10.50	11.06	9.15
10.75	11.21	9.34
11.00	11.37	9.53
11.25	11.53	9.72
11.50	11.69	9.91
11.75	11.85	10.10
12.00	12.01	10.29
12.25	12.17	10.48
12.50	12.33	10.68
12.75	12.49	10.87
13.00	12.66	11.07

Example
What is the monthly payment on a $60,000 loan at 9 percent for 30 years?

8.05

Solution
Refer to the mortgage factor chart above. Move down the "Rate" column to 9%. Then move to the right to the column headed "30 Years" to find the payment on a $1,000 loan ($8.05). To find the monthly payment on the $60,000 loan:

$$\text{Monthly Payment} = \frac{\text{Amount of Mortgage}}{\$1,000} \times \begin{array}{c} \text{Payment for } \$1,000 \text{ Loan} \\ \text{(from monthly payment factors chart)} \end{array}$$

$$\frac{\$60,000}{\$1,000} \times \$8.05 = 60 \times \$8.05 = \$483.00$$

The $483 monthly payment is for the principal and interest only. The lender might add an amount for homeowner insurance premiums and for real estate taxes.

If it is known how much a borrower has available to spend on a monthly loan payment, one may use the mortgage factor chart to determine the amount of the loan that the borrower can afford.

Assume that a prospective buyer can afford $800 per month for principal and interest and the lender will make a loan for 30 years at 8 percent. To find the amount of the loan move down column 1, "Rate," to find the interest rate; then move to the right to find where the rate and the 30-year column meet; you will find $7.34. Every $7.34 of monthly payment will support a loan of $1,000.

$$\text{Amount of Loan} = \begin{array}{c} \text{Amount borrower has available to spend each month for} \\ \text{principal and interest} \end{array} = \$800 \div \$7.34 \begin{array}{c} \text{Monthly payment per } \$1,000 \end{array}$$

108.991 thousands or $108,991

The mortgage factor chart also can be used to determine how much interest will be paid over the life of the loan.

Using the $800 monthly payment figure, what is the total interest paid over the life of this loan?

$$\$800 \text{ (monthly payment)} \times 360 \text{ months} = \$288,000$$

$288,000	(Total principal and interest)
−108,991	(Amount of principal)
$179,009	(Total interest paid over life of loan)

MATH REVIEW TEST

P. 233 white book

1. A broker sold a home for $62,000. The broker charged the seller a 7 percent commission and will pay 25 percent of that amount to the listing salesperson and 30 percent to the selling salesperson. What amount of commission will the listing salesperson receive from the sale of the home?
   1. $1,085
   2. $1,302
   3. $4,340
   4. None of the above

2. A man signed an agreement to purchase a home. The contract stipulated that the seller replace the damaged bedroom carpet. The carpet the buyer has chosen costs $14.95 per square yard plus $3.50 per square yard for installation. If the bedroom dimensions are as illustrated in Figure 13.8, how much will the seller have to pay for the job?
   1. $164.45   3. $222.50
   2. $173.62   4. $256.27

Figure 13.8

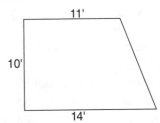

3. Three investors decided to pool their savings and purchase some commercial real estate for $150,000. If one invested $40,000 and the second contributed $20,000, what percentage of ownership was left for the third investor, if ownership interests were allocated on the basis of capital investment?
   1. 60 percent   3. 26 percent
   2. 40 percent   4. 13 percent

4. A father is curious to know how much money his son and daughter-in-law still owe on their mortgage loan. The father knows that the interest portion of their last monthly payment was $582.84. If they are paying interest at the rate of 12 percent, what was the approximate outstanding balance of their loan before the last payment was made?
   1. $48,520   3. $63,583
   2. $58,284   4. $69,941

   annual interest

5. You bought a house one year ago for $102,900. Property in your neighborhood is said to be increasing in value at a rate of 4 percent annually. If this is true, what is the current market value of your real estate?
   1. $171,600   3. $107,188
   2. $170,160   4. $107,016

6. You own a home valued at $75,000. Property in your area is assessed at 80 percent of its value and the local tax rate is $3.25 per $100. What is the amount of your monthly taxes?
   1. $1950.002.   3. $195.00
   2. $243.75   4. $162.50

   60,000 AV ÷ 100 = 600

7. You are planning to construct a patio in your backyard. An illustration of the surface area to be paved appears in Figure 13.9. If the cement is to be poured as a six-inch slab, how many cubic feet of cement will be poured in your patio?
   1. 64 cubic feet
   2. 244 cubic feet
   3. 384 cubic feet
   4. None of the above

Figure 13.9

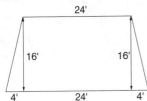

8. You receive a monthly salary of $500 plus 3 percent commission on all of your listings that sell and 2.5 percent on all of your sales. None of the listings you took sold last month, but you received $7,350 in salary and commission. What was the value of the property you sold?
    1. $245,000   3. $274,000
    2. $247,000   4. $294,000

9. A residence has proved difficult to sell. The salesperson suggests that it might sell faster if the owners enclosed a portion of the backyard with a privacy fence. If the area to be enclosed is as illustrated in Figure 13.10, how much would the fence cost at $7.25 per linear foot?
    1. $1,051.25   3. $1,486.25
    2. $1,232.50   4. $1,667.50

Figure 13.10

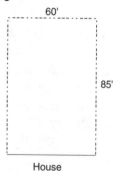

House

10. An owner leases the 24 apartments in his building for a total monthly rental of $6,000. If this figure represents a 9 percent annual return on the owner's investment, what was the original cost of the property?
    1. $800,000
    2. $720,000
    3. $666,667
    4. None of the above

For the following questions regarding closing statement prorations, base your calculations on a 30-day month. Carry all computations to three decimal places and round off after all computations have been made.

11. A sale is to be closed on April 15. Real estate taxes for the current year are $1,860 and have not been paid. What amount of the real estate tax proration will be credited to the buyer?
    1. $434   3. $1,317.49
    2. $542.51   4. $1,860

12. You sell your house to a married couple. The buyers are assuming your outstanding mortgage, which had an unpaid balance of $65,400 after the last payment on September 1 and an annual interest rate of 11 percent. Interest is paid in advance each month. The sale is to be closed on September 14. What is the amount of mortgage interest proration to be credited to you at the closing?
    1. $185.44   3. $319.73
    2. $279.77   4. $501.98

13. Your brother sells a home on October 10. At the closing, the buyer assumes the seller's three-year fire and hazard insurance policy, which is due to expire at the end of May of next year. The original cost of the premium was $740. What is the amount of insurance proration that will be charged to the buyer at the closing?
    1. $144.76
    2. $158.28
    3. $255.49
    4. None of the above

14. In a sale of residential property, real estate taxes for the current year amounted to $1,630 and already have been paid by the seller. The sale is to be closed on November 4. What is the settlement sheet entry for the tax proration?
    1. $237.19 debit to seller; $237.19 credit to buyer
    2. $253.56 credit to seller; $253.56 debit to buyer
    3. $1,476.05 debit to seller; $153.95 credit to buyer
    4. $253.56 credit to seller, only

15. You are buying a house and assuming the seller's mortgage. The unpaid balance after the most recent payment (August 1, the first of the month) was $64,750. Interest is paid in arrears each month at an annual rate of 12 percent. The sale is to be closed on August 18. What is the amount of the mortgage interest proration to be credited to you at the closing?
    1. $140.72
    2. $388.49
    3. $539.19
    4. None of the above

16. A 200-acre farm is divided into house lots. The streets require one-eighth of the whole farm, and there are 220 lots. How many square feet are there in each lot?
    1. 34,650 square feet
    2. 39,784 square feet
    3. 43,916 square feet
    4. None of the above

17. The taxes of $2,140 have been paid for the entire calendar year. The seller sells on November 1. What is the amount of the remaining prepaid proration?
    1. $1,961.67   3. $356.67
    2. $1,783.30   4. $178.33

18. A broker received a $28,000 commission check for the sale of a house. The broker's commission was 6 percent of the total sale price. What was the total sale price of the house?
    1. $560,000   3. $297,872
    2. $466,667   4. $168,000

19. A seller wants to sell his house and realize $80,000 from the sale. If his only cost of selling would be a 7 percent commission, what is the minimum amount he could sell his house for and realize his desired net?
    1. $85,600
    2. $86,022
    3. $87,400
    4. None of the above

20. You have been making constant payments of $623 per month on your mortgage. The balance after your last payment was $59,200. The interest rate on your mortgage is 7 percent. What will be the balance of your mortgage after your next payment?
    1. $55,056
    2. $58,577
    3. $58,922.33
    4. None of the above

21. Using the mortgage factor chart on page 127, what is the monthly payment for a $150,000 loan at 11.5 percent for 30 years?
    1. $1,429.50   3. $1,525.50
    2. $1,486.50   4. $1,543.50

22. Using the numbers in question 21, what is the total interest paid over the life of the loan?
    1. $150,000
    2. $385,140
    3. $533,653
    4. None of the above

23. A young couple want to purchase a home and feel that they can afford to pay $990 per month on a loan. They have saved enough to make a $14,000 down payment and pay closing costs. If lenders are offering 30-year loans at 8.25 percent interest, what is the maximum amount this couple can pay for a home? (Refer to the mortgage factor chart on page 127.)
    1. $131,800   3. $145,800
    2. $141,300   4. $155,400

24. An appraiser has estimated the replacement cost of an office building at $300,000. The building is 18 years old and has an estimated useful life of 50 years. What is the current total depreciation of the property?
    1. $96,000   3. $108,000
    2. $102,000   4. $114,000

25. What is the value of an apartment building expected to produce a net annual income of $40,000, if the owner estimates that she should receive a return of 9 percent on her investment?
    1. $444,444
    2. $500,000
    3. $571,428
    4. $666,666

ANSWER KEY WITH EXPLANATIONS

1. $62,000 sales price × 7% commission = $62,000 × 0.07 = $4,340, broker's commission
   $4,340 × 25% = $4,340 × 0.25 = $1,085
   Correct answer: **1** (120)
2. See Figure 13.11.

Figure 13.11

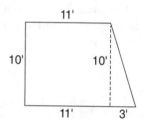

11' × 10' = 110 square feet, area of rectangle
½ (3' × 10') = ½ (30') = 15 square feet, area of triangle
110 + 15 = 125 square feet, total area
Divide by 9 to convert square feet to square yards.
125 ÷ 9 = 13.89 square yards
$14.95 + $3.50 installation = $18.45, cost per square yard
$18.45 × 13.89 square yards = $256.27
Correct answer: **4** (121–23)
3. $40,000 first investor + $20,000 second investor = $60,000
   $150,000 – $60,000 = $90,000 third investor's contribution

$$\frac{\text{part}}{\text{total}} = \text{percent}$$

$90,000 ÷ $150,000 = 0.60, or 60%
Correct answer: **1** (120)

4. $582.84 × 12 = $6,994.08 annual interest

$$\frac{\text{part}}{\text{percent}} = \text{total}$$

$6,994.08 ÷ 12% = $6,994.08 ÷ 0.12 = $58,284 (120)
Correct answer: **2**
5. $102,900 × 4% = $102,900 × 0.04 = $4,116, annual increase in value.
   $102,900 + $4,116 = $107,016, current market value
   Correct answer: **4** (120)
   Read your calculator carefully.
   Answer choices with the same number combinations can be misleading.
6. $75,000 × 80% = $75,000 × 0.80 = $60,000, assessed value
   Divide by 100 because tax rate is stated per $100.
   $60,000 ÷ 100 = $600
   $600 × $3.25 = $1,950, annual taxes
   Divide by 12 to get monthly taxes.
   $1,950 ÷ 12 = $162.50
   Correct answer: **4** (121)
7. See Figure 13.12.

Figure 13.12

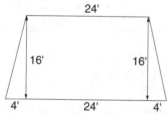

24' × 16' = 384 square feet, area of rectangle
½ (4' × 16') = ½ (64') = 32 square feet, area of triangle
32 × 2 = 64 square feet, area of two triangles
384 + 64 = 448 square feet, surface area to be paved
6" deep = ½'
448' × ½' = 224 cubic feet of cement needed for patio
Correct answer: **4** (121–23)
8. $7,350 – $500 salary = $6,850 commission on sales
   $6,850 ÷ 2.5% = $6,850 ÷ 0.025 = $274,000 value of property sold
   Correct answer: **3** (120)

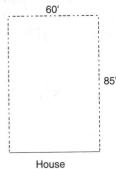

9. See Figure 13.13.

Figure 13.13

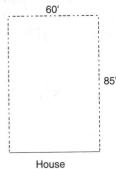

House

Two sides of 85' plus one side of 60'
85' × 2 = 170 feet
170 + 60 = 230 linear feet
230 × $7.25 = $1,667.50
Correct answer: **4** (121–23)

10. $6,000 × 12 = $72,000 annual return
$72,000 ÷ 9% = $72,000 ÷ 0.09 =
$800,000, original cost of property
Correct answer: **1** (124–25)

11. $1,860 ÷ 12 months = $155 per month
$155 ÷ 30 days= $5.167 per day
$155 × 3 months = $465
$5.167 × 15 days = $77.505
$465 + $77.505 = $542.505, rounds to
$542.51
Correct answer: **2** (125–26)

12. $65,400 × 11% = $65,400 × 0.11 = $7,194
$7,194 ÷ 12 months = $599.50 per month
$599.50< ÷ 30 days = $19.983 per day
30-day month – 14 days = 16 days
$19.983 × 16 days = $319.728, rounds
to $319.73
Correct answer: **3** (125–26)

13. $740 ÷ 3 years = $246.667 per year
$246.667 ÷ 12 = $20.556 per month
$20.556 ÷ 30 days = $.685 per day
$20.556 × 7 months = $143.892
$.685 × 20 days = $13.70
$143.892 + $13.70 = $157.592, rounds
to $157.59
Correct answer: **4** (125–26)

14. $1,630 ÷ 12 months = $135.833 per
month
$135.833 ÷ 30 days = $4.528 per day
$4.528 × 26 days = $117.728
$135.833 + $117.728 = $253.561, rounds
to $253.56
Correct answer: **2** (125–26)

The taxes have been paid. The seller is entitled to a refund for 1 month and 26 days. He therefore will receive a credit and the buyer will be charged (debited) for the same amount.

15. $64,750 × 12% = $64,750 × 0.12 = $7,770
$7,770 ÷ 12 months = $647.50
$647.50 ÷ 30 days = $21.583 per day
$21.583 × 18 days = $388.494, rounds
to $388.49
Correct answer: **2** (125–26)

16. 43,560 square feet/acre × 200 acres =
8,712,000, total square feet
8,712,000 square feet × ⅛ = 8,712,000 ×
0.125 = 1,089,000 square feet for streets
8,712,000 – 1,089,000 = 7,623,000
square feet for lots
7,623,000 square feet ÷ 220 lots =
34,650 square feet per lot
Correct answer: **1** (121–23)

17. Time period: 2 months (November/
December)
$2,140 per year ÷ 12 = $178.33 per
month
$178.33 × 2 = $356.67
Correct answer: **3** (125–26)

18. Part = $28,000, Percent = 6%
Part ÷ Percent = Total
$28,000 ÷ .06 = $466,667
Correct answer: **2** (120)

19. Part ÷ Percent = Total
$80,000 ÷ .93 = $86,021.5, rounds to
$86,022
Correct answer: **2** (120)

20. $59,200 × .07 = $4,144.00 annual interest
$4,144 ÷ 12 = $345.33 interest for one
month
$623.00 P&I – 345.33 = $277.67 principal payoff
$59,200 – $277.67 = $58,922.33 balance
after next payment
Correct answer: **3** (126–27)

21. $1,486.50 (150,000 × 9.91)
Correct answer: **2** (126–28)

22. $1,486.50 × 360 months = $535,140
total P&I – $150,000 P = $385,140
Correct answer: **2** (126–28)

23. The payment chart indicates 8.25 percent loans are 7.51 per $1,000.
$990 affordable monthly payment / 7.51 = 131.82423
$131.82423 × 1,000 = $131,824.33 maximum loan amount
$131,824.33 plus down payment = $145,824.33 maximum selling price of house.
Correct answer: **3** (127)

24. $300,000 ÷ 50 years = $6,000 annual depreciation charge
$6,000 × 18 years = $108,000 current total depreciation
Correct answer: **3** (124)

25. $I \div R = V$
$40,000 ÷ 9% (0.09) = $444,444
Correct answer: **1** (124–25)

PART 14

Specialty Areas

OUTLINE OF CONCEPTS TO UNDERSTAND

I. Property management and landlord/tenant

A. A lease is a contract between the lessor (owner) and the lessee (tenant) and a transfer of possession to the tenant.

B. Leasehold estate—less-than-freehold estate involving the tenant's right to occupy the real estate during the term of the lease, usually considered personal property (nonfreehold)

  1. Estate for years—lease for a definite period of time terminating automatically without notice by either party
  2. Periodic estate (estate from year to year)—lease for an indefinite period of time without a specific expiration date; notice must be given to terminate.
  3. Tenancy at will—lease that gives the tenant the right to possess with the consent of the landlord for an indefinite period of time; terminated by giving notice or by the death of either the landlord or the tenant.
  4. Tenancy at sufferance—tenant continues to hold possession without the consent of the landlord.

C. Types of leases

  1. Gross lease—tenant pays a fixed rent, while landlord pays all taxes, insurance, etc.
  2. Net lease—tenant pays rent plus all or part of property charges.
  3. Percentage lease—usually provides for minimum fixed rent plus a percentage of the portion of tenant's business income that exceeds a stated minimum
  4. Graduated lease—provides for rent increase at set future dates
  5. Index lease—allows rent to be increased or decreased periodically based on agreed index such as the change in the government cost of living index

D. Requirements of a valid lease

  1. Offer and acceptance—mutual agreement of parties on contract terms
  2. Consideration—generally takes the form of rent for right of occupancy
  3. Capacity to contract—legal capacity
  4. Legal objectives

E. Breach of lease

  1. Tenant breach

   a. Landlord may sue tenant to obtain judgment to cover amount due.
   b. Landlord may retake possession through actual eviction.
2. Landlord breach—tenant may terminate lease through constructive eviction, if breach causes premises to be untenantable.
3. Death of parties or sale of property generally will not terminate a lease.

F. Management Agreement

   1. Creates an agency relationship between property manager and owner.
   2. Property manager is a general agent.
   3. Management agreement
      a. Defines manager's responsibilities
      b. States owner's purpose
      c. Identifies extent of manager's authority

G. Management functions

   1. Develop an operating budget
   2. Rent property
   3. Select tenants and collect rents
   4. Maintain good relations with tenants
   5. Maintaining the property

II. **Common interest ownership properties**

A. Cooperatives

   1. Title to the land and the building held by the corporation
   2. Each purchaser becomes a stockholder and receives a proprietary lease; each purchaser holds a personal property interest except in states that have adopted Common Interest Ownership Act, which converts this to a real estate interest.
   3. Taxes and the mortgage are liens against the corporation generally given to the shareholders.
   4. Owners-occupants may be forced to pay expenses for the shareholders who are unable to pay, to prevent foreclosure on the entire building.

B. Condominiums

   1. Generally created under a horizontal property act
   2. The owner holds fee-simple title to one unit and a specified share in the common elements.
   3. Default in payment of taxes, mortgage payments, or monthly assessments by one unit owner may result in a foreclosure sale of that owner's unit; this does not affect the titles of the remaining owners.

C. Time-shared ownership

   1. Allows multiple buyers to buy interests in real estate with each buyer receiving the right to use the facilities for a specified period of time.
   2. Owners' use and occupancy is limited to the contractual period that was purchased.
   3. The owner is assessed for common expenses and maintenance based on the ratio of the ownership period to the total number of ownership periods in the property.
   4. Time-share estate includes a fee-simple interest in condominium ownership or a leasehold estate.

5. Time-share use is a contractual right under which the developer owns the real estate.

III. Subdivisions

A. Subdividers versus developers

1. Subdivider—buys undeveloped land and divides it into smaller lots for sale
2. Developer—improves land, constructs buildings on land, and sells them

B. Regulation of land development

1. Land development plan—must comply with municipality's comprehensive plan, zoning regulations, and environmental regulations.
2. Plats—map that illustrates the geographic boundaries of specific lots.
   a. Plat shows block, streets, etc., in prospective subdivision.
   b. Plat must present restrictive covenants and engineering data established by deeds, declarations, etc.
   c. Plat must be approved by appropriate boards of the municipality before being recorded.
3. Subdivision plans
   a. Lot size is generally regulated by local zoning ordinances.
   b. Plan must provide for water, sewer, and utility easements.

C. Private land-use controls

1. Establish standards for all lots within a subdivision.
2. Restrictive covenants control many aspects including type and construction methods.

D. Federal Interstate Land Sales Full Disclosure Act

1. Regulates unimproved parcels sold through an interstate sale.
2. Objective is to avoid fraudulent marketing schemes.
3. Law requires developers to file reports with HUD prior to offering unimproved lots in interstate commerce through the mail or by telephone.
4. The reports must contain disclosure about the properties.
5. Buyer or lessee may be able to void contract, if not provided copy of report before signing.
6. Law does not cover subdivisions with fewer than 25 lots or lots of 20 acres or more.

IV. Business opportunities (brokers only)

A. Forms used

1. Inventory and equipment are personal property and are transferred by bill of sale rather than by deed.
2. A written document of assignment is used to assign accounts receivable.
3. Business sales are regulated by the Uniform Commercial Code, which governs documents and forms when personal property is used as security for a loan.
   a. The UCC requires the borrower to sign a security agreement in order for a lender to create a security interest in personal property; the security interest includes personal property that will become fixtures and must contain a complete list of the items against which the lien applies.

       b. A financing statement or UCC-1 (a short notice of the security agreement) must be filed usually in the Security of States office; it identifies any real estate involved when personal property is made part of the real estate.

       c. When the financing statement has been recorded, subsequent lenders and buyers are placed on notice with regard to the security interest in fixtures and personal property.

       d. Lenders generally require that a security agreement be signed and a financing statement filed when chattels are being financed and subsequently will be affixed to the real estate.

  B. Issues involved in the sale of a business

    1. Contract should be comprehensive and in writing.

    2. The buyer (vendee) should be aware of any representations and warranties made by the seller (vendor).

    3. The offer to purchase should make the sale of the business contingent upon the issuance of the appropriate franchise (if applicable), licenses and permits, approval by vendee of existing leases, and landlord's consent, if required by terms of lease.

    4. Where an ongoing business is being sold, the buyer may want the seller to commit to a covenant not to compete. The covenant should be limited as to territory and time so that the restrictive effect is no more than is necessary to protect the goodwill for which the buyer is paying. More than this is usually unenforceable in a court of law.

    5. If the sale of a business includes the unpaid accounts receivable, the assignment of these accounts should be in writing and the buyer should notify the customers of the assignment and that all payments should be made to the buyer. Prior thereto the buyer should determine the authenticity of such account receivables.

    6. If the seller has a lease, the buyer will generally want a new lease or an assignment of the existing lease; the buyer's preference should be a contingency in the offer to purchase.

    7. If the sale includes fixtures, the buyer should check to be sure that they belong to the seller.

    8. If the sale includes a building, the buyer should be sure that the business complies with zoning, building codes, and other governmental laws and regulations such as environmental laws, as well as marketable title.

  C. Bulk transfers

    1. The sale of a business must comply with the Uniform Commercial Code (UCC).

    2. The UCC applies whenever an owner sells a substantial portion of his inventory.

    3. If the buyer fails to comply with the law, the buyer's title to equipment and inventory may be subject to the claims of the creditors created while the seller operated the business.

V. Commercial property/income property

  A. Advantages of real estate investment

    1. Serves as a hedge against inflation

    2. Rates of return exceed the average rate of return.

    3. Leverage—using other people's money to finance an investment

B. Disadvantages of real estate investment

    1. Lack of liquidity
    2. Investing is generally expensive
    3. Requires active management
    4. Involves substantial risk

C. Investment objectives

    1. Appreciation in value of investment
    2. Cash flow—spendable income generated by income properties
    3. Leverage—financing an investment by using borrowed money
    4. Equity buildup resulting from paying off mortgage plus increase in property value
    5. Pyramiding—using currently owned property as a catalyst to purchase additional properties through either sale or refinance of currently owned property

D. Tax benefits

    1. Capital gains—difference between net selling price and adjusted basis of property; a portion of capital gains is excluded from income tax.
    2. Exchanges
        a. A method of deferring taxation of capital gains
        b. Property involved in a tax-deferred exchange must be like-kind—real estate for real estate of equal value
        c. Any additional personal property or capital needed to even out the exchange is called boot.
        d. *Boot* is taxed at the time of the exchange.
    3. Depreciation
        a. Allows investor to recover cost of asset through tax deductions over useful life of asset
        b. Depreciation may be deducted only if property produces income or is used in trade or business.
        c. Land may not be depreciated.
        d. Straight-line depreciation takes equal periodic amounts over an asset's useful life.
    4. Deductions
        a. Losses may be deducted by investors in certain circumstances.
        b. Tax credits (direct reduction) are allowed for renovation of older buildings, historic properties, etc.
    5. Installment sales
        a. Payments received are taxed only on profit portion.
        b. Interest received is taxed as ordinary income.

VI.   **Agricultural property (broker only)**

A. Property types

    1. General farming properties
    2. Irrigated—includes orchard, vineyard, pasture, and raw crop-land
    3. Livestock ranches—used for grazing livestock
        a. Ranch—business enterprise that depends mainly on range forage for production of livestock and related products.

4. Range—includes all grasslands and shrub lands and those forest lands that will continually or periodically, naturally or through management support vegetation that provides forage for grazing and browsing animals

5. Dairy farms—improvements generally contribute significantly to the value of the operating dairy farm.

6. Permanent plantings: orchards and vineyards
   a. Vary in size from small family-owned and operated grove or vineyard to large agribusiness endeavors
   b. Requires substantial knowledge about the particular varieties of trees or vines
   c. Generally have a high value per acre, dependent on quality of management the permanent plantings have received over a period of time
   d. Require a startup period of several years before a cash flow is realized

7. Timberland
   a. Considered agricultural because it produces a crop-merchantable timber that is periodically harvested.
   b. Timber crop is harvested every 20 to 80 years, unlike other farm properties, which usually have an annual crop to harvest.
   c. Standing timber is legally considered to be real property, but once severed, becomes personal property.

8. Value of agricultural real estate is affected by
   a. Climatic conditions
   b. Management expertise
   c. Productivity

REVIEW LIST

The student should have an understanding of the following specialty areas:

1. Property management and landlord/tenant

2. Common interest ownership properties

3. Subdivisions

4. Commercial property/income property

5. Business opportunities (broker only)

6. Agricultural properties (broker only)

DIAGNOSTIC TEST

1. A man signed a lease for six months. This is an example of a(n)
    1. estate for years.
    2. periodic estate.
    3. tenancy at will.
    4. tenancy at sufferance.

2. You purchased the right to live in an apartment in a resort for the 32nd complete week of each calendar year for the next 30 years. The type of interest you have called a(n)
    1. joint tenancy
    2. time-share estate.
    3. tenancy in common.
    4. estate for years.

3. An owner in a condominium project does not
    1. hold a fee simple title on his or her unit.
    2. have an undivided proportionate interest in the common elements.
    3. have to pay mortgages, taxes, and assessments that are liens against other units in the project.
    4. have a real property interest.

4. Which of the following statements does NOT correctly describe a cooperative development in a state that does NOT recognize the Common Interest Ownership Act?
    1. Title to the land and building is owned by a corporation.
    2. Mortgage and taxes are liens against the corporation.
    3. Each buyer of an apartment becomes a shareholder in the corporation.
    4. The owner holds a real property interest.

5. You have entered into a lease that requires you to pay all or part of the landlord's operating expenses. You have signed a(n)
    1. index lease.
    2. gross lease.
    3. net lease.
    4. graduated lease.

6. A woman's two-year lease had expired when she decided to continue living in her apartment without the consent of her landlord. The woman now has a(n)
    1. estate for years.
    2. periodic estate.
    3. tenancy at will.
    4. tenancy at sufferance.

7. A man bought undeveloped land and divided it into smaller lots for sale. The man would be classified as a(n)
    1. appraiser.
    2. broker.
    3. developer.
    4. subdivider.

8. Which of the following statements does NOT correctly describe the Interstate Land Sales Full Disclosure Act?
    1. It regulates unimproved parcels sold through an interstate sale.
    2. It is aimed at avoiding fraudulent marketing schemes.
    3. It covers subdivisions with fewer than 25 lots.
    4. It requires developers to file reports with HUD prior to offering unimproved lots in interstate commerce by telephone.

9. Which of the following would not be an advantage of investing in real estate?
   1. It serves as a hedge against inflation.
   2. It does not require active management.
   3. It allows for leverage.
   4. It produces a rate of return that exceeds the average rate of return.

10. The term *boot* is related to
    1. appreciation in the value of an investment.
    2. cash flow generated by income property.
    3. pyramiding.
    4. an exchange.

11. Using borrowed money to finance an investment is known as
    1. appreciation.   3. leverage
    2. cash flowing.   4. pyramiding.

12. Which of the following may NOT be depreciated?
    1. A motel
    2. Land
    3. An office building
    4. An apartment building

13. Inventory and equipment sold as part of a business would be transferred to the buyer by a
    1. bargain and sale deed.
    2. bill of sale.
    3. quitclaim deed.
    4. warranty deed.

14. The law that governs documents and forms when personal property is used as security for a loan is the
    1. Interstate Land Sales Full Disclosure Act
    2. Horizontal Property Act.
    3. Real Estate Settlement Procedures Act.
    4. Uniform Commercial Code.

15. Standing timber is legally considered to be
    1. emblements.
    2. chattels.
    3. real property.
    4. personal property.

ANSWER KEY WITH EXPLANATIONS

1. **(1)** An estate for years is a lease with a definite duration. (135)

2. **(2)** A time-share use is a right under which the developer owns the real estate as opposed to a time-share estate, which is a fee-simple interest in condominium ownership. (136)

3. **(3)** The financial hazard of having to pay liens against other units exists in a cooperative development. (136)

4. **(4)** The buyer of a cooperative unit receives stock in the corporation that owns the unit and a proprietary lease; it is a personal property interest. The buyer would have a real property interest if the unit was located in a state that has adopted the Common Interest Ownership Act. (136)

5. **(3)** The lessee is responsible for paying all or part of the landlord's expense. (135)

6. **(4)** In a tenancy at sufferance, the tenant is a trespasser. (135)

7. **(4)** A developer improves land, constructs buildings on the land, and sells them. (137)

8. **(3)** The Interstate Land Sales Full Disclosure Act covers subdivisions with 25 or more lots. (137)

9. **(2)** Real estate investments require active management. (138–39)

10. **(4)** Boot is any additional cash or personal property needed to even out an exchange. (139)

11. **(3)** Cash flow refers to spendable income generated by an income property. Pyramiding is selling or refinancing currently owned

properties in order to purchase additional properties. (139)

12. **(2)** Buildings are depreciated. It is assumed that land value will be recovered at the end of the economic life of the property. (139)

13. **(2)** A deed is used to convey title to real property. (137)

14. **(4)** The Horizontal Property Act is related to condominium development. (137–38)

15. **(3)** Emblements and chattels are considered to be personal property. (142)

SPECIALTY AREAS

TEST SCORE

RATING	RANGE	YOUR SCORE	
Good = 80% to 100%	12-15	Total Number	15
Fair = 70% to 79%	10-11	Total Wrong	-
Needs Improvement = Lower than 70%	9 or less	Total Right	

Passing Requirement: 10 or better

PART 15

Brokerage Management

OUTLINE OF CONCEPTS TO UNDERSTAND

I. **Types of ownership**

    A. Sole proprietorship

        1. Provides broker with flexibility and control, while trading off protection against personal liability

        2. Appropriate for the broker who desires a small operation and sales staff

    B. Joint or multiple ownership—appropriate for the broker interested in growth and expansion as well as joint ownership; five primary forms of multiple ownership

        1. Corporation

            a. Advantages

                1. Limited liability—any liability incurred by a corporation through judgments, bankruptcies, etc., limited to the investment of a shareholder in a corporation; does not affect a shareholder's personal assets

                2. Centralized management—shareholders elect a board of directors, who elect officers to manage the company; a licensed broker-director is responsible for the real estate brokerage phase of the business.

                3. Continuity of life—a corporation is a legal entity that never dies; its officers may be continually replaced if necessary.

                4. No income limitations—no upper limit on the amount of income a corporation may earn or the number of shareholders it may have

                5. Transferability—corporate stock may be freely transferred from one shareholder to another.

            b. Disadvantages

                1. Double taxation—profits taxed at both the corporate and individual levels

                2. Treatment of losses—corporation losses may not be passed on to shareholders; they may be applied to future earnings of the corporation.

                3. Capital gains—passed on to shareholders as ordinary income

        2. S corporation

            a. Advantages

        1. No double taxation—income, losses and capital gains passed directly to the shareholders

        2. Centralized management and continuity of life—similar to the typical corporation

        3. Limited liability with shareholders' interests freely transferable

    b. Disadvantages

        1. Ownership limited to 35 shareholders

        2. Not more than 20 percent of income may be from passive investments, that is, investments that are income-related, such as stock dividends or interest from deposits.

3. General partnership

    a. Advantages

        1. No double taxation—income directly taxable to each partner

        2. Capital gains or losses pass directly to the partners.

    b. Disadvantages

        1. Problems arising from the death, bankruptcy, etc., of the partner(s)

        2. Personal liability

        3. Ownership not freely transferable

4. Limited partnership

    a. Rarely used in an active brokerage firm

    b. Used primarily to acquire investments such as syndicates, joint ventures

    c. One or more general partners have unlimited liability; are responsible for the operation of the business

    d. Limited partners generally have no say in the business operation.

    e. Limited partners' liability is limited to the amount of the investment, unless the partners take an active role in management.

5. Limited liability companies

    a. Offer advantages of the single-level taxation of a partnership and the limited liability of a corporation

    b. Avoid some of the restrictions that are imposed on an S corporation

    c. Must generally have at least one member; members may be corporations, individuals, limited or general partnerships, a trust or foreign persons

    d. May be directly managed by members, or responsibility may be delegated to a property manager

C. Franchises and alternatives—the broker may choose among various types of operations.

1. Remain independent—provides pride of ownership

2. Become a member of a referral system

3. Franchise membership—for example, Century 21 and Electronic Realty Associates (ERA)

    a. Advantages

        1. Approaches to management and marketing—members pay an initial fee and a percentage of the profits in return for franchise "expertise."

        2. Client referral system

        3. Economics of volume purchasing of equipment, signs, etc.

        4. National advertising and promotion

    b. Disadvantages

        1. Loss of individual identity

      2. High initial fees and franchise fees

      3. Possibly limited geographic area

    4. Quasi-franchise membership—for example: Better Homes and Gardens and Gallery of Homes

      a. The broker may retain the name as part of the firm identification.

      b. Offer varied services that are less extensive than those of a franchise operation—for example: Help-U-Sell

      c. The owner is guided by a broker on how to sell property.

      d. The seller takes on part of the broker's responsibility such as showing the property.

    5. The seller generally pays a commission less than that charged by a traditional broker.

    6. Advantages

      a. The broker's monetary investment and time are less.

      b. Greater exposure to FSBOs (For Sale by Owner)

    7. Disadvantages

      a. Lower fees require increased business activity.

      b. Increased pressure to earn a profit

      c. May retain offices while pooling advertising outlays and sharing in the profits of the cooperative

    8. Membership in broker association—single office composed of a group of individual brokers who share office space and expenses

    9. 100-percent commission office

      a. Landlord-broker owns the office and facilities; rents the office to other brokers or associates on a per-desk basis

      b. Each broker or associate pays a monthly fee to cover the landlord's office expenses and a small percentage of the commission for the benefit of all the brokers and associates; the 100-percent concept often is used in combination with other forms of operation.

  D. Internal structure of organization

    1. One-person organization

    2. One-agent to ten-agent organization

      a. A small, centralized operation in which the capacity for doing business grows as the size of the organization grows

      b. Management responsibility, as well as the need for office space and equipment, will increase the cost of doing business.

    3. Monolithic organization

      a. Functions as single unit, though it normally consists of a number of work groups

      b. There is a single source of authority at the top of the organization.

    4. Decentralized organization—fewer levels of management, thus the managers have the authority to operate essentially as individual business units

II.   Sales associate relationship

  A. Independent contractor

    1. Salesperson under limited supervision

    2. The salesperson contracts with the broker to produce specific outcomes—for example, leasing commissions and real estate sales.

3. The process by which a salesperson produces a commission cannot be controlled by the broker except within the guidelines of the contract.
4. The broker may not unduly restrict the methods that the associate may use.
5. The broker may not withhold federal and state income taxes, Social Security taxes, or state unemployment insurance from commissions.
6. The broker may not provide health insurance or pension plans.
7. The salesperson must pay his or her own license fees and board dues.
8. The salesperson is responsible for car and transportation expenses.
9. The salesperson may not be required to attend sales meetings.
10. The salesperson may not be required to follow a set work schedule.

B. Employee

1. The broker can employ, guide the activities of, maintain the standards of conduct of, or terminate an employee at will.
2. The broker is required to withhold federal and state income taxes, pay an employee's share of Social Security taxes, and withhold state unemployment insurance from commissions.
3. The broker may choose to provide fringe benefits such as health insurance.
4. The broker may require attendance at sales meetings.

C. Federal income tax requirements to be classified as an independent contractor—see "VIII. IRS regulations," in *Outline of Concepts to Understand* for Part 11.

III. Agent supervision (broker only)

A. A broker is responsible for supervising the activities of any salesperson employed by the broker.

B. Supervision includes but is not limited to

1. Reviewing all documents related to transactions.
2. Providing all licensed employees with written statement of procedures under which the office and employees shall operate with respect to handling documents related to transactions.
3. Assuming responsibility for preparation, custody, safety, and correctness of all entities on real estate forms, closing statements, and other records even though another person may be

C. Antitrust guidelines include but are not limited to

1. Broker should provide ongoing education on antitrust.
2. Salespeople must promote company and base fees of services provided rather than comparison with competitive forms.
3. Salespeople must avoid communication with competing forms that might be interpreted as boycotts or price fixing.
4. Policy and procedures manual must include polices for antitrust compliance.

D. In carrying out fair housing guidelines

1. Broker should provide ongoing education on fair housing.
2. Broker should be sure that salespeople do not provide assistance reluctantly to members of protected classes.
3. Salespeople should not differentiate in the quality of service offered to members of protected classes.

4. Salespeople should not represent that a property is sold or refuse to write an offer for members of protected classes.
5. Salespeople should not suggest that members of protected classes would not be comfortable in a neighborhood.

E. Americans with Disabilities Act guidelines

1. Salespeople should avoid referring to a person's disability.
2. Avoid using the word "special" in dealing with someone who is disabled.
3. Avoid patronizing people with disabilities.
4. Brokers should make sure office is accessible to those with disabilities.
5. Be able to communicate with people hard-of-hearing.

IV. Developing plans

A. Purpose—to commit broker's financial and human resources to those activities that will produce highest return on investment

1. Plans tell what broker's company wants to accomplish and provide general framework for how organization will follow through.
2. The broker must have specific goals for the company to accomplish.

B. Business plan—generally a three-year to five-year blueprint for the organization.

C. Short-range plan—tells company what it should be doing in the coming year.

D. Mission statement—states what a company's purpose is for doing business, specifically, what the business does and where the company intends to be in the future

V. Risk management

A. Management styles

1. Dictatorial style—the manager has total control over the organization.
2. Autocratic style—managers are authoritarian but more benevolent than dictatorial managers.
3. Participative style—more democratic than above styles; utilizes talents of people to a greater extent than is common in other styles of management
4. Laissez-faire—manager doesn't exercise any authority; style characterized by nonintervention and indifference

B. Benefits of training program

1. Reputation—reputation for good program attracts new salespeople
2. Supervision—need for close supervision reduced
3. Selection—helps the broker select the most promising salespeople
4. Motivation—motivates salespeople to try out what they have learned
5. Morale—aids the retention of salespeople by helping them to be productive as quickly as possible
6. Less turnover—provides the knowledge that is necessary for salespeople to succeed, thus reducing the need to terminate the unproductive

C. Objectives of a training program

1. Good habits—primary objective to develop good working habits in trainees
2. Increased profits—provides well-chosen salespeople with greater profits
3. Better production—providing salespeople with training as well as attention increases their productivity.

4. Better time management—lessens the need for salespeople to depend on brokers, thus allowing greater sales production
5. Learning from mistakes—makes salespeople aware of the need to learn from mistakes

D. Personal assistants

1. Personal assistants may handle the non-sales-related aspects of real estate transactions.
2. Personal assistants have enhanced the productivity of salespeople as well as the profitability of brokerage firms.
3. State licensing laws may address the numerous issues posed by the use of personal assistants.
4. Personal assistants generally are hired and supervised by a salesperson.
5. The broker's policies and procedures should define how salespersons' assistants are handled in an organization.

E. Recordkeeping

1. Method of keeping financial records
   a. Cash method—records income as received and expenses when actually paid
   b. Accrual method—records income when earned and expenses when incurred (Most firms begin operating under the cash method because the accrual method is more complicated.)
2. Financial analysis guidelines
   a. Provides standardized method of classifying income and expenses; accounting functions are becoming computerized.
   b. After expense categories have been established and income categories assigned, the coding of deposit slips and checks written can provide the basis for the development of financial statements, balance sheets, and profit-and-loss statements.
3. Typical bookkeeping system
   a. Records of income—can be entered on a ledger page as in a checkbook register or on a computer.
   b. Record of payments—carbon copy of entries, duplicate of check, or computer record is sufficient.
   c. Accounts payable—list all the bills received and the date of payment in the file or book.
   d. Payroll card—shows the gross and net salaries plus the federal and state tax deductions for all employees.
   e. Commission records—indicate the amounts of all commissions paid to each salesperson, with each transaction identified.
   f. Advertising—newspaper, Internet, cable TV, etc., ads are checked for accuracy and charted to keep track of calls received.
   g. Telephone—outgoing personal calls should be discouraged as much as possible by logging incoming and outgoing calls or by computer print-outs.
   h. Supplies—a sign-in/sign-out sheet should be used to keep track of such items as lawn signs and lock boxes.
4. Miscellaneous
   a. Licensing requirements—brokers should make sure that salespeople are licensed properly.

       b. Contracts—each person in the office should sign the contract; this is essential for the independent contractor.

       c. Policy manual—the office policy and procedure manual should be ready when a brokerage office is opened.

       d. Legal advice—brokers should retain good attorneys for sound legal advice.

VI. Trust accounts

A. Commingling business monies with escrow monies is illegal.

B. Trust account records must be kept of the names of parties for whose benefit the trust account is created; most brokers maintain trust account records on computer.

C. Notation of the date of receipt of any sum and the record of the date and manner of disbursement of funds held in trust should be maintained.

D. All disbursement notations should include the check number and the name of the payee.

E. Trust funds should be deposited in a checking account maintained especially for this purpose.

VII. Basic financial concepts

A. Cash flow—net spendable income from the investment calculated by deducting all the operating and fixed expenses from the gross income

B. Company dollar—amount of income that remains after subtracting all the commissions from the gross income

C. Gross income—revenue earned from all sources, including sales, appraisals, management fees, etc.

D. Budget—a quantified business plan

E. Budgeting process—mechanism through which a broker can design a firm's activities and assign dollar costs and anticipated revenues to their implementation

F. Zero-base budgeting—requires that all budgeted costs for the planning period be justified each time a new budget is developed

G. Desk cost—the cost of providing the opportunity for salespeople to conduct business is calculated by dividing the total operating expenses of the firm (including salaries, rent, insurance, etc.) by the number of salespeople. (The number of desks is not considered in the calculation. For example, if the broker's annual overhead is $60,000 and there are two desks, each accommodating two salespeople, the desk cost for the firm is $15,000. On a 50/50 split, each salesperson does not begin to earn a profit for the broker until each has brought in a total of $30,000 in gross commissions for the year.)

REVIEW LIST

The student should have an understanding of the following areas of brokerage management:

1. Types of ownership

2. Sales associate relationships

    a. Independent contractor
    b. Employee

3. Risk management

    a. Agent supervision
    b. Record keeping

4. Trust accounts

5. Basic financial concepts

DIAGNOSTIC TEST

1. Ownership in S corporations is limited to
   1. 20 stockholders.
   2. 25 stockholders.
   3. 35 stockholders.
   4. 100 stockholders.

2. Which of the following is NOT an advantage of the corporation form of ownership?
   1. Limited liability
   2. Centralized management
   3. No income limitations
   4. Double taxation

3. Which of the following statements does NOT correctly describe a limited partnership?
   1. A limited partnership is a popular form of ownership for active brokerage firms.
   2. Limited partners generally have no say in business operations.
   3. The general partner has unlimited liability.
   4. Limited partnerships are used primarily to acquire investments such as syndicates.

4. Which of the following is a quasi-franchise?
   1. Electronic Realty Associates (ERA)
   2. Better Homes and Gardens
   3. Century 21
   4. Re/Max

5. A landlord-broker generally would be found in a
   1. sole proprietorship.
   2. limited partnership.
   3. general partnership.
   4. 100-percent commission office.

6. Which of the following statements does NOT correctly describe the independent contractor relationship?
   1. The salesperson is under limited supervision.
   2. The salesperson is responsible for car and transportation expenses.
   3. The broker must provide health insurance.
   4. The broker may not withhold federal income taxes from commissions.

7. A broker has an annual overhead of $300,000, and there are ten desks, each accommodating two salespeople. The broker's desk cost is
   1. $15,000.   3. $25,000.
   2. $20,000.   4. $30,000.

8. The person who manages your brokerage firm exercises total control over the organization. This type of management style would be called
   1. autocratic.
   2. dictatorial.
   3. participative.
   4. laissez-faire.

9. Which of the following statements does NOT correctly describe the methods of keeping financial records?
   1. The cash method records income as it is received.
   2. The accrual method records income when it is earned.
   3. Most firms begin operating under the accrual method.
   4. The accrual method records expenses when they are incurred.

10. Which of the following is NOT an objective of a training program?
    1. Increased profits
    2. Better time management
    3. Good habits
    4. Preparation for passing the license exam

11. Which of the following is NOT a benefit of a training program?
    1. Supervision
    2. Motivation
    3. Morale
    4. Handling of personal problems

12. Which of the following is NOT included in a typical bookkeeping system?
    1. Records of income
    2. Accounts payable
    3. Payroll cards
    4. A policy manual

13. Which of the following is NOT included in trust account notations?
    1. The receipt of any monies belonging to others
    2. A record of the date of the disbursement of the funds
    3. The manner in which the funds are disbursed
    4. A record of appointments to show homes

14. Which of the following statements does NOT correctly describe trust accounts?
    1. Commingling of business funds with escrow funds is illegal.
    2. Trust funds should be deposited in a business account.
    3. Trust account records must be kept of the names of the parties for whose benefit the trust account is created.
    4. All disbursement notations should include the check number and the name of payee.

15. Which of the following is NOT a part of a broker's miscellaneous record?
    1. Providing a policy manual
    2. Ensuring sure that salespeople are properly licensed
    3. Retaining an attorney to provide sound legal advice
    4. Ensuring that salespeople are staying up-to-date in their field

ANSWER KEY WITH EXPLANATIONS

1. **(3)** This is a disadvantage of S corporations as compared to a limited liability company. (145)

2. **(4)** Other disadvantages of a corporation include how capital gains and losses are treated. (144)

3. **(1)** The limited partners liability is limited to the amount of the investment. (145)

4. **(2)** ERA, Century 21 are franchises while RE/MAX is a 100 percent commission office. (146)

5. **(4)** The landlord-broker owns the office and rents the space to other brokers on a per-desk basis. (146)

6. **(3)** The broker may not provide fringe benefits such as health insurance or pension plans. (146–47)

7. **(1)** 10 desks × 2 salespeople = 20 salespeople
   $300,000 annual overhead ÷ 20 salespeople = $15,000 (150)

8. **(2)** Laissez-faire is the least authoritarian management style. (148)

9. **(3)** The accrual method is more complicated than the cash method. (149)

10. **(4)** Some of the larger firms maintain prelicensing classes from which they recruit salespeople. (148–49)

11. **(4)** Personal problems are handled by the manager or owner on an individual basis. (148)

12. **(4)** The policy and procedure manual must be made available to new salespeople. (150)

13. **(4)** Maintaining a record of showings would be included in the policy and procedures manual. (150)

14. **(2)** Trust funds must be deposited in a special checking account. (150)

15. **(4)** Brokers generally provide periodic meetings to present information allowing salespeople to stay up-to-date in their field. This type of material could also be included in advanced training programs. (149–150)

BROKERAGE MANAGEMENT

TEST SCORE

RATING	RANGE	YOUR SCORE	
Good = 80% to 100%	12-15	Total Number	15
Fair = 70% to 79%	10-11	Total Wrong	-_____
Needs Improvement = Lower than 70%	9 or less	Total Right	

Passing Requirement: 10 or better

PART 16

Salesperson Examinations

The sample examinations that follow evaluate your general real estate knowledge and test-taking ability. Simulate as closely as possible the actual test conditions (see Part 1, "Use of the Manual"); avoid distractions; and use only those tools permitted by your state. These exams contain 80 questions or 100 questions. Circle your answer for each question. Remember that the PSI exam includes an additional 40-question to 50-question portion that tests your knowledge of your state's real estate laws and specific real estate practices.

After completing and grading the sample exams, carefully analyze your results. Did you complete all the questions in the allotted time? Did you answer a minimum of 65 or 81 questions correctly? It will be useful to mark in the answer key all the questions you missed. The answers and explanations are keyed to pages in the concepts-to-understand outlines for each part. The pattern of your errors should immediately suggest which areas require additional study.

As a final check, you may wish to review all the exam questions in the *Guide* that relate to a specific topic. Feel free to test and retest yourself. The greater your familiarity with the scope and style of the PSI exam, the better you are likely to perform.

SALESPERSON EXAMINATION I

1. Which of the following would NOT be considered real property?
   1. Mineral rights
   2. A leasehold estate
   3. Fixtures
   4. Air

2. The servient estate in an easement appurtenant is the property
   1. owned by the landlord.
   2. on which the easement is placed.
   3. owned by the tenant.
   4. that benefits from the easement.

3. Which of the following statements concerning encumbrances is NOT true?
   1. All encumbrances are liens.
   2. All liens are encumbrances.
   3. Restrictions beneficial to the grantee are encumbrances.
   4. An easement is a physical encumbrance.

4. Which of the following is NOT a specific lien?
   1. Mortgage lien
   2. State inheritance taxes
   3. Real estate taxes
   4. Mechanic's lien

5. You have entered into a lease that requires you to pay 20 percent of the owner's expenses. Your lease would be an example of a
   1. variable lease.
   2. net lease.
   3. percentage lease.
   4. gross lease.

6. A husband and wife own an apartment building. The husband owns an undivided three-fourths interest and the wife owns a one-fourth interest. This type of tenancy is a
   1. leasehold estate
   2. joint tenancy.
   3. tenancy in common
   4. tenancy by the entirety.

7. The highest form of ownership interest a person may hold in real estate is
   1. life estate
   2. fee simple.
   3. legal life estate.
   4. base fee.

8. Two unrelated people own a three-unit apartment building as tenants in common. One wants to sell but the other does not. Which of the following statements describes the legal rights of the party who wants to sell?
   1. The party may request a court to partition the building.
   2. The party may require the co-owner to sell.
   3. The party may record a lis pendens on the property.
   4. The party may refinance the mortgage in her or his own name, thus eliminating the co-owner's interest in the property.

9. Your aunt died intestate and you inherited her house. The way in which you acquired the title to her house is by
   1. curtesy.
   2. descent.
   3. escheat.
   4. laches.

10. Which of the following statements does NOT correctly describe a legal life estate?
    1. The life tenant generally is answerable to the holder of the future interest.
    2. The life tenant may not commit any acts that would permanently injure the property.
    3. There may be a reversionary interest.
    4. There may be a remainder interest.

11. Which of the following is NOT a leasehold estate?
    1. An estate for years
    2. Periodic estate
    3. Time-share estate
    4. Estate from year to year

12. You are married and own a house under a form of ownership that prohibits you from selling it without the signature of your spouse. Your form of ownership is LEAST likely to be
    1. in severalty.
    2. a joint tenancy.
    3. a tenancy in common.
    4. a tenancy by the entirety.

13. A state wants to build a publicly owned convention center to attract private development in its largest city. Can the state use eminent domain to acquire the land?
    1. No, because private investments would not be allowed.
    2. Yes, if just compensation is paid to the owners of the land.
    3. No, because eminent domain can only be used for highway expansion.
    4. Yes, if the owners hold fee simple interest in the land.

14. Which of the following grants zoning authority to municipal governments?
    1. Eminent domain
    2. State enabling acts
    3. Laches
    4. Escheat

15. The city in which you live has a zoning ordinance. The basis for the city to have such an ordinance is
    1. eminent domain.
    2. escheat.
    3. police power.
    4. riparian rights.

16. Which of the following terms are NOT related?
    1. Freehold estate–fee simple
    2. Grantor–person conveying title
    3. Leasehold estate–personal property
    4. Police power–deed restriction

17. Strict liability under Superfund means that
    1. each of the individual owners is personally responsible for the damages in whole.
    2. the owner is responsible to the injured party without excuse.
    3. the liability is not limited to the person who currently owns the property but also includes people who have owned the site in the past.
    4. the owner is not responsible to the injured party unless it can be proved that the owner was aware of the problem.

18. Which of the following does NOT correctly describe how real estate licensees should handle the possibility of hazardous substances on a property being sold?
    1. Clients should be asked about the possibility of hazardous substances being on the property.
    2. Licensees should consider the consequences of potential liability.
    3. Licensees should be scrupulous in considering environmental issues.
    4. Licensees should not disclose the problem because it might harm the seller.

19. Sources of groundwater contamination do NOT include
    1. waste disposal sites.
    2. underground storage tanks.
    3. use of pesticides in farming communities.
    4. radon.

20. Your neighbor has given you permission to go hunting on his farm. He has also stated that he reserves the right to cancel the agreement. You have a(n)
    1. leasehold estate.
    2. easement appurtenant.
    3. license.
    4. defeasible fee estate.

21. A claim based on adverse possession of property must NOT be
    1. notorious.   3. hostile.
    2. open.   4. secretive.

22. A man gives his friend the right to go hunting on his property for just one day. This is an example of
    1. a license.
    2. an easement in gross.
    3. an easement appurtenant.
    4. an easement by prescription.

23. A person who receives property by will is called a
    1. trustee.
    2. devisee.
    3. testator.
    4. hypothecator.

24. Riparian rights would exist in a
    1. condominium on a bay.
    2. house on a bay.
    3. hotel whose land abuts a large lake.
    4. cooperative on a river.

25. A developer was able to buy two adjoining single-family lots for $20,000 each. He combined the lots into one parcel with a value of $90,000. The developer's action reflects the process of
    1. accession.   3. exchange.
    2. attachment.   4. plottage.

26. A McDonald's restaurant opened in a neighborhood and was enjoying substantial profits. Within a year a Burger King was built across the street from McDonald's and resulted in McDonald's losing 30 percent of its profits in the next year. This is an example of the principle of
    1. competition.
    2. conformity.
    3. highest and best use.
    4. progression.

27. A meat-packing plant has just been built one block from your house. The strong odors are lowering property values in your neighborhood. The loss in value would be classified as
    1. functional obsolescence.
    2. physical deterioration.
    3. the principle of change.
    4. external obsolescence.

28. In the appraisal of a public building, an appraiser would use the
    1. cost approach.
    2. income capitalization approach.
    3. sale comparison approach.
    4. gross rent multiplier.

29. A four-bedroom house with one bathroom would be an example of
    1. physical deterioration.
    2. functional obsolescence.
    3. economic obsolescence.
    4. environmental obsolescence.

30. Which of the following is NOT a stage in the appraisal process?
    1. State the problem.
    2. Analyze the tax consequences of the property owner.
    3. Reconcile the data for the final value estimate.
    4. Analyze and interpret the data.

31. An appraiser uses the cost approach in appraising a home. The appraiser should NOT use which of the following types of information?
    1. Physical deterioration
    2. Cost of replacement of house
    3. Depreciation of land
    4. Economic obsolescence

32. A house that is the least expensive home in its neighborhood has nevertheless grown significantly in value over the years because of an increasing number of larger, more expensive houses being built nearby. This growth in value is an example of the principle of
    1. regression.
    2. competition.
    3. progression.
    4. highest and best use.

33. You are preparing a competitive market analysis on a house that you hope to list for sale. Which of the following approaches to value will be used in the development of the estimated value?
    1. Cost approach
    2. Gross rent multiplier
    3. Income approach
    4. Sales comparison approach

34. A competitive market analysis reflects the use of the
    1. cost approach.
    2. income approach.
    3. sales-comparison approach.
    4. gross-rent-multiplier method.

35. Bank *A* holds a lien on a home on which Bank *B* already had a lien. The lenders subsequently entered into an agreement in which Bank *A* moved into a first lien position. This is an example of a(n)
    1. hypothecation agreement.
    2. disintermediation agreement.
    3. reverse annuity mortgage.
    4. subordination agreement.

36. If the Federal Reserve Board raises its discount rate, which of the following is likely to occur?
    1. Mortgage money will become more available.
    2. Interest rates will stay the same.
    3. Mortgage money will become less available.
    4. Interest rates will decline.

37. You have a mortgage in which you make the same payment each month for principal and interest, with the principal payment increasing and the interest payment decreasing from month-to-month. This is called a(n)
    1. amortized mortgage.
    2. term mortgage.
    3. reverse annuity mortgage.
    4. partially amortized mortgage.

38. Which of the following agencies would be involved in administering special assistance program for housing?
    1. Fannie Mae
    2. Ginnie Mae
    3. Freddie Mac
    4. The "Fed"

39. Which of the following agencies is NOT included in the secondary mortgage market?
    1. FHA
    2. FNMA
    3. GNMA
    4. FHLMC

40. All loans subject to the Real Estate Settlement Procedures Act (RESPA) require lenders to
    1. charge the seller for all loan discount points.
    2. document any reason for declining credit to a loan applicant.
    3. deliver a Uniform Settlement Statement (HUD-1) form to both buyer and seller.
    4. allow the buyer to rescind the contract any time prior to the first payment due date.

41. You financed your property with a two party mortgage and just made the final mortgage payment on your property. Recording which of the following documents will provide notice that the mortgage lien has been removed?
    1. Reconveyance deed
    2. Satisfaction of mortgage
    3. Alienation of the mortgage instrument
    4. Reversion of the "deed"

42. When a loan is subject to the provisions of the Real Estate Settlement and Procedures Act (RESPA), which of the following elements of a real estate transaction need NOT observe RESPA guidelines?
    1. The commission structure for licensees
    2. The type of settlement statement used at the closing
    3. Who receives a good-faith estimate of closing costs
    4. The payment of referral fees to licensees by providers of closing-related services

43. Regulation Z of the Truth-in-Lending Act provides which of the following penalties for licensees who willfully fail to comply with its advertising guidelines for real estate financing?
    1. Fines only
    2. License revocation
    3. Fines and/or imprisonment
    4. None, all violations of Regulation Z are referred to state licensing agencies.

44. Salesperson A for broker B has listed a home. Salesperson C for broker D is trying to sell the home to his own buyer. Salesperson C is primarily responsible to
    1. his own buyer.   3. broker B.
    2. salesperson A.   4. broker D.

45. In some states, the listing broker owes a fiduciary duty to
    1. the customer.
    2. the listing salesperson.
    3. the client.
    4. the buyer.

46. A broker was employed by an owner to sell her home. Which of the following statements does NOT correctly describe the broker's relationship to the owner?
    1. The broker has become the seller's agent.
    2. The broker owes fiduciary duty to the seller.
    3. The broker is a special agent.
    4. The broker is a general agent.

47. You are a licensee holding an open house on one of your listings. An old friend sees the sign and stops in, and ultimately asks you to write an offer to purchase. At this point, which of the following statements about agency relationships is correct?
    1. Your friend is your customer.
    2. Your position as seller's agent prohibits you from writing the offer.
    3. The request automatically creates an express dual agency relationship.
    4. The relationship with your friend presents an irreconcilable conflict of interest.

48. You listed a home that was subsequently shown by six cooperating brokers and two buyer's brokers. How many single-agency relationships were involved in the transaction?
    1. One   3. Seven
    2. Three   4. Nine

49. A salesperson listed a home for sale and transferred to another brokerage firm two weeks later. Which of the following statements describes the status of the listing?
    1. The listing is terminated.
    2. The listing is transferred to the new broker.
    3. The two brokers will negotiate to decide who will hold the listing.
    4. The listing will stay with the former broker of the salesperson.

50. A salesperson received an earnest money payment for $2,000. The salesperson should
    1. hold the payment until the buyer has received a financing commitment.
    2. give the earnest money to his broker.
    3. open up a trust account and deposit the payment in it.
    4. deposit the payment in the seller's checking account.

51. You are working as a buyer's broker for a client. Which of the following would NOT describe your role as a buyer's broker?
    1. You should show the buyer properties in which your commission is protected.
    2. You should counsel the buyer about developing accurate objectives.
    3. You should search for the best properties for your buyer to inspect, widening the marketplace to include homes for sale by owners (FSBOs).
    4. You should help the buyer prepare the strongest offer.

52. According to the law of agency, a real estate broker does NOT owe the principal the duty of
    1. exercising reasonable care.
    2. acting in good faith.
    3. conforming with the principal's legal instructions.
    4. offering legal advice.

53. A broker acting as the agent of a principal
    1. can agree to a change in price without the principal's approval.
    2. may share her commission with the salesperson of another broker.
    3. must report all offers to the principal unless instructed otherwise.
    4. must maintain as confidential all information the principal says not to disclose.

54. A broker listed a property under a valid written listing agreement. After the sale was completed the owner refused to pay the broker's fee. Which of the following can the broker do?
    1. She can take the seller to court and sue for the commission.
    2. She is entitled to a lien on the seller's property for the amount of the commission.
    3. She can go to court and stop the transaction until she is paid.
    4. She can collect the commission from the buyer.

55. Commissions and fees paid by the seller to a listing agency are determined by
    1. standards promulgated by the local board of REALTORS®.
    2. negotiations between the seller and the listing licensee.
    3. applying the prevailing customary fees charged in that area.
    4. an industry index computed monthly from multiple listing service data.

56. A listing broker is MOST likely to have earned a commission from a principal when which of the following events occur?
    1. An offer to purchase has been presented to the client.
    2. Title has been transferred to the buyer.
    3. The seller accepts and signs an offer to purchase.
    4. A "ready, willing, and able buyer" signs an offer to purchase that meets the terms of the listing contract.

57. A broker listed an owner's home and later received an offer from another licensee that met all of the listing terms and conditions. After considering the offer, the owner informed the broker that the owner no longer wished to sell, and asked to be released from the listing agreement immediately. Which of the following is a TRUE statement about the broker's position in this situation?
    1. The broker must release the owner without obligation.
    2. The broker must tell the owner that the offeror may sue for specific performance.
    3. The broker may succeed in collecting an earned commission from the owner.
    4. The broker may keep the earnest money that accompanied the offer as liquidated damages.

58. On July 1, an owner and a salesperson entered into a six month exclusive-right-to-sell agreement for a residential property. On July 15, the owner rejected a low offer and fired the listing agent. On August 1, there was a house fire that required extensive kitchen repairs. On September 12 the owner entered into another exclusive-right-to-sell agreement with a salesperson from a different agency. On January 1 the property was still unsold. On which date was the first listing agreement MOST likely to terminate and why?
    1. July 15, because the salesperson was dismissed
    2. August 1, because the listed property suffered material damage
    3. September 12, because the owner breached the first listing agreement by signing a second
    4. January 1, because the first listing agreement ended at midnight on December 31

59. An option, prior to being exercised, is an example of
    1. an assignable contract.
    2. a unilateral contract.
    3. a bilateral contract.
    4. an executed contract.

60. Which of the following is a similarity between an exclusive-right-to-sell listing and an exclusive-agency listing?
    1. Under both, the seller avoids paying the broker a commission if the seller sells the property without the help of the broker.
    2. Both give the responsibility of representing the seller to just one broker.
    3. Both are net listings.
    4. Under both, the seller authorizes one specific salesperson to show the property.

61. A buyer has entered into an agreement with more than one buyer's agent at the same time but owes compensation only if she uses the services of a buyer's broker. This arrangement is known as a(n)
    1. multiple-listing agreement.
    2. exclusive right agreement.
    3. exclusive agency agreement.
    4. open agreement.

62. Which of the following types of clauses governs the right of a listing broker to collect a commission from an owner who waits until the listing period expires and then personally contracts to sell the property to a party the broker had shown the property to during the listing period?
    1. Alienation   3. Defeasance
    2. Protection   4. Habendum

63. You wrote an offer on a house for $214,000. The seller gave you a counteroffer for $218,000. The seller may withdraw the counteroffer
    1. within 72 hours after acceptance.
    2. prior to the buyer's acceptance.
    3. prior to removal of all contingencies in the offer.
    4. prior to closing.

64. You signed a lease for one year and took possession of an apartment. When the lease expired, you continued to live in the apartment without the owner's consent. Your tenancy would be considered to be a(n)
    1. estate for years.
    2. estate from year to year.
    3. tenancy at will.
    4. tenancy at sufferance.

65. A lease that allows rent to be increased or decreased periodically based on changes in economic indicators is a(n)
    1. graduated lease.
    2. gross lease.
    3. percentage lease.
    4. index lease.

66. Which of the following types of deeds gives a property buyer the MOST protection against problems that may arise with the title?
    1. Quitclaim
    2. Bargain and sale
    3. Special warranty
    4. General warranty

67. You have entered into a land contract for the sale of your home. Which of the following is NOT correct?
    1. The buyer is the vendee.
    2. The buyer will take possession when the contract is signed by both parties, if the contract so provides.
    3. The buyer will hold legal title during the term of the contract.
    4. The buyer will hold equitable title during the term of the contract.

68. Personal property is generally conveyed by a
    1. bill of sale.
    2. certificate of title.
    3. quitclaim deed.
    4. trust deed.

69. The loss of land because of an earthquake would be an example of
    1. accretion.
    2. avulsion.
    3. erosion.
    4. hypothecation.

70. When property transfers from one party to another, recording the deed provides what is called
    1. validation of the agreement between the parties.
    2. a writ of attachment.
    3. certificate of title.
    4. constructive notice.

71. The IRS has how many requirements for establishing an independent-contractor status?
    1. One   3. Three
    2. Two   4. Four

72. Brokers who violate the Sherman Antitrust Act may be punished by a maximum fine of
    1. $10,000.
    2. $25,000.
    3. $50,000.
    4. $100,000.

73. Which of the following is NOT a violation of antitrust laws?
    1. Two brokers agree that they both will pay 2.5 percent of the sales price to cooperating brokers on all listings published in an MLS after the date of the specified agreement.
    2. Two brokers agree to pay just $40 to the Reliance Title Company for closings
    3. Two brokers agree not to cooperate with a flat-fee broker.
    4. A broker refuses to cooperate with a flat-fee broker.

74. The Civil Rights Act of 1866 prohibits discrimination based on
    1. handicap.
    2. familial status.
    3. race.
    4. sex.

75. Broker X is showing buyer Y, an Asian, homes only in Asian neighborhoods. The broker may be guilty of
    1. arbitrage.
    2. block busting.
    3. redlining.
    4. steering.

76. Which of the following is NOT a category protected by federal Fair Housing laws against discrimination in housing?
    1. Race
    2. National origin
    3. Sexual orientation
    4. Familial status

77. You sign an agreement to purchase a home. The contract requires that the seller replace the damaged living room carpet. The carpet you have chosen costs $16.95 per square yard plus $4.50 per square yard for installation. If the living room dimensions are as illustrated in Figure 16.1, how much will the seller have to pay for the job?
    1. $357.50
    2. $314.60
    3. $353.93
    4. None of the above

Figure 16.1

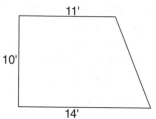

78. A house has been difficult to sell. The salesperson suggests it might sell faster if the owner enclosed a portion of the backyard with a privacy fence. If the area to be enclosed is as illustrated in Figure 16.2, how much would the fence cost at $8.40 per linear foot?
    1. $546
    2. $1,512
    3. $2,058
    4. None of the above

Figure 16.2

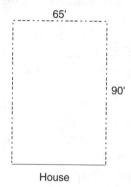

79. A sale is to close on June 23. Real estate taxes of $2,640 for the current year have NOT been paid. What is the amount of the real estate tax proration to be credited to the buyer? (Use a 30-day month for calculation.)
    1. $168.67
    2. $868.67
    3. $1,268.66
    4. None of the above

80. A home is valued at $92,000. Property in this city is assessed at 70 percent of its value and the local tax rate is $3.40 per $100. What is the amount of the owner's monthly taxes?
    1. $182.47
    2. $260.67
    3. $2,189.60
    4. None of the above

81. A mother wants to know how much money her son owes on his mortgage loan. The mother knows that the interest part of the last monthly payment was $473.26. If her son is paying interest at the rate of 9 percent, what was the outstanding balance of the loan before the last payment was made?
    1. $52,584.44
    2. $55,921.03
    3. $63,101.33
    4. None of the above

82. You are selling your house to two brothers. The buyers will assume your outstanding mortgage, which has an unpaid balance of $58,700 after the last payment on August 1 and an annual interest rate of 9 percent. Interest is paid in advance each month. The sale is to be closed on August 18. What is the amount of mortgage interest to be credited to you at closing?
    1. $161.43
    2. $176.10
    3. $190.78
    4. None of the above

83. Using the mortgage factor chart on page 127, what is the monthly payment for a $150,000 loan at 11.5 percent for 30 years?
    1. $1,429.50   3. $1,525.50
    2. $1,486.50   4. $1,581.00

84. Using the information in question 83, what is the total interest paid over the life of the loan?
    1. $297,300
    2. $371,625
    3. $535,140
    4. None of the above

85. A broker sold a home for $146,000. The broker charged the owner 6 percent commission and will pay 25 percent of that amount to the listing salesperson and 30 percent to the selling salesperson. What amount of commission will the listing salesperson receive from the sale?
    1. $2,058
    2. $2,190
    3. $2,628
    4. None of the above

86. You receive a monthly salary of $600 plus 3.5 percent commission on all of your listings that sell and 2.5 percent on all of your sales. None of the listings that you took sold last month, but you receive $8,460 in salary and commission. What was the value of the property you sold?
    1. $131,000
    2. $224,571
    3. $314,400
    4. None of the above

87. You bought a home one year ago for $83,500. Property in your neighborhood is said to be increasing in value at a rate of 6 percent annually. If this is true, what is the current value of your real estate?
    1. $86,840
    2. $87,675
    3. $88,510
    4. None of the above

88. What is the actual value of your property if the annual taxes are $2,880 and real estate is assessed at 30 percent of actual value? (Figure a levy of 48 mills per $1 of assessed value.)
    1. $86,400
    2. $120,000
    3. $200,000
    4. None of the above

89. Three investors decided to pool their savings and buy some commercial real estate for $180,000. If one invested $60,000 and the second invested $40,000, what percentage of ownership was left for the third investor, if the percentage is based on capital investment rather than services rendered?
    1. 22.2 percent
    2. 33 percent
    3. 44.4 percent
    4. None of the above

90. A farmer was unable to secure credit from other sources, so he probably got a mortgage loan from which of the following?
    1. FHA
    2. Savings and loan
    3. Farm Service Agency
    4. Commercial bank

91. A and B, a married couple, bought a home in 1991 for $200,000. The sold their home in 1999 with a capital gain of $150,000. Capital gains tax on their profit will be
    1. nothing.   3. $150,000.
    2. $50,000.   4. $200,000.

92. As of 1999, the required holding period for a non-corporate taxpayer with regard to long term capital gains is
    1. 6 months.   3. 18 months.
    2. 12 months.   4. 24 months.

93. Which of the following home related expenses would NOT generally be tax deductible for a homeowner?
    1. Interest paid on a second mortgage
    2. Penalties for late payment of real estate taxes
    3. Prepayment penalties on loans
    4. Real estate taxes

94. Which of the following types of loans would be considered to be conventional?
    1. A privately insured loan
    2. A FHA loan
    3. A Freddie Mac loan
    4. A VA loan

95. Which of the following agencies administers special assistance programs in the secondary mortgage market?
    1. FDIC   3. FHLMC
    2. FNMA   4. GNMA

96. A margin is added to an index to determine the interest rate in which of the following types of mortgage?
    1. Adjustable rate
    2. Blanket
    3. Graduated payment
    4. Package

97. Which of the following statements would NOT be a material fact to be disclosed by a seller's agent?
    1. Presentation of all offers
    2. A relationship which the agent has with the buyer
    3. Buyer's ability to make a lower offer
    4. Discussion of disadvantages of an offer

98. Under the new capital gains tax law, a single person may take up to $250,000 in capital gains tax free on the sale of a home if that person has lived in the house for at least
    1. the past year.
    2. two of the past five years.
    3. one of the past three years.
    4. two of the last four years.

99. Losing a right to the court's injunction by inaction is an example of the doctrine of
    1. accession.
    2. eminent domain.
    3. annexation.
    4. laches.

100. *A* gave *B* a deed with an implied warranty. The deed was most likely a(n)
    1. general warranty deed.
    2. special warranty deed.
    3. bargain and sale deed.
    4. quitclaim deed.

ANSWER KEY WITH EXPLANATIONS

NOTE: The number in parentheses at the end of each explanation refers to the page number where this material is discussed.

1. **(2)** A leasehold estate is a non-freehold estate involving the tenant's right to occupy the real estate during the term of the lease. (135)
2. **(2)** A servient estate also is referred to as a servient tenement. The property that benefits from the easement is known as the dominant tenement. (29)
3. **(1)** Encumbrances may be liens, which affect the title, or physical encumbrances, which affect the condition of the land. (28–29)
4. **(2)** State inheritance taxes are a general lien and affect all the debtor's property. (29)
5. **(2)** A tenant in a net lease pays rent plus all or part of the property charges. A tenant in a gross lease pays a fixed rent, while the landlord pays all her own expenses. (135)

6. **(3)** A leasehold estate is a personal property interest. Joint tenancy and tenancy by the entirety require equal interests in most states. (31)
7. **(2)** A fee simple is the highest form of interest. A base fee is subject to certain limitations imposed by the owner. A life estate is limited to the life of an owner or some other person. Legal life states are created by state law. (30)
8. **(1)** Tenants in common may partition the property by agreement and, if no agreement, by judicial determination. (31)
9. **(2)** When a person dies intestate, the decedent's real estate and personal property pass to his or her heirs according to the statutes. (99)
10. **(1)** The life tenant generally is not answerable to the holder of the future interest. (31)
11. **(3)** A time-share estate includes a fee simple interest in condominium ownership. (135)
12. **(1)** Severalty refers to one owner, while joint tenants and tenants in common may convey individual interests. (31)
13. **(2)** The government has the right to acquire private property for public use while paying just compensation to the owner. The convention center would attract private development of hotels and retail establishments. The type of estate held by owners would not prevent the state from acquiring the land. (41)
14. **(2)** Eminent domain, laches, and escheat were defined earlier. (41)
15. **(3)** Police power is the power of the state to establish legislation to protect public health and safety and promote general welfare. (41)
16. **(4)** Police power is a public-land-use control; a deed restriction is a private-land-use control. (41–47)

17. **(2)** Joint and several liability means that each owner is personally responsible for the damages in whole; if only one owner is financially able to handle the total damage, that owner will have to pay all and attempt to collect from the other owners their proportionate shares. Retroactive liability means that liability also extends to people who have owned the site in the past. (46)

18. **(4)** The first three answers describe how licensees should handle that type of transaction. (44)

19. **(4)** Radon is an odorless radioactive gas released from rocks under the earth's surface that finds its way to the surface; it usually is released into the atmosphere. (46)

20. **(3)** License is permission to enter the land of another for a specific purpose. (29)

21. **(4)** A claim based on adverse possession must be notorious, open, and hostile. (99)

22. **(1)** An easement in gross is the personal interest to use the land of another. An easement appurtenant requires two tracts of land with one of the tracts benefitting from the easement. An easement by necessity is used where the owner is landlocked, and an easement by prescription involves hostile use of another's land. (29)

23. **(2)** A testator is a person who makes a will. Devise refers to a transfer of real property under a will. (99)

24. **(4)** Riparian rights are water rights granted to owners along a river or stream. (41)

25. **(4)** Accession refers to acquiring title to real property through the annexation of a fixture. Attachment is the act of placing a lien upon a person's property by a court. An exchange is a transaction in which part or all of the consideration is the transfer of like-kind property. (54)

26. **(1)** The principle of competition states that excess profits create ruinous competition. (54)

27. **(4)** Functional obsolescence and physical deterioration refer to a loss of value within the property, while external obsolescence refers to a loss of value outside the property. (55)

28. **(1)** The cost approach is considered most reliable in the appraisal of special-purpose buildings such as churches and schools. (55)

29. **(2)** Functional obsolescence is a loss in the value of a property resulting from a deficiency in the floor plan of a house. One bathroom would be inadequate for a four-bedroom house. (55)

30. **(2)** Tax consequences would be analyzed in a feasibility study exploring the potential for profitability in a proposed project. (56)

31. **(3)** Depreciation generally is applied to a wasting asset such as a building. Land is not considered a wasting asset. (55)

32. **(3)** The principle of progression states that the value of the most expensive home in a neighborhood will be lessened by the presence of less expensive homes being built nearby. The principle of competition states that excess profits create ruinous competition. Highest and best use states that each parcel of land should be developed to its most profitable use subject to legal constraints such as zoning. (54)

33. **(4)** The cost approach is most applicable to the appraisal of special purpose properties such as a church. The gross rent multiplier is used as a substitute for the income approach in the valuation of a single family home. The income approach is, of course, used in the appraisal of an income-producing property. (53)

34. **(3)** The sales comparison approach relies on comparable sales as well as sales that involve willing buyers and sellers, with neither under abnormal pressure. (55)

35. **(4)** Hypothecation refers to the pledging of property as security for a loan in which the borrower retains possession of the property pledged as security. Disintermediation results in less availability of mortgage money for lenders. A reverse annuity mortgage allows the borrower to receive periodic payments from the lender on the equity in the home. (69)

36. **(3)** Raising the discount rate would increase the interest rates and make mortgage money less available because of the increased cost of borrowing. (67)

37. **(1)** A term mortgage allows for payment of interest only with a lump-sum payment at maturity. A partially amortized loan also involves a lump-sum or balloon payment at maturity. (63)

38. **(2)** Ginnie Mae administers special assistance programs and works with Fannie Mae in secondary market activities. (69)

39. **(1)** The FHA insures mortgages made in the primary mortgage market. FNMA, GNMA, and FHLMC are major warehousing agencies in the secondary mortgage market. (69)

40. **(3)** RESPA provides for use of a HUD form. (102)

41. **(2)** An alienation clause states that if the borrower sells the property, the lender has the choice of either declaring the entire debt due and payable or allowing the buyer to assume the loan. A reconveyance clause is used in a trust deed. A reversion clause could be used in a deed and stipulates that if not complied with, the property reverts to the owner. (64)

42. **(1)** The commission agreement between the broker and client is negotiable and not subject to RESPA. (102)

43. **(3)** *Willful* violation is a misdemeanor punishable by a fine of up to $5,000, one year of imprisonment, or both. (114)

44. **(4)** Salesperson *C* is an agent of his broker *D* and a subagent of the listing broker *B*. (77)

45. **(3)** The fiduciary relationship of trust and confidence exists between the agent and the principal (client). The listing salesperson is a subagent of the client. The listing broker does not have a fiduciary responsibility to the buyer or customer. (75)

46. **(4)** A real estate broker is a special agent authorized to represent the principal in one specific transaction. (75–76)

47. **(1)** The seller is your client. The customer is a third party for whom a service is provided. (75)

48. **(2)** The six cooperating brokers were subagents of the seller. (75)

49. **(4)** The salesperson's listing of the home created an agency relationship between the seller and the salesperson's broker. The listing belongs to the broker. (77)

50. **(2)** Earnest money must be placed in the broker's trust account. (77)

51. **(1)** The buyer's broker has a fiduciary relationship with the buyer. (76)

52. **(4)** The broker may not offer legal advice—only a licensed attorney may do so. (75)

53. **(3)** Unless instructed otherwise, the broker is responsible for submitting all offers to his or her principal. (76)

54. **(1)** In most states, the broker has no lien on a property for a commission due on negotiating the sale of that property. Accordingly, the broker may not go to court to stop the transaction. The broker

cannot collect the commission from the buyer because the buyer is not in the agency relationship between the seller and broker. You should be aware that in Connecticut, a broker may place a lien on property if in compliance with the statute. (76)

55. **(2)** The broker is not required to charge a commission; the commission is negotiable. (76)

56. **(4)** The broker generally earns the commission when he or she produces a "ready, willing, and able" buyer. (76)

57. **(3)** The owner has the power to terminate the listing contract but not necessarily the right; the broker may be able to sue the owner for damages. The offeror would not be able to sue for specific performance because the offer was not accepted; the owner is not obligated to accept the offer. The broker would not be entitled to the earnest money because the offer was never accepted; the earnest money would have to be returned to the offeror. Finally, the point at which a commission is earned is no longer an absolute in all jurisdictions. (76)

58. **(3)** Dismissal of the salesperson does not affect the listing because the salesperson is not a party to the contract. Material damage is not destruction. Signing a second listing while the first listing is in effect is a clear breach of contract. Expiration of the listing was too late, in light of the second listing's having been signed. (92)

59. **(2)** An option is an example of a unilateral contract. An option is an agreement to keep open for a specified period an offer to sell or purchase property. When an option is exercised by the optionee, it becomes a bilateral contract. (89)

60. **(2)** The exclusive-agency listing allows the seller to sell his or her own house without paying the broker a commission. The broker under an exclusive-right-to-sell listing receives a commission regardless of who sells the property. Either type is given to only one broker. (90)

61. **(4)** The buyer agency open agreement is similar to an open listing seller agency agreement. (91)

62. **(2)** Standard listings contain a clause that stipulates that if the property is sold to someone who was introduced to the property by the broker, even after the listing has expired, the broker is entitled to a commission. Usually, there is a time period written into the clause. This is called the protection clause. Alienation and defeasance are related to mortgages while the habendum clause is found in a deed. (77)

63. **(2)** Any offer or counteroffer may be withdrawn at any time prior to acceptance by the offeree. (92)

64. **(4)** A tenant at sufferance continues to hold possession without consent of the landlord. (135)

65. **(4)** An index lease is adjusted periodically based on changes in a government cost-of-living index. (135)

66. **(4)** The quitclaim deed is the least protective. (100)

67. **(3)** The buyer (vendee) will not receive the deed to the property until the entire land contract has been paid in full. (92–93)

68. **(1)** Real property is conveyed by deed. (27)

69. **(2)** Erosion is the gradual wearing away of land by natural forces such as wind while avulsion is the sudden removal of soil by an act of nature. (48)

70. **(4)** Deeds are recorded to establish priority and provide protection against third parities. (102)

71. **(3)** The three IRS requirements for establishing independent contractor status are: 1.) the individual must have a current real estate license; 2.) the individual must have a written contract with broker that states that the salesperson will not be treated as a salesperson for federal tax purposes; and 3.) ninety percent or more of the individual's income as a licensee must be based on sales production rather than the number of hours worked. (104)

72. **(4)** In addition to the maximum fine, the broker may have to serve up to three years in prison. (78)

73. **(4)** The first three choices are examples of price fixing or boycotts. (78)

74. **(3)** Sex became a protected class in 1974; familial status and handicap became protected classes in 1989. (109)

75. **(4)** Blockbusting and redlining are violations of the Federal Fair Housing Act of 1968, which was discussed. Arbitrage refers to the difference between interest rates in financing arrangements. (111)

76. **(3)** The fair housing laws do not include age, martial status, or sexual orientation in their protected arrangements. (109)

77. **(4)** See Figure 16.3.

Figure 16.3

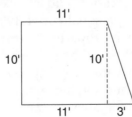

11' × 10' = 110 square feet, area of rectangle

½ (3' × 10' = ½ (30') = 15 square feet, area of triangle

110 + 15 = 125 square feet

To convert square feet to square yards, divide by 9

125 ÷ 9 = 13.888 square yards

$16.95 + $4.50 installation = $21.45, cost per square yard

$21.45 × 13.888 square yards = $297.92 (121–123)

78. **(3)** See Figure 16.4

Figure 16.4

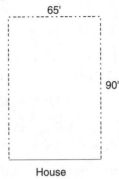

House

2 sides of 90' + one side of 65'

180' + 65' = 245 linear feet

245 × $8.40 = $2,058 (121–123)

79. **(3)** $2,640 ÷ 12 months = $220 per month

$220 ÷ 30 days = $7.333 per day

$220 × 5 months = $1,100

$7.333 × 23 days = $168.66

$1,100 + $168 = $1,268.66 (125)

80. **(1)** $92,000 × 70% (0.70) = $64,400 assessed value

Divide by 100 because the tax rate is stated per $100

$644 ÷ 100 = $644

$644 × $3.40 = $2,189.60, annual taxes

Divide by 12 to get the monthly taxes

$2,189.60 ÷ 12 = $182.47 (121)

81. **(3)** $473.26 × 12 = $5,679.12 annual interest

part ÷ percent = total

$5,679.12 ÷ 9% (0.09) = $63,101.33 (126–127)

82. **(2)** $58,700 × 9% (0.09) = $5,283

$5,283 ÷ 12 months = $440.25 per month

$440.25 ÷ 30 days = $14.675 per day

30-day month - 18 days = 12 days

$14.675 × 12 days = $176.10 (125–126)

83. **(2)** $150,000 ÷ 1,000 = $150 x 9.91 = $1,486.50 (128)

84. **(4)** $1,486.50 × 360 months =

$535,140 Total principal and interest − $150,000 Amount of loan =

$385,140 Total interest paid over the life of the loan (128)

85. **(2)** $146,000 sales price × 6% commission

$146,000 × 0.06 = $8,760 × 0.25 = $2,190 (120)

86. **(3)** $8,460 − $600 = $7,860 commission on sales

$7,860 ÷ 2.5% (0.025) = $314,400 value of property sold (120)

87. **(3)** $83,500 × 6% (0.06) = $5,010, annual increase in value

$83,500 + $5,010 = $88,510, current market value (120)

88. **(3)** $2,880 ÷ 0.048 = $60,000 assessed value

$60,000 ÷ 30% (0.30) = $200,000 market value (120)

89. **(3)** $60,000 first investor + $40,000 second investor = $100,000

$180,000 − $100,000 = $80,000 third investor's contribution

part ÷ total = percent

$80,000 ÷ $180,000 = 44.4% (120)

90. **(3)** The Farm Service Agency provides loans in communities of 10,000 or fewer. (66)

91. **(1)** A married couple may exclude $500,000 from capital gains tax for profits on the sale of a principal residence if they file jointly. (103)

92. **(2)** The holding period was lowered to 12 months in 1988. (103)

93. **(2)** Real estate taxes, but not penalties for late payments of taxes, are deductible. (103)

94. **(1)** A conventional loan is neither insured nor guaranteed by the government agency. (65)

95. **(4)** GNMA also works with FNMA in the tandem plan. (69)

96. **(1)** Most of the indexes used in adjustable rate mortgages are related to U.S. Treasury securities. The margin reflects the lender's cost of doing business. (67)

97. **(3)** A seller's agent would disclose, in most states, that the buyer was able to make a higher offer. (86)

98. **(2)** A married couple may take up to $500,000 in capital gains tax free in a similar situation. (103)

99. **(4)** Accession and annexation relate to personal property's becoming real property. Eminent domain allows the government to take private property for public use while paying just compensation to the owner. (47)

100. **(3)** General and warranty deeds contain promises or covenants while the quitclaim deed provides no warranty. A quitclaim deed, the grantor is only releasing or quitting an interest possessed; no warranty is provided to grantee. (100)

SALESPERSON EXAMINATION II

1. A grantor wishes to convey title to a grantee in a deed that creates the least protection for the grantee. The grantor should give the grantee a
    1. bargain and sale deed.
    2. quitclaim deed.
    3. general warranty deed.
    4. special warranty deed.

2. Of the following liens, which generally would be given the highest priority?
    1. A judgment issued last year
    2. A mortgage recorded four years ago
    3. A special assessment
    4. A mechanic's lien for work begun two months ago

3. You are showing a property described as being in the "nicest neighborhood in town" when, in fact, other neighborhoods are arguably as nice. A statement such as this is MOST likely to be categorized as
    1. fraud.
    2. puffery.
    3. misrepresentation.
    4. professional negligence.

4. You are chairperson of the Democratic party in your state and you also own an eight-unit apartment building you currently rent out. You are taking a rental application from a prospective tenant when she informs you that she works for the Republican party of your state. You inform her that all the apartments have been rented even though you know they have not been rented. Which of the following statements correctly describes your situation?
    1. You have violated Regulation Z.
    2. You have violated the federal fair housing law.
    3. You have exercised your rights as an owner of private property.
    4. You have violated RESPA.

5. When a listing agreement includes a broker protection clause, the clause
    1. protects the broker against any lawsuits filed by the client.
    2. allows the broker to buy the listed property if the broker is unable to sell it.
    3. automatically extends the listing for six months if the broker is unable to see the property.
    4. states that the owner will pay a commission to the listing broker if the property is sold to a buyer with whom the broker negotiated during the listing term within a specific time after the listing expires.

6. Which of the following would not be considered to be real property?
    1. Trees
    2. Buildings
    3. Trade fixtures
    4. Water rights

7. A sale is to be closed on June 23. Real estate taxes of $3,760 for the current year have NOT been paid. What is the amount of real estate tax proration to be credited to the buyer? (Use a 30-day month for calculation.)
    1. $1,566.65
    2. $1,806.86
    3. $1,879.98
    4. None of the above

8. The giver of an option is called the
    1. vendor.　　　　3. vendee.
    2. optionor.　　　 4. optionee.

9. Which of the following types of depreciation is generally incurable?
    1. Physical deterioration
    2. Economic obsolescence
    3. Functional obsolescence
    4. Physical depreciation

10. Three investors decided to pool their savings and buy a motel for $330,000. If one invested $90,000 and the second contributed $50,000, what percentage of ownership was left for the third investor?
    1. 14.1
    2. 27.3
    3. 57.6
    4. None of the above

11. Which of the following clauses gives a lender the right to declare the entire debt due and payable if the mortgaged property is sold?
    1. Acceleration clause
    2. Equitable redemption
    3. Defeasance clause
    4. Alienation clause

12. A woman owns a tract of land that also is a servient tenement. The easement over, through, or under the tract is a(n)
    1. lien.
    2. encumbrance.
    3. license.
    4. encroachment.

13. In the traditional exclusive right-to-sell listing agreement, how many agents are involved?
    1. Two
    2. One
    3. As many as the owner/listed chooses
    4. As many salespeople as the broker has in his or her office

14. The broker has listed an owner's home. This agreement will be terminated by all of the following **EXCEPT**
    1. death of the listing salesperson.
    2. death of the owner.
    3. death of the broker.
    4. bankruptcy of the broker.

15. A drunken man signed an offer to purchase. The contract that he signed is
    1. valid.
    2. void.
    3. voidable.
    4. unenforceable.

16. You sign an agreement to purchase a home. The contract requires that the seller replace the damaged living room carpet. The carpet you have chosen costs $18.95 per square yard plus $5.50 per square yard for installation. If the living room dimensions are as illustrated in Figure 16.5, how much will the seller have to pay for the job?
    1. $315.82
    2. $407.34
    3. $490.81
    4. None of the above

Figure 16.5

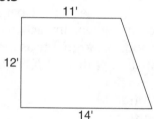

17. All of the following agency relationships could be classified as a cooperating broker in a real estate transaction **EXCEPT**
    1. a subagent.
    2. a buyer's broker.
    3. a selling broker.
    4. a listing broker.

18. An appraiser is trying to determine the value of an income property by capitalizing the income stream. Which of the following factors will the appraiser use?
    1. Mortgage interest
    2. Net income
    3. Replacement cost
    4. Income taxes

19. A partial release clause generally is found in a
    1. construction mortgage.
    2. package mortgage.
    3. blanket mortgage.
    4. wraparound mortgage.

20. Which of the following scenarios would NOT be considered discriminatory under the federal fair housing law?
    1. A man owns and lives in his four-unit apartment building, and he refuses to rent to families with children.
    2. A landlord charges higher security deposits to tenants with children.
    3. A landlord places all families in selected buildings in his apartment complex.
    4. A landlord refuses to rent to a pregnant woman.

21. Which of the following is a requirement for a valid deed?
    1. The grantee must sign the deed.
    2. The consideration must be in dollars.
    3. It must contain a subordination clause.
    4. It must contain a granting clause.

22. You bought a home one year ago for $115,900. Property in your neighborhood is said to be increasing in value at a rate of 8 percent annually. If this is true, what is the current value of your real estate?
    1. $125,172
    2. $134,444
    3. $144,063
    4. None of the above

23. An enforceable contract may contain any of the following as consideration EXCEPT
    1. money.   3. affection.
    2. love.   4. duress.

24. Which of the following is an economic characteristic of land?
    1. Immobility
    2. Situs
    3. Non-homogeneity
    4. Indestructibility

25. You have just given an option to buy your restaurant to your friend. Which of the following statements is NOT correct?
    1. Your friend is the optionee.
    2. Your are the optionor.
    3. Your friend is obligated to buy your restaurant.
    4. You friend may pay a non-refundable fee for the option right.

26. A broker listed a home under the condition that the owner receive $210,000 from the sale, with the broker being able to sell the property for as much as possible and to keep the difference as the commission. This agreement is an example of
    1. an exclusive-agency listing.
    2. an exclusive-right-to-sell listing.
    3. a net listing.
    4. an option listing.

27. A broker was offered a listing by homeowners who stated that they would not sell to a minority. The broker should
    1. accept the listing and allow the owners the right to choose the buyer.
    2. file a complaint with the local board of Realtors.
    3. accept the listing and make sure that no minorities are shown the property.
    4. refuse to accept the listing based on this condition.

28. All of the following would be public land use controls EXCEPT
    1. zoning.
    2. environmental protection laws.
    3. subdivision regulations.
    4. deed restrictions.

29. A home is valued at $103,000. Property in this city is assessed at 80 percent of its value and the local tax rate is $3.60 per $100. What is the amount of the owner's monthly taxes?
    1. $247.20
    2. $824
    3. $2,966.40
    4. None of the above

30. Who of the following persons would NOT be protected under the familial status definition according to the federal fair housing law?
    1. A 19-year-old girl living with her mother
    2. A 17-year-old boy living with his father
    3. A 14-year-old girl living with a person who is seeking legal custody of her
    4. A 21-year old woman who is pregnant

31. You are working as a salesperson for a broker and you have just sold a home. You will receive your share of the commission on the sale from
    1. the cooperating broker.
    2. the seller.
    3. your broker.
    4. the buyer.

32. You have been given oral permission to park in a friend's driveway while attending a football game. This right is a(n)
    1. easement appurtenant.
    2. encroachment.
    3. license.
    4. littoral right.

33. Charging a rate of interest in excess of the maximum rate allowed by law is
    1. novation.   3. laches.
    2. subordination.   4. usury.

34. Which of the following categories represents the FIRST one to be protected by federal law against discrimination in housing?
    1. Familial status
    2. Sex
    3. Race
    4. Sexual orientation

35. Using the mortgage factor chart on page 127, what is the monthly payment for a $170,000 loan at 8.5 percent for 30 years?
    1. $1,247.80   3. $1,307.30
    2. $1,276.70   4. $1,337.90

36. Using the information in question 35 above, what is the total interest paid over the life of the loan?
    1. $279,208
    2. $300,628
    3. $311,644
    4. None of the above

37. A broker listed a home for sale under an exclusive-right-to-sell listing. A second broker cooperated with the listing broker and sold the home. The house was sold and the commission split between the listing broker and the selling broker. Which of the following is FALSE?
    1. The selling broker is an agent of the listing broker.
    2. The listing broker is an agent of the seller.
    3. The selling broker is a subagent of the seller.
    4. A broker who is not the seller's agent cannot receive any part of the commission.

38. The requirement that a lender use the Uniform Settlement Statement form (HUD-1) for certain government-related loans is a requirement of
    1. IRS regulations.
    2. RESPA.
    3. Regulation Z.
    4. Federal Housing Administration (FHA) regulations.

39. All of the following would be considered a lien except a(n)
    1. encroachment.
    2. judgment.
    3. mechanic's lien.
    4. mortgage.

40. The borrower under a note secured by a mortgage is the
    1. mortgagor.
    2. trustee.
    3. mortgagee.
    4. vendee.

41. Which of the following licensees is MOST likely to act as a general agent for a client?
    1. Broker
    2. Property manager
    3. Cooperative broker
    4. Listing salesperson

42. The relationship of trust and confidence that a broker has with a principal is called a(n)
    1. fiduciary relationship.
    2. hypothecation.
    3. escrow.
    4. trustor relationship.

43. You received a real estate loan from a bank in which the lender was privately insured against loss in the event of default and foreclosure. The loan would have been which of the following?
    1. Conventional
    2. Federal Housing Authority (FHA)
    3. Veterans Administration (VA)
    4. Rural Development

44. A 500-acre farm is divided into house lots. The streets require one-eighth of the whole farm and there are 300 lots. How many square feet are in each lot?
    1. 48,636
    2. 55,584
    3. 63,525
    4. 72,600

45. Which of the following real estate loans is guaranteed against loss by the government?
    1. Conventional
    2. Veterans Administration (VA)
    3. Federal Housing Authority (FHA)
    4. Seller carries back in excess of $100,000

46. The agency that serves as the nation's banker and fiscal manager is the
    1. United States Treasury
    2. Federal Reserve System
    3. Federal National Mortgage Association (FNMA) or "Fannie Mae"
    4. Federal Home Loan Mortgage Corporation (FHLMC) or "Freddie Mac"

47. You receive a monthly salary of $1,200 plus a 3 percent commission on all of your listings that sell and 2.5 percent on all of your sales. None of the listings that you took sold last month, but you receive $6,300 in salary and commission. What is the value of the property that sold?
    1. $170,000
    2. $204,000
    3. $252,000
    4. None of the above

48. A mortgage in which the lender receives an equity position as well as interest on the mortgage is a(n)
    1. adjustable-rate mortgage.
    2. participation mortgage.
    3. reverse annuity mortgage.
    4. wraparound mortgage.

49. A sale closed on July 21. Real estate taxes of $3,420 for the current year have not been paid. What is the settlement sheet entry for the proration of the real estate taxes?
    1. Credit seller $1,985.50; debit buyer $1,988.50.
    2. Debit seller $1,995; credit buyer $1,995.
    3. Debit seller $1,909.50; credit buyer $1909.50.
    4. Debit buyer $00.00; credit seller $1,710.

50. *A*, who works for broker *C* on a 50-50 basis, sold a house listed by broker *E* for $193,950. The seller agreed to pay a 6 percent commission but stipulated in the listing that 60 percent was to go to the selling broker. How much commission (to the nearest dollar) will *A* make on this sale?
    1. $2,327.40
    2. $2,909.25
    3. $3,491.10
    4. $4,189.32

51. You tore out an old furnace and installed a new furnace with central air conditioning in your home. This newly installed personal property becomes a
    1. trade fixture.
    2. chattel fixture.
    3. fixture.
    4. physical trade fixture.

52. An easement would generally be utilized in which of the following?
    1. Accession
    2. Novation
    3. Partition
    4. Right of way

53. You had an exclusive right-to-sell listing with a seller who openly negotiated with a prospective buyer that you showed the property to during the listing term to wait until the listing had expired to buy the property so there would be a commission savings on the transaction. You found out that the property was sold to the prospective buyer within a month of the time the listing expired. Are you entitled to a commission? Why or why not?
    1. No; because the entire transaction occurred after the listing expired.
    2. No; because exclusive right-to-sell listings allow the seller to sell the property themselves without owing a commission.
    3. Yes; because you were the procuring cause of the sale.
    4. Yes; because you are entitled to a commission if the property is sold by anyone within a year of the listing period.

54. Which of the following would not be an example of economic obsolescence?
    1. Changing land uses in a neighborhood.
    2. The major employer in the city going out of business.
    3. A poor floor plan.
    4. A nearby landfill contaminating the ground waste.

55. A lender that refuses to provide loans on properties located in a minority neighborhood regardless of the ethnicity of the applicant would be engaged in a discriminatory practice known as
    1. steering.
    2. redlining.
    3. blockbusting.
    4. hypothecating.

56. A house located next to an airport would be an example of
    1. functional obsolescence.
    2. economic obsolescence.
    3. physical deterioration.
    4. physical depreciation.

57. You have sold your home and taken back a mortgage from the buyer for part of the balance due. The type of mortgage you hold is a
    1. blanket mortgage.
    2. purchase money mortgage.
    3. participation mortgage.
    4. wraparound mortgage.

58. An odorless radioactive gas produced by the decay of other radioactive materials in rocks under the earth's surface is which of the following?
    1. Asbestos
    2. UFFI
    3. Lead
    4. Radon

59. Within the field of real estate finance, what does the *secondary mortgage market* refer to?
    1. Placing of junior liens
    2. Transferability of mortgages among mortgagees
    3. Transferability of mortgages among mortgagors
    4. None of the above

60. Which of the following types of depreciation contains elements that are incurable only?
    1. Physical deterioration
    2. Economic obsolescence
    3. Functional obsolescence
    4. Physical depreciation

61. A woman wants to know how much money she owes on her mortgage loan. She knows that the interest part of the last monthly payment was $647.91. If she was paying an interest rate of 9 percent, what was the outstanding balance of her loan before the last payment was made?
    1. $64,791.10   3. $86,388
    2. $77,749.20   4. $97,186.50

62. Which of the following types of listings establishes a broker-compensation arrangement whereby the broker gets to keep all proceeds in excess of a stated minimum sales price?
    1. Net
    2. Open
    3. Exclusive agency
    4. Exclusive right-to-sell

63. Which of the following factors would NOT be considered by an appraiser in conducting a neighborhood analysis?
    1. Relation to the rest of the community
    2. Rent levels
    3. Racial characteristics of the residents
    4. Zoning

64. A contract in which the intentions of the parties are shown by their conduct is
    1. an express contract.
    2. an implied contract.
    3. a bilateral contract.
    4. an executory contract.

65. Who of the following is NOT considered an agent?
    1. A broker who has listed an owner's home for sale
    2. A property manager
    3. A salesperson employed by a broker
    4. A personal assistant

66. A swollen, rushing river sweeps away an outcropping of land with several trees on it. The term that most accurately identifies this kind of property loss is
    1. erosion.
    2. avulsion.
    3. accretion.
    4. disenfranchisement.

67. You have purchased three lots zoned for single-family use and combined them into one large parcel to build an apartment building. This is an example of
    1. the principle of progression.
    2. assemblage.
    3. the principle of substitution.
    4. plottage value.

68. A summary of all the recorded instruments affecting the title to a property is called a(n)
    1. abstract of title.
    2. certificate of title.
    3. escrow.
    4. title insurance policy.

69. A contract in which one party promises to do something if the other party performs a specific act is a(n)
    1. unenforceable contract.
    2. unilateral contract.
    3. void contract.
    4. bilateral contract.

70. Federal Fair Housing laws prohibit housing discrimination against all of the following groups of people **EXCEPT**
    1. women.
    2. college students.
    3. ethnic minorities.
    4. families with minor children.

71. The form of listing that provides the most protection to the broker is the
    1. exclusive agency.
    2. exclusive right-to-sell.
    3. net listing.
    4. open listing.

72. All of the following represent environmental hazards that may affect the marketability of a residential property **EXCEPT**
    1. xenon.
    2. radon gas.
    3. lead-based paint.
    4. underground storage tanks.

73. Brokers who violate the Sherman Antitrust Act may be punished by a maximum prison term of
    1. one year.   3. three years.
    2. two years.   4. five years.

74. *M*, a real estate broker, was renting *P*'s apartments as *P*'s property manager. *M* showed the remaining vacant apartment to *S*, a African-American woman. *M* checked *S*'s job, credit, and housing references and was about to inform *S* that she would be able to sign a lease when *P* called and inquired about *S*. *P* wanted to know *S*'s color. *M* should
    1. tell *P* because *M* has a fiduciary responsibility of loyalty to *P*.
    2. tell *P* only on the condition that *P* keeps the information in confidence.
    3. not tell *P* because it is not a material fact.
    4. not tell *P* because *S* is a member of a protected class.

75. An appraiser has estimated the replacement cost of an office building at $300,000. The building is 22 years old and has an estimated useful life of 60 years. What is the current total depreciation of the building?
    1. $90,000
    2. $110,000
    3. $130,000
    4. None of the above

76. What is the value of an apartment building expected to produce a net annual income of $20,000, if the owner estimates that he should receive a return of 8 percent on his investment?
    1. $120,000   3. $200,000
    2. $160,000   4. $250,000

77. *A* and *B*, a married couple, sold their home in 1999 and made a profit on the sale of $600,000. *A* and *B* had lived in that home since 1987. *A* and *B* will have to pay capital gains tax on
    1. $100,000   3. $500,000
    2. $250,000   4. $600,000

78. First time homebuyers may make penalty free withdrawals from their tax-deferred IRAs up to
    1. $5,000.   3. $20,000.
    2. $10,000.   4. $50,000.

79. A portion of *A*'s land is protected from judgment for unsecured debts. *A*'s protection is based on
    1. riparian rights.
    2. downer rights.
    3. littoral rights.
    4. homestead rights.

80. *A* has given *B* permission to park in *A*'s driveway during the month of July. *B* has
    1. an easement appurtenant.
    2. a life estate.
    3. a license.
    4. a easement by prescription.

ANSWER KEY WITH EXPLANATIONS

NOTE: The information in parentheses at the end of each explanation refers to the page number where this material is discussed.

1. **(2)** The general warranty and special warranty deed contain an express warranty. A bargain and sale deed has an implied warranty. A quitclaim deed contains no form of warranty. (100)

2. **(3)** Special assessments and real estate taxes take priority over all other liens, regardless of the date of recording. (29)

3. **(2)** Your opinion would be an example of puffing. (78)

4. **(3)** Political belief is not a protected class under the federal fair housing laws. (109)

5. **(4)** The broker protection clause refers to the broker's commission. The broker protection clause does not exist in Connecticut. In addition, the automatic extension of listing agreements is against the law in most states. (77)

6. **(3)** Trade fixtures are items installed by a tenant for conducting a business. (27)

7. **(2)** $3,760 ÷ 12 months = $313.33 per month

   $3,13.33 ÷ 30 days = $10.444 per day

   $313.33 × 5 months = $1,566.65

   $10.444 × 23 = $240.21

   $1,566.65 + $240.21 = $1,806.86 (125)

8. **(2)** The giver of an option is the optionor, while the buyer is the optionee. The vendor is a seller of realty; the vendee is the purchaser of realty. (92)

9. **(2)** Physical deterioration or depreciation and functional obsolescence may be incurable, while economic obsolescence generally is incurable. (55)

10. **(3)** $90,000 (first investor) + $50,000 (second investor) = $140,000

    $330,000 – $140,000 = $190,000 third investor's contribution

    part + total = percent

    $190,000 ÷ $330,000 = 0.5757 or 57.6% (132)

11. **(4)** An acceleration clause states that if the borrower defaults, the lender has the right to declare the entire debt due and payable. The defeasance clause requires the lender to execute a satisfaction of mortgage when the note is fully paid. Equitable redemption refers to the right of the borrower to redeem his interest in his property prior to a public foreclosure sale. (64)

12. **(2)** The tract of land over which an easement appurtenant runs is the servient tenement; an easement appurtenant is an encumbrance as are the lien, license and encroachment. (29)

13. **(2)** In an exclusive right-to-sell listing, there is only one agent. All other brokers and salespeople involved in the transaction are subagents of the seller. (90)

14. **(1)** The listing salesperson is a subagent whose death will not affect the listing contract. (91)

15. **(3)** A voidable contract may be disaffirmed because one of the parties signed when under duress. (90)

16. **(2)** See Figure 16.6.

Figure 16.6

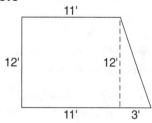

$11' \times 12' = 132' = 132$ square feet, area of rectangle

$\frac{1}{2}(3' \times 12') = \frac{1}{2}(36') = 18$ square feet, area of triangle

$132 + 18 = 150$ square feet

To convert square feet to square yards divide number of square feet by 9

$150 \div 9 = 16.666$ square yards

$\$18.95 + \$5.50 = \$24.45$ cost per square yard

$\$24.45 \times 16.66$ square yards $= \$407.34$ (132)

17. **(4)** The listing broker would be the agent of the seller and thus not be the cooperating broker. (75)

18. **(2)** The net income in an operating statement does not reflect interest and taxes. (55)

19. **(3)** A blanket mortgage covers more than one property or lot; it is typically used to finance the development of a subdivision. (66)

20. **(1)** Rentals of rooms in an owner-occupied one-family to four-family dwelling are exempt from the federal fair housing law. (111)

21. **(4)** The grantor must sign the deed. Consideration can be monetary or non-monetary. Subordination clauses are used in mortgages. (101)

22. **(1)** $\$115,900 \times 8\%(0.08) = \$9,272$ annual increase in value

$\$115,900 + \$9,272 = \$125.172$ current market value (132)

23. **(4)** A valid contract must be based on good and valuable consideration. If duress is involved, however, there would not be a meeting of the minds; the contract would thus not be valid. (89)

24. **(2)** Immobility, non-homogeneity, and indestructibility are physical characteristics of land. (27)

25. **(3)** The optionee (prospective buyer) pays for the option right but assumes no obligation to make any other payments until she decides whether or not to exercise her option right. (92)

26. **(3)** The other listings would include a commission agreed on in advance in terms of a percentage dollar amount. (90–91)

27. **(4)** The federal fair housing law provides that it is unlawful to discriminate on the basis of race, when selling residential property. The broker must refuse to accept the listing based on this condition. (109)

28. **(4)** Zoning, environmental protection laws and subdivision regulations are public land-use controls. (41–42)

29. **(1)** $\$103,000 \times 80\% (0.80) = \$82,400$ assessed value

Divide by 100 because the tax rate is stated per $100.

$\$82,400 \div 100 = \$842.00$

$\$824 \times \$3.60 = \$2,966.40$ annual tax

$\$2,966.40 \div 12 = \$247.20$ (121)

30. **(1)** The familial status category protects individuals who have not reached the age of 18, under certain circumstances. (109)

31. **(3)** A salesperson can only receive compensation from the broker for whom she works. (77)

32. **(3)** A license provides permission to enter the land of another for a specific purpose. Littoral rights involve water rights. An en-

croachment is an illegal extension of the building beyond the land of its owner. An easement appurtenant requires two tracts of land. (29)

33. **(4)** Charging a rate of interest in excess of the maximum rate allowed by law is known as usury. Novation refers to an agreement in which a new debtor is accepted in place of an old one. Laches is a court doctrine used to bar a legal claim because of undue delay in asserting the claim. Subordination refers to an agreement that changes the order of priority of liens between two creditors. (69)

34. **(3)** Race became a protected class in 1968; sex in 1974. Sexual orientation is not a protected class under federal fair housing law. (109)

35. **(3)** $170,000 ÷ 1,000 = 170 × 7.69 = $1,307.30 (13) (128)

36. **(2)** $1307.30 × 360 months =
$470,628 Total principle and interest
−170,000 Amount of loan
$300,628 Total interest paid over life of the loan (128)

37. **(4)** The cobroker is an agent of the listing broker as well as a sub-agent of the seller. A broker need not be the seller's agent to receive part of the commission. (75)

38. **(2)** The other choices do not have requirements on what closing form should be used. (102)

39. **(1)** An encroachment is an encumbrance. (28–29)

40. **(1)** The borrower under a note secured by a mortgage is a mortgagor. The lender is a mortgagee. The trustee holds the real estate as a security for the loan under a trust deed. The vendee is the buyer in a real estate contract. (63)

41. **(2)** The broker is a special agent while the cooperative broker and listing salesperson are subagents. (75–76)

42. **(1)** Hypothecation is the pledging of property as security for a loan without losing possession of it. Escrow is a third party agreement while the trustor is the borrower in a trust deed. (75)

43. **(1)** Privately insured loans are conventional loans. All non-FHA and non-DVA loans are conventional loans. (65)

44. **(3)** 43,560 sq. ft. per acre × 500 acres

21,780,000 × (0.125) = 2,772,500 sq. ft. for streets

21,780,000 − 2,722,500 = 19,057,500 sq. ft. for lots

19,057,500 sq. ft. ÷ 300 lots = 63,525 sq. ft. per lot (28)

45. **(2)** The DVA loan provides a guarantee to the lender. An FHA loan is insured. (65)

46. **(2)** The U.S. Treasury is responsible for supervising the daily fiscal operations of the federal government. FHLMC and FNMA are warehousing agencies in the secondary mortgage market. The Federal Reserve regulates the flow of money through member banks. (67)

47. **(2)** $6,300 − $1,200 = $5,100 commission on sales

$5,100 ÷ 2,5%(0.025) = $204,000 value of property sold (76)

48. **(2)** A participation mortgage provides the lender with a percentage of cash flow beyond the interest paid by the borrower. (67)

49. **(3)** $3,420 ÷ 12 months = $285 per month

$285 ÷ 30 days = $9.50 per day

$286 × 6 months = $1,710

$9.50 × 21 days = $199.50

$1,710 + $199.50 = $1,909.50

The taxes for the year have not been paid. When they are paid, the buyer will be in possession and have to pay the bill. The seller, therefore, must pay (be debited) for the portion of the year that she occupied the property. The buyer receives a credit for the same amount. (125)

50. **(3)** $193,950 sales price × 6% (0.06) commission = $11,367 broker commission

    $11,637 × 60% (0.60) = $6,982.20 × 0.05 = $3,491.10 selling salesperson's commission (76)

51. **(3)** A trade fixture is attached to real property for the purpose of carrying on a business. A chattel fixture is an item of personal property. (27)

52. **(4)** A commercial easement in gross would be used for right-of-way. (29)

53. **(3)** The broker's commission would be protected by the broker protection clause in the listing contract. (77)

54. **(3)** Economic obsolescence is a loss in value due to factors outside the property. (55)

55. **(2)** Redlining refers to discriminatory denial of loans to people in selected areas, regardless of their qualifications. (111)

56. **(2)** Economic or environmental obsolescence is a loss in value resulting from a factor external to the property, such as being located next to an airport. (55)

57. **(2)** A purchase money mortgage involves seller financing in which the legal title passes to the buyer. (66)

58. **(4)** Asbestos is a material used for many years as insulation on heating pipes and ducts. UFFI is a synthetic material generally used to insulate buildings. Lead is a material used to impede water flow. (44)

59. **(2)** The secondary mortgage market deals only with the first mortgages of mortgagors (borrowers) transferred among mortgagees (lenders). (68–69)

60. **(2)** Economic obsolescence occurs outside the property. (55)

61. **(3)** $647.91 × 12 = $7,774.92

    $7,774.92 ÷ 9% (0.09) = $86,388 (126–27)

62. **(1)** Under a net listing, the broker may retain as compensation all money received in excess of the "net" set by the seller; the compensation is not definitely specified. This type of listing is either prohibited or discouraged by licensing authorities in many states. (90–91)

63. **(3)** Appraisers are not allowed to discuss racial characteristics in an appraisal report. (56)

64. **(2)** A contract in which the parties show their intentions by conduct is an implied contract; intention is shown by words in an expressed contract. Promises are exchanged in a bilateral contract. Something remains to be performed in an executory contract. (89)

65. **(4)** A personal assistant would be an employee of the broker. (75)

66. **(2)** Avulsion is the *sudden* tearing away of land by action of water while erosion is the *gradual* wearing away of land by water and wind. (47–48)

67. **(2)** Plottage is the value increment resulting from assemblage. (54)

68. **(1)** A buyer's attorney examines the abstract for flaws and prepares a written opinion of the condition of ownership. (100)

69. **(2)** An unenforceable contract appears to be valid but neither party may sue the other to force performance. A void contract lacks an essential element of a valid contract and thus has no legal effect. A bilateral contract is a contract in which both parties promise to do something. (89)

70. **(2)** Sex, race, and familial status are protected classes under the Federal Fair Housing Law. (109)

71. **(2)** Under an exclusive right-to-sell listing, the broker receives the commission regardless of who sells the property. (90–91)

72. **(1)** Xenon is an inert gas and trace element in air. (44–46)

73. **(3)** The Sherman Antitrust Act also provides for a maximum $100,000 fine. (78)

74. **(4)** A license may not disclose that a prospective tenant is a member of a protected class. (110)

75. **(2)** $300,000 ÷ 60 = $5,000 annual depreciation charge

    $5,000 × 22 = $110,000 current total depreciation (124)

76. **(4)** $I ÷ R = V$
    $20,000 ÷ .08 = $250,000 estimated value (125)

77. **(1)** *A* and *B* would be entitled to an exclusion of $500,000. (103)

78. **(2)** The withdrawals must be used for down payments on their homes. (103)

79. **(4)** Riparian and littoral rights are water rights, while dower rights is a legal life estate. (31)

80. **(3)** An easement appurtenant requires a dominant tenement while an easement by prescription requires use without the owner's approval. A life estate is limited to the lifetime of the owner of the life estate or the lifetime of another (pur autrie vie). (29)

SALESPERSON EXAMINATION III

1. Which of the following terms would include the interests, benefits, and rights inherent in the ownership of real estate?
   1. Chattels
   2. Personal property
   3. Real property
   4. Trade fixtures

2. Which of the following is a physical characteristic of land?
   1. Scarcity
   2. Situs
   3. Permanence of investment
   4. Immobility

3. C and D held title as joint tenants. Which of the following statements would NOT correctly describe the requirements for them to own as joint tenants?
   1. C and D have the right of survivorship.
   2. C and D must have equal interests.
   3. C and D must be married.
   4. C and D may partition the land.

4. Which of the following statements would NOT correctly describe easements?
   1. An easement is an encumbrance.
   2. An easement appurtenant must have a dominant tenement and a servient tenement.
   3. An easement in gross must have a dominant tenement.
   4. An easement constitutes an interest in land.

5. D has a property that is a servient tenement in an easement appurtenant. D is considering selling his property to F. Which of the following statements would NOT correctly describe their potential transaction?
   1. The easement is an encumbrance.
   2. The easement may have a negative effect on the value of the property.
   3. The easement is very likely to prevent D from selling his property to F.
   4. The easement may have an impact on F's use of the property.

6. Contractor R replaced the roof on T's house. If T refuses to pay R for the work, R has the right to
   1. remove the roof.
   2. take T's personal property and hold it as compensation should the lien be unpaid.
   3. file a mechanic's lien.
   4. record a judgment.

7. The local utility company holds an easement to install power lines on a vacant lot. This is an easement
   1. appurtenant.
   2. in gross.
   3. by necessity.
   4. by prescription.

8. A wife and husband may NOT hold title to their home as
   1. tenants by the entirety.
   2. tenants at will.
   3. tenants in common.
   4. joint tenants.

9. L, M, and P are joint tenants. If L dies
   1. L's interest will go to his surviving spouse.
   2. L's interest will go to M or P depending on the terms of L's will.
   3. L's interest will escheat to the state.
   4. L's interest will go to M and P.

10. The SE¼ of the SW¼ of the NE¼ of Section 23 contains
    1. 10 acres.
    2. 40 acres.
    3. 160 acres.
    4. 320 acres.

11. *V* has been informed that his land is being taken by the state for the development of a new highway. The state will pay *V* for his land. This process illustrates the right of
    1. escheat.
    2. police power.
    3. taxation.
    4. eminent domain.

12. Which of the following would NOT be a governmental restriction on land?
    1. Police power
    2. Deed restriction
    3. Eminent domain
    4. Taxation

13. *K* builds an office building on commercially zoned land that is subsequently rezoned by the city to residential. *K* will
    1. have to close his office building.
    2. have to get his land rezoned by the city to continue operating his building.
    3. need a conditional use permit to continue operating his property.
    4. be able to continue with his office building which is now a nonconforming use.

14. *T* wants to build a medical clinic in a neighborhood that is zoned residential. *T* will need to obtain a
    1. non-conforming use.
    2. down zoning.
    3. variance.
    4. conditional use permit.

15. EMFs are created by
    1. peeling paint.
    2. the movement of electrical currents.
    3. contaminated groundwater.
    4. the decay of radioactive materials in rocks under the earth's surface.

16. Which of the following hazardous substances enters a house through the foundation of a house?
    1. Asbestos
    2. Radon
    3. Lead
    4. Urea-formaldehyde foam insulation

17. *C* objected to the violation of a deed restriction in his subdivision but waited one year to request a court injunction to enforce the restriction. The judge subsequently ruled that *C* had waited too long to request court action. The judge would not issue the injunction. *C's* loss is an example of
    1. accession.
    2. reliction.
    3. annexation.
    4. laches.

18. The water rights of a landowner adjacent to a stream are known as
    1. equitable rights.
    2. littoral rights.
    3. riparian rights.
    4. prior appropriation rights.

19. A Holiday Inn was developed just outside a city and within six months was operating at 95 percent occupancy. One year later a Marriott was built across the street. This would be an example of the principle of
    1. competition.
    2. contribution.
    3. progression.
    4. increasing and decreasing returns.

20. A four-bedroom house with a one-car garage is an example of
    1. physical deterioration.
    2. functional obsolescence.
    3. environmental obsolescence.
    4. locational obsolescence.

21. The most reliable approach for appraising a single-family home would be the
    1. cost approach.
    2. income approach.
    3. sales comparison approach.
    4. gross income multiplier.

22. Which of the following statements correctly describes how effective gross income is calculated in the operating statement?
    1. Annual potential gross income minus annual operating expenses.
    2. Annual potential gross income minus vacancy and rent loss.
    3. Annual potential gross income ÷ the capitalization rate.
    4. Annual potential gross income ÷ annual operating expenses.

23. An example of a governmental factor to consider in a neighborhood analysis would be
    1. the street pattern.
    2. new construction.
    3. population density.
    4. special assessments.

24. Which of the following would NOT be a characteristic of value?
    1. Effective demand   3. Plottage
    2. Utility   4. Scarcity

25. Deposits in commercial banks are insured by
    1. BIF.   3. FNMA.
    2. SAIF.   4. GNMA.

26. Which of the following statements does NOT correctly describe the secondary mortgage market?
    1. FNMA buys conventional, FHA, and VA loans.
    2. GNMA works with FNMA in the tandem plan.
    3. FHLMC administers special assistance programs.
    4. FNMA sells government guaranteed bonds.

27. Deposits in commercial banks are insured for up to
    1. $10,000.   3. $50,000
    2. $20,000.   4. $100,000.

28. Which of the following lenders does NOT provide its own money for loans on real estate?
    1. Commercial banks
    2. Mortgage brokers
    3. Savings and loan associations
    4. Life insurance companies.

29. A trust deed generally is released by a
    1. satisfaction document.
    2. release document.
    3. reconveyance document.
    4. acceleration document.

30. Using the mortgage factor chart on page 127, what is the monthly payment for a $200,000 loan at 9.5 percent for 15 years?
    1. $1,682   3. $2,090
    2. $2,060   4. $2,120

31. Using the information in question 30, what is the total interest paid over the life of the loan?
    1. $176,200   3. $463,200
    2. $181,600   4. $552,400

32. Which of the following mortgages utilizes an "equity kicker"?
    1. Blanket mortgage
    2. Package mortgage
    3. Wraparound mortgage
    4. Participation mortgage

33. Which of the following laws would utilize a "trigger"?
    1. Statute of limitations
    2. Regulation Z
    3. RESPA
    4. Statute of frauds

34. Reserve requirements for banks are controlled by the
    1. BIF.
    2. FDIC.
    3. FED.
    4. U.S. Treasury.

35. Salesperson *A* is employed by Broker *C* to sell *E*'s house, which is listed with *C*. *A* is
    1. *C*'s subagent
    2. *E*'s agent.
    3. a general agent.
    4. *C*'s agent.

36. Broker *P* listed *S*'s house. *P* has the authority to
    1. modify the listing price.
    2. accept an offer for *S*.
    3. encourage prospective buyers to make an offer at less than list price.
    4. market the property.

37. Broker *Q* listed *W*'s house, which was sold by broker *Y*. Which of the following would NOT describe *Y*'s role in the transaction?
    1. *Y* was a buyer's agent.
    2. *Y* was a cooperating broker.
    3. *Y* was a listing agent.
    4. *Y* was a subagent.

38. You listed a home that was subsequently shown by four cooperating brokers and five buyer's brokers. How many single-agency relationships were involved in this transaction?
    1. One
    2. Four
    3. Six
    4. Ten

39. You listed a home for $200,000 and agreed to a 7 percent commission on the selling price. You and the seller subsequently amended the list price to $190,000 with a commission of 6 percent of the selling price. The house sold two weeks later for $180,000. Your commission was
    1. $10,800.
    2. $11,400.
    3. $12,600.
    4. $14,000.

40. Broker *A* listed *B*'s house for sale. The next day, *A* was contacted by *C* and *D* about the availability of homes in the city. On the following day, *A* showed *B*'s house to *C* and *D*. Which of the following statements correctly describe this situation.
    1. *A* has created a fiduciary relationship with *B*, *C*, and *D*.
    2. When *A* showed *B*'s house to *C* and *D*, *A* was entering into a dual agency.
    3. *B*, *C*, and *D* are *A*'s customers.
    4. *B* is a client of *A* and *C* and *D* are *A*'s customers.

41. Broker *M* listed the home of owner V who indicated that she was very anxious to sell her house. *M* may
    1. disclose to prospective buyers that the seller will take less that the list price.
    2. not disclose the seller's motivation unless he has the owner's permission to do so, in writing.
    3. not disclose the seller's motivation under any condition.
    4. disclose the seller's motivation only if he is showing *V*'s house to a buyer with whom he has a buyer agency agreement.

42. Which of the following statements would NOT be a violation of the antitrust law?
    1. Two brokers agree not to share listings with a third broker.
    2. A broker in a listing presentation informs a prospective client that he would have to receive a 7 percent commission because that is the local board rate.
    3. A broker refuses to sell his listed house to a customer unless the customer lists her present home with the broker.
    4. A broker refuses to give another broker the same MLS commission as she offered to the rest of the brokers on MLS.

43. *Y*, who works for broker *T* on a 50-50 basis, sold a house listed by broker *S* for $206,000. The seller agreed to pay a 7 percent commission but stipulated in the listing that 55 percent was to go to the selling broker. How much commission (to nearest dollar) will *Y* make on this sale?
    1. $3,966
    2. $7,931
    3. $14,420
    4. None of the above

44. Which of the following would not be classified as a latent defect?
    1. Nonconforming use of property
    2. Inadequate electrical outlets
    3. A sagging roof
    4. An inadequate furnace

45. Which of the following statements correctly describes the status of dual agency?
    1. Dual agency is always allowed as long as the broker tells the parties.
    2. Dual agency is legal in every state.
    3. Disclosure of dual agency should be made subsequent to completing an offer to purchase.
    4. Dual agency is not allowed unless all parties agree to it.

46. Which of the following statements would be a material fact to be disclosed by the seller's agent?
    1. Presentation of all offers.
    2. The buyer's ability to make a higher offer.
    3. Disclosure of property's deficiencies.
    4. Disclosure of how long the property has been listed.

47. Broker *F* listed owner *Z*'s house with the condition that *F*'s commission would be the excess received over $160,000. *F* has a(n)
    1. exclusive agency listing.
    2. exclusive right-to-sell listing.
    3. open listing.
    4. net listing.

48. *P* signed an offer to purchase in a state of obvious drunkenness. The next morning he realized what he had done and told the broker that he did not want to be bound by the terms of the contract. This would be an example of a(n)
    1. valid contract.
    2. void contract.
    3. voidable contract.
    4. unenforceable contract.

49. Which of the following would NOT terminate a listing contract?
    1. The listing broker dies.
    2. The salesperson dies.
    3. The listed property is destroyed.
    4. Bankruptcy of the owner of the listed property.

50. *G* and *J* entered into a contract to purchase subject only to *G*'s getting the designated financing. The contract would be classified as a(n)
    1. bilateral contract.
    2. executed contract.
    3. unilateral contract.
    4. executory contract.

51. Buyer *S* and seller *T* have entered into a binding offer to purchase. Which of the following would correctly describe the rights of the parties at this point in the transaction?
    1. *T* holds equitable title.
    2. *S* is entitled to immediate possession.
    3. *S* holds equitable title.
    4. *T* may terminate the contract.

52. Which of the following require certain real estate contracts to be in writing in order to be enforceable?
    1. Statute of descent and distribution
    2. Statute of frauds
    3. Statute of limitations
    4. Uniform commercial code

53. Seller *D* entered into a land contract with buyer *L*. Which of the following correctly describes the parties?
    1. *D* is the grantor; *L* is the grantee.
    2. *L* is the vendor; *D* is the vendee.
    3. *D* is the grantee; *L* is the grantor.
    4. *D* is the vendor; *L* is the vendee.

54. *A* gave *C* an option on her home. *C* has 30 days to inform *A* as to whether he will exercise his option. At this point in the transaction the contract is a(n)
    1. bilateral contract.
    2. unenforceable contract.
    3. unilateral contract.
    4. anticipatory contract.

55. *M* and *O* wish to change the closing date on their binding offer to purchase (agreement or contract). They should generally use which of the following forms to modify the language?
    1. An amendment
    2. A counteroffer
    3. An addendum
    4. A multiple counteroffer

56. A seller and buyer entered into an instrument of conveyance in which the buyer immediately received legal title. Which of the following instruments would have been used by the parties?
    1. An offer to purchase
    2. A deed
    3. A land contract
    4. An option

57. A man forged his wife's name on a deed and sold their home. The wife subsequently was able to have the title insurance company give her a check for one-half the market value of the home. Which type of deed would the wife usually give to the title company upon receipt of the check?
    1. A warranty deed
    2. A bargain and sale deed
    3. A special warranty deed
    4. A quitclaim deed

58. One of the covenants in a general warranty deed promises that the grantor has title and the right to convey. This is the covenant of
    1. further assurance.
    2. quiet enjoyment.
    3. seisin.
    4. warranty forever.

59. Which of the following parties must sign the deed in order for it to be a valid conveyance?
    1. The listing broker
    2. The director of the Public Record office
    3. The grantor
    4. The grantee

60. Which of the following types of title evidence would prevent a property from being acquired through adverse possession?
    1. Abstract and opinion
    2. Torrens system
    3. Certificate of title
    4. Title insurance

61. A married couple sold their home for $400,000 in 1999 after living in it for 10 years. They purchased their home in 1987 for $190,000. The balance of their mortgage when they sold was $30,000. The capital gains tax on their profit will be
    1. $42,000
    2. $52,500
    3. zero
    4. $160,000

62. Which of the following laws prohibits the payment of referral fees by lenders when no services are actually rendered?
    1. Regulation Z
    2. RESPA
    3. Statute of frauds
    4. Statute of limitations

63. *B* had been diagnosed as mentally ill when his rental application was rejected by a landlord based on his mental health problems. Which of the following statements correctly de-scribes *B*'s status under the Federal Fair Housing Law?
    1. *B*'s illness does not provide him with protected class status.
    2. Once *B* has signed a lease he may not be evicted because he is a member of a protected class.
    3. *B* is protected under the law but must file a complaint within one year after the alleged discriminatory housing practice.
    4. *B* is not protected unless he is currently receiving treatment for his illness.

64. Which of the following would NOT be a protected class under the Federal Equal Credit Opportunity Act?
    1. Sex
    2. Marital status
    3. Dependency on public assistance
    4. Sexual orientation

65. Which of the following would NOT be protected under the Federal Fair Housing Law?
    1. A person diagnosed as mentally ill
    2. A convicted drug dealer
    3. An alcoholic who has been diagnosed, treated, and is not currently addicted
    4. A drug addict who has been diagnosed, treated, and is not currently addicted

66. Which of the following laws regulate the advertising of credit terms by lenders?
    1. Regulation Z
    2. RESPA
    3. Federal Equal Credit Opportunity Act
    4. Statute of frauds

67. Which of the following properties would NOT be exempt from the Federal Fair Housing Law?
    1. The rental of an owner-occupied one-family home
    2. The Elk's Club renting only to members on a non-profit basis
    3. The Lutheran Church renting its own dwelling units on the condition that they be occupied by only Lutherans
    4. The rental of an owner-occupied five-family apartment building

68. Which of the following laws utilizes "trigger terms"?
    1. Federal Equal Credit Opportunity Act
    2. RESPA
    3. Regulation Z
    4. Statute of frauds

69. A broker sold a home for $154,000. The broker charged the seller a 6 percent commission and will pay 30 percent of that amount to the listing salesperson and 35 percent to the selling salesperson. What amount of commission will the listing salesperson receive from the sale of the home?
    1. $2,310
    2. $2,772
    3. $3,234
    4. None of the above

70. Buyer *A* bought a house for $200,000. She was required to pay her bank a discount fee of $9,600 for points on her $160,000 loan. How many points did *A* pay for the loan?
    1. 4   3. 6
    2. 5   4. 7

71. You want to know how much money you owe on your mortgage loan. You know that the interest portion of your last monthly payment was $619.73. If you are paying interest at the rate of 9 percent, what was the outstanding balance of your loan before the last payment was made?
    1. $82,631
    2. $92,960
    3. $106,239
    4. None of the above

72. You own a home valued at $146,000. Property in your area is assessed at 70 percent of its value and the local tax rate is $2.84 per $100. What is the amount of your semiannual taxes?
    1. $241.87
    2. $1,451.24
    3. $2,902.48
    4. None of the above

73. You bought a house one year ago for $172,900. Property in your neighborhood is said to be increasing at a rate of 5 percent annually. If this is true, what is the current market value of your real estate?
    1. $179,816
    2. $181,545
    3. $183,279
    4. None of the above

74. You receive a monthly salary of $600 plus 2 percent commission on all of your listings that sell and 3 percent on all of your sales. None of the listings you took sold last month, but you received $7,940 in salary and commission. What was the value of the property you sold?
    1. $146,800
    2. $244,667
    3. $367,000
    4. None of the above

75. An owner leases the 16 apartments in his building for a total monthly rental of $12,800. If this figure represents an 8 percent annual return on the owner's investment, what was the original cost of the property?
    1. $153,600
    2. $1,706,667
    3. $1,920,000
    4. $2,194,286

For the next two questions regarding closing statement prorations, base your calculations on a 30-day month. Carry all computations to three decimal places and round off after all computations have been made.

76. A sale is to be closed on March 14. Real estate taxes for the current year are $3,170 and have not been paid. What amount of the real estate tax proration will be credited to the buyer?
    1. $651.62
    2. $660.42
    3. $642.81
    4. None of the above

77. In a sale of residential property, real estate taxes for the current year amounted to $2,840 and already have been paid by the seller. The sale is to be closed on December 3. What is the settlement sheet entry for the tax proration?
    1. $220.87 debit to seller, $220.87 credit to buyer
    2. $212.98 credit to seller, $212.98 debit to buyer
    3. $2,627.02 debit to seller, $205.09 credit to buyer
    4. $212.98 credit to seller only

78. The tenant is a trespasser in which of the following leases?
    1. Estate for years
    2. Periodic estate
    3. Tenancy at will
    4. Tenancy at sufferance

79. *A* purchased a fee simple interest in one of 40 units in a property development. *A* also received a 2 percent share of the ownership in all of the grounds and facilities outside the units. *A* owns which of the following types of property?
     1. Partnership
     2. Time-share
     3. Cooperative
     4. Condominium

80. *C* borrowed from several banks to get into an investment he could not have financed on his own. This is an example of
     1. Appreciation
     2. Leverage
     3. Equity buildup
     4. Pyramiding

ANSWER KEY WITH EXPLANATIONS

NOTE: The information in parenthesis at the end of each explanation refers to the page number where the material is discussed.

1. **(3)** Chattels and trade fixtures are personal property. (27)
2. **(4)** Scarcity, situs and performance of investment are economic characteristics. (27)
3. **(3)** Joint tenants do not have to be married. (31–32)
4. **(3)** An easement in gross does not have a dominant tenement; it has a servient tenement only. (29)
5. **(3)** An easement would have to be disclosed to a potential buyer, but is unlikely to affect the transfer of title to the property. (29)
6. **(3)** *R* would have to give notice of the lien and then file a court suit within the time required by state law. (29)
7. **(2)** The easement held by the utility company is a commercial easement in gross. (29)

8. **(2)** In a tenancy at will, a person continues occupancy of the real estate with the owner's permission. (31–32)
9. **(4)** *L*'s interest will automatically go to *M* and *P* under the right of survivorship. (31–32)
10. **(1)** $4 \times 4 \times 4 = 64$

    640 acres ÷ 64 = 10 acres (28)
11. **(4)** Escheat is a state law which provides for ownership to transfer to the state when an owner dies intestate (without a will) leaving no heirs and no will. Police power is used to enact laws such as zoning ordinances and building codes. Taxation on real estate is used to raise funds to meet the needs of the government. (41)
12. **(2)** A deed restriction is a private land use control. The other answers were discussed in the preceding question. You should be aware that in the event of a conflict between a zoning ordinance and a deed restriction, the more restrictive of the two takes precedence. (42)
13. **(4)** Zoning ordinances are not retroactive; *K*'s property was appropriately zoned when he developed it, thus he can continue to operate his building. (41–42)
14. **(4)** A conditional use permit allows for a use specifically permitted. Here, a commercial use is desired in a residential zone which is not permitted. (42)
15. **(2)** EMFs are suspected of causing cancer and related diseases. (46)
16. **(2)** Asbestos is used in insulation. Lead was used as an ingredient in oil-based paint. Urea-formaldehyde was used primarily in building insulation. (44)
17. **(4)** Accession occurs when tenants leave their trade fixtures on the rented premises after the lease expires; the tenant's trade fixtures (personal property) become

the real property of the landlord. Reliction refers to the increase in land resulting from the gradual recession of water from the usual water area. Annexation occurs when personal property such as strips of lumber are used to build the floor of the house. (48)

18. **(3)** Water rights are discussed on pages 47–48. You should be aware that littoral rights are granted to owners along a large lake or ocean.

19. **(1)** The principle of competition states that excess profits create ruinous competition. (54)

20. **(2)** Functional obsolescence is a loss in value due to a deficiency in the floor plan or design of a house. (55)

21. **(3)** The cost approach is the most applicable to the appraisal of a special purpose property such as a school. The income approach is most reliable for income-producing property. The gross income multiplier is also used in appraising income property. (55)

22. **(2)** Annual net operating income is calculated by subtracting annual operating expenses from effective gross income. Annual net operating income is then capitalized to arrive at an estimate. (55)

23. **(4)** Zoning would also be a governmental factor. (56)

24. **(3)** Plottage is the additional value created by assembling parcels of land to create a higher and better use. (54)

25. **(1)** The bank insurance fund is part of the Federal Deposit Insurance Corporation. (68)

26. **(3)** Special assistance programs are administered by GNMA. (69)

27. **(4)** Deposits in commercial banks are insured by BIF. (68)

28. **(2)** Mortgage brokers generally originate loans for other lenders; they do not use their own money. (68)

29. **(3)** Mortgages are released by a satisfaction or release of mortgage documents while an acceleration clause is used in a mortgage to deal with default on the part of the borrower. (63)

30. **(3)** $200,000 ÷ 1,000 = 200 × 10.45 = $2,090 (126–128)

31. **(1)** $2,090 × 180 months = $376,200 - $200,000 = $176,200 total interest paid on the life of the loan (128)

32. **(4)** A participation mortgage provides the lender with a return on the loan which exceed the rate of interest. The different types of mortgages are discussed on page 67.

33. **(2)** Regulation Z regulates real estate ads relating to mortgage financing terms. Specific credit terms such as down payment are referred to as "trigger" terms and may not be advertised unless the ad includes five categories of information including cash price and required down payment. (113)

34. **(3)** The Federal Reserve controls reserve requirements of member banks as part of its monetary policy authority. (67)

35. **(4)** *A* is also a subagent of 3; a general agent would be a property manager. (77)

36. **(4)** *P* is a special agent responsible for finding a buyer for the seller's property. (76)

37. **(3)** *Y* could have represented the buyer as an agent or the seller as a subagent. (75)

38. **(3)** Cooperating brokers would be subagents of your seller. (75)

39. **(1)** $180,000 ×. 06 = $10,800 (120)

40. **(4)** *A* has not entered into a fiduciary relationship with *C* and *D*; there cannot be a dual agency. (75)

41. **(2)** The listing broker has a fiduciary relationship with the seller including loyalty. A buyer agency relationship would not affect the listing broker's loyalty to the seller. (75)

42. **(4)** An individual broker can react negatively to another broker; this is not a violation of the antitrust law. (78)

43. **(1)** $206,000 sales price × 7% (0.07) commission = $14,420 broker commission
    $14,420 × 55% (0.55) = $3,965.50 selling salesperson's commission (120)

44. **(3)** A latent defect is a hidden structural defect that would not be discovered by an ordinary inspection. (85)

45. **(4)** The risks of dual agency have resulted in the practice being illegal in some states. Disclosure alerts the parties that they may have to assume greater responsibility for protecting their interests than would be the case if they had agents representing only their own interests. (85)

46. **(2)** Material facts refer to relevant information that the agent is aware of or should have known. For example, the seller's agent has a duty to disclose the identity of prospective buyers as well as any relationships existing between the buyer and the broker such as being related to the buyer. (86)

47. **(4)** Net listing is either illegal or discouraged in most states because of the potential conflict of interest between broker's profit motive and broker's fiduciary responsibility to this seller. (90–91)

48. **(3)** *P* did not have the mental capacity to be bound by the terms of a binding contract, thus he may disaffirm it, if he wishes. *P* has a voidable contract. (90)

49. **(2)** The salesperson is not a party to the listing contract. (91)

50. **(4)** In an executory contract something remains to be done by one or both parties. (89)

51. **(3)** *S* receives equitable title and will receive legal title at closing. (92)

52. **(2)** The time period varies for the different types of legal actions, however, the right must be enforced within the prescribed time period in order to avoid the loss of enforcement rights. (33)

53. **(4)** The vendee receives possession and equitable title and also agrees to pay real estate taxes, insurance premiums, and expenses for maintaining the property. The vendee will not receive legal title until the land contract has been paid in full. (92–93)

54. **(3)** The option becomes a bilateral contract if the optionee chooses to exercise the option right. (92)

55. **(1)** The addendum adds additional language to the approved forms. The counteroffer and multiple counteroffer can only modify language prior to the offer becoming binding on all parties. (93)

56. **(2)** The seller withholds legal title to the property until the terms of the contract are fulfilled in a land contract, offer to purchase, and option. (100)

57. **(4)** A quitclaim deed contains no warranties; the grantor simply quits or releases any claim she has against the property. (100)

58. **(3)** The covenant of seisin also promises that the grantor has possession. (100)

59. **(3)** The grantee has to be identified but does not have to sign the deed for it to be valid. (101)

60. **(2)** The Torrens System is a system of public title registration. (100)

61. **(3)** A married couple may exclude up to $500,000 from capital gains on the sale of their principal residence if they file jointly. The couple must have occupied the property as their residence for the last two of the past five years. (103)

62. **(2)** Referral fee would take the form of anything of value for services

such as mortgage loans or title insurance. (102)

63. **(3)** Mentally ill people do not have to be currently receiving treatment to be protected under the law. However, they would have to file their complaint within the one year period to be protected under the law. (110)

64. **(4)** You should be aware that sexual orientation is not a protected class under the Federal Fair Housing Act. (112)

65. **(2)** Convicted drug dealers are not protected under the federal fair housing laws under any condition. (110)

66. **(1)** Regulation Z requires full disclosure of all finance charges and the true interest rate before the completion of a transaction. (113)

67. **(4)** The rental of an owner-occupied apartment building of four units or less is exempt from the Federal Fair Housing Law. (111)

68. **(3)** The statute of frauds is a law that requires certain contracts to be in writing in order to be enforceable. (113)

69. **(2)** $154,000 × 6% (0.06) commission = $9,240 brokers commission

    $9,240 × 30% (0.30) = $2,772 (120)

70. **(3)** $9,600 ÷ $160,000 = .06 or 6 percent

    1 point equals 1 percent of the loan amount

    6 percent = 6 points (65)

71. **(1)** $619.73 × 12 = $7,436.76 annual interest

    $$\frac{\text{Part}}{\text{Percent}} = \text{Total}$$

    $7,436.76 ÷ 9% (0.09) = $82,630.67 (120)

72. **(2)** $146,000 × 70 percent (0.70) = $102,200 assessed value
    Divide by 100 because tax rate is stated per $100
    $102,200 ÷ 100 = $1,022

$1,022 × $2.84 = $2,902.48 annual taxes
Divide by 2 to get semiannual taxes
$2,902.48 ÷ 2 = $1,451.24 (121)

73. **(2)** $172,900 × 5% (0.05) = $8,645 annual increase in value
    $172,900 + $8,645 = $181,545 current market value (120)

74. **(2)** $7,940 − $600 salary = $7,340 commission sales
    $7,340 ÷ 3% (0.03) = $244,667 value of property sold (120)

75. **(3)** $12,800 × 12 = $153,600 annual return
    $153,600 ÷ 8% (0.08) = $1,920,000 original cost of property (125)

76. **(1)** $3,170 ÷ 12 months = $264.166 per month
    $264.166 ÷ 30 days = $8.806 per day
    $264.166 × 2 months = $528.332
    $8.806 x 14 days = $123.284
    $528.332 + 123.284 = $651.616 rounds to $651.62 (125–126)

77. **(2)** $2,840 ÷ 12 months = $236.666 per month
    $236.666 ÷ 30 days = $7.888 per day
    $7.888 × 27 days = $212.976, rounds to $212.98
    The taxes have been paid. The seller is entitled to a refund for 27 days. He, therefore, will receive a credit and the buyer will be charged (debited) for the same amount. (125–126)

78. **(4)** The other leases allow the tenant to possess with the landlord's consent. (135)

79. **(4)** An owner of a condominium unit holds fee-simple title to the unit and a specified share (as a tenant in common) in the common elements. (136)

80. **(2)** Leverage is using borrowed money to finance an investment. The amount of leverage used by an investor is in direct proportion to the risk. (139)

BROKER EXAMINATIONS

The PSI broker examination, like the salesperson exam, consists of two parts: an 80 or 100-question national exam and 25 to 50 question state exam. Both tests must be completed within a period of up to five hours. The national exam for Wisconsin covers generic real estate brokerage practices on a national scale. The state exam covers the listing contract, sales contract and settlement statement, as well as state real estate practices, license law, and rules and regulations.

The national portion of the broker examination contains 80 or 100 questions and closely resembles the national salesperson exam in that with the exception of broker management, both exams cover the same categories. The differences between the two exams involve slight variations in weighing the categories, and brokerage management is covered only on the Wisconsin broker's exam. The subject area and number of questions in each area on the broker examination varies from state to state but in general they are as follows:

Property Ownership	13 questions
Land Use Controls and Regulations	10 questions
Valuation and Market Analysis	7 questions
Financing	13 questions
Laws of Agency	11 questions
Mandated Disclosure	4 questions
Contracts	13 questions
Transfer of Property	7 questions
Practice of Real Estate	7 questions
Mathematics	11 questions
Specialty Areas	4 questions
Brokerage Management (Wisconsin only)	

The two sample broker examinations that follow evaluate your general real estate knowledge and your test taking ability.

BROKER EXAMINATION I

1. Which of the following would be considered to be real property?
   1. A leasehold estate
   2. Fixtures
   3. Chattels
   4. Trade fixtures

2. Your uncle died without a will and you inherited his real estate. The way in which you would acquire his estate is by
   1. accession.
   2. the statute of descent and distribution.
   3. escheat.
   4. novation.

3. Loans to low-income people in rural areas are made and guaranteed by
   1. The Federal Home Loan Mortgage Corporation (FHLMC).
   2. Rural Development.
   3. Farm Service Agency.
   4. The Federal Housing Administration (FHA).

4. A man receives possession of property under a deed that states that he will own the property as long as the present building standing on the property is not torn down. The type of estate the man holds is which of the following?
   1. Life estate
   2. Non-destructible estate
   3. Fee simple estate
   4. Determinable fee estate

5. You would like to hire more than one broker to sell your house and be able to sell the house yourself without paying a commission to a broker. Which of the following listing agreements should you choose?
   1. Net
   2. Open
   3. Exclusive agency
   4. Exclusive right-to-sell

6. Which of the following is responsible for investigating and prosecuting violations of federal fair housing laws?
   1. National Association of REALTORS® (NAR)
   2. Equal Employment Opportunity Commission (EEOC)
   3. Department of Housing and Urban Development (HUD)
   4. Associate of Real Estate License Law Officials (ARELLO)

7. You have been making constant payments of $635 per month on your mortgage. The balance after your last payment was $80,300. The interest rate on your mortgage is 8 percent. What will the balance of your mortgage be after your next payment?
   1. $79,647.00
   2. $80,067.32
   3. $80,182.33
   4. $80,300.00

8. Using the mortgage factor on page 127, what is the monthly payment for $121,000 at 7 percent for 30 years.
   1. $733.19
   2. $804.65
   3. $816.75
   4. $847.00

9. Using the numbers in question 8, what is the total interest paid over the life of the loan?
   1. $166,709.23
   2. $167,514.74
   3. $168,319.46
   4. $168,674.00

10. Which of the following statements correctly identifies a defining characteristic of conventional mortgages?
    1. They are assumable.
    2. There is no down payment.
    3. They are guaranteed by the federal government.
    4. Their interest rates are set by the lender.

11. A home valued at $92,000 is assessed at 70 percent of its value and is taxed at a rate of $3.40 per $400. What are the semi-annual taxes on this property?
    1. $1,094.80
    2. $1,564.80
    3. $2,189.60
    4. None of the above

12. A broker has been showing homes to some prospects. The prospects have learned of a home for sale by its owner, which they are interested in visiting. The broker calls the owner to arrange a showing, although the owner will not list with the broker. The broker shows the home and writes the offer to purchase, which is accepted by the owner. Which of the following statements correctly describes this situation?
    1. The owner is legally bound to pay the broker a commission.
    2. The prospects are responsible for paying a commission to the broker.
    3. The owner and the prospects are legally bound to pay a commission to the broker.
    4. Neither the owner nor the prospects are legally bound to pay a commission to the broker.

13. A veteran wishes to receive a loan for $70,000 to buy a home. The home has been appraised buy the VA at $68,000. Which of the following statements most accurately describes the veteran's situation?
    1. The veteran may buy the home with a VA loan only if he is able to lower the price to $68,000.
    2. The veteran may buy the home with a VA loan if the seller agrees to hold a second mortgage of $2,000.
    3. The veteran may buy the home with a VA loan if he makes a down payment of $2,000.
    4. The veteran may not buy the home.

14. You are paying interest on a $75,000 mortgage for three years after which the entire loan is due. This is called a(n)
    1. amortized mortgage.
    2. graduated payment mortgagee.
    3. purchase money mortgage.
    4. term mortgage.

15. A farmer is unable to pay the county taxes on his farm. The delinquent taxes would be considered
    1. a lien.
    2. an attachment.
    3. an easement.
    4. an appurtenance.

16. A licensee's relative asks the licensee for information about one of the licensee's listings. After reviewing it, the relative arranges to see the property with the licensee. Two weeks later, the relative submitted an offer through another agency on the licensee's listing. Which of the following statements about this situation is CORRECT?
    1. The listing licensee should disclose the family relationship with the buyer to the seller.
    2. The selling licensee should refuse to continue with the transaction if the buyer mentions the listing licensee's family status.
    3. The buyer has breached an express agency relationship with the listing licensee and must resubmit the offer using the listing licensee.
    4. The listing licensee is entitled to a portion of the selling licensee's compensation for having introduced the buyer to the property.

17. Which of the following Internal Revenue Service (IRS) forms is used to report commissions paid to salespeople by brokers?
    1. W-9
    2. 1031
    3. 1040
    4. 1099 Misc.

18. A retired woman owns her home free and clear and is looking for a mortgage that would provide her with monthly payments until she dies. This type of mortgage is called a
    1. guaranteed payment mortgage.
    2. blanket mortgage.
    3. participation mortgage.
    4. reverse annuity mortgage.

19. A man leased a store with the agreement that he would pay a fixed rent and the landlord would pay all operating expenses. This is an example of a
    1. gross lease.
    2. graduated lease.
    3. net lease.
    4. percentage lease.

20. You have entered into a land contract for the sale of your home. Which of the following statements is NOT correct?
    1. The seller is the vendor.
    2. The buyer is the vendee.
    3. The seller will hold legal title during the term of the contract.
    4. The seller will retain possession during the term of the contract.

21. Which of the following terms identifies the practice of charging loan interest rates in excess of the maximum allowed by law?
    1. Usury   3. Arbitrage
    2. Leverage   4. Novation

22. Which of the following statements correctly describes the way in which a listing broker should represent her client?
    1. The listing broker can tell a prospective buyer the lowest price her client will accept.
    2. The listing broker may choose which offers to present to her client.
    3. The listing broker with two offers may hold back on presenting the second offer until her client has responded to the first offer.
    4. The listing broker must present all offers to her client promptly when received.

23. Which of the following is true as it relates to an easement appurtenant?
    1. This easement may be acquired by prescription only.
    2. The easement right cannot be terminated.
    3. The dominant tenement owner pays taxes only on the dominant estate.
    4. The easement right reverts to the owner of the servient estate on the death of the owner of the dominant estate.

24. *A* died and left a will which transferred one-half of his 36 unit apartment building to his wife, one-fourth to his son and one-fourth to his daughter. The devisees will be holding title as
    1. tenants in common.
    2. tenants by the entirety.
    3. joint tenants.
    4. tenants at will.

25. A licensee has entered into a written buyer-broker agreement with a client whereby the licensee will be compensated if the client buys a property of the type described in the agreement within the agreement period, regardless of whether or not the licensee located the property for the buyer. This type of agreement as known as
    1. dual agency.
    2. open buyer agency.
    3. exclusive buyer agency.
    4. exclusive-agency buyer agency.

26. A mortgage is all of the following **EXCEPT**
    1. an encumbrance.
    2. a lien on real property.
    3. a recordable legal document.
    4. an example of involuntary alienation.

27. Three investors decided to pool their savings and buy an office building for $200,000. If one invested $70,000 and the second contributed $40,000, what percentage of ownership was left for the third investor?
    1. 20 percent
    2. 35 percent
    3. 45 percent
    4. None of the above

28. A broker is selling a home for $85,900. The owner tells the broker that the roof needs repair, the basement leaks, the house is a nonconforming use and that she will accept an offer well below $85,900. The broker now is negotiating with a prospect for the sale of the home. The broker should NOT tell the prospect that the
    1. roof needs repair.
    2. basement leaks.
    3. house is a nonconforming use.
    4. seller will accept an offer well below $85,900.

29. You listed a home for sale under an exclusive right-to-sell agreement and showed the property to a man who wrote an offer that was rejected by the owner. The owner subsequently sold the house to a woman who then sold it immediately to the man for whom you had written the offer. The MOST LIKELY description of your right to compensation from these transactions is that you are entitled to compensation for
    1. the first transaction only.
    2. both transactions, if you had a broker protection clause in the listing agreement.
    3. both transactions regardless of whether or not you had a broker protection clause in the listing agreement.
    4. the first transaction and perhaps to damages from the second if the first one was conducted under fraudulent circumstances to reduce your original commission.

30. An investor finds that the cost of installing an air-conditioning system in an office building is greater than is justified by the rental increase that might result from the improvement of the property. However, the investor installs the air-conditioning to avoid having tenants move to comparable office space nearby that is air-conditioned. The investor's decision is most reflective of the principle of
    1. anticipation.
    2. compensation.
    3. contribution.
    4. highest and best use.

31. *A* loaned money to her sister and in return took a mortgage as security for the debt. He immediately recorded the mortgage. Thereafter, *B* loaned money to her sister, took a mortgage and recorded it. The sister later defaulted, and a court determined that *B*'s interest had priority over *A*'s interest. Under these circumstances, chances are that
    1. *A* knew *B* was going to make a loan before *A* made his own loan.
    2. *B*'s loan was larger than *A*'s loan.
    3. *A* had signed a subordination agreement in favor of *B*.
    4. *B* had signed a satisfaction.

32. A sale closed on July 29. Real estate taxes of $2,380 for the current year have not been paid. What is the settlement sheet entry for the proration of real estate taxes?
    1. Credit seller $1,381.70; debit buyer $1,381.70
    2. Debit seller $998.30; credit buyer $1,381.70
    3. Debit seller $1,381.70; credit buyer $1,381.70
    4. Debit buyer $00,00; credit seller $2,380.00

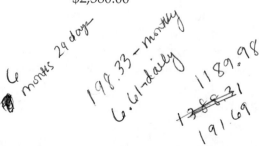

33. You receive a monthly salary of $600 plus 3 percent commission on all your listings that sell and 3.5 percent on all of your sales. None of the listings that you took sold last month, but you received $4,100 in salary and commission. What was the value of the property you sold?
    1. $100,000
    2. $116,666
    3. $117,142
    4. None of the above

34. A broker has been asked to serve as an agent of a friend who wishes to sell his home. Prior to listing the friend's home, the broker is asked by another friend to serve as her agent in finding a home. Relatives of the two friends also have asked the broker to serve as their agent in helping them find homes. Which of the following statements is correct?
    1. The broker is not allowed to work with the relatives because he would have a conflict of interest.
    2. The broker may not serve as agent to the various parties unless he gets permission from all of the parties.
    3. The broker may serve only as an agent of the seller.
    4. The broker may serve as agent for any of the buyers and sellers.

35. Which of the following types of depreciation is incurable?
    1. A leaky roof
    2. A worn-out water heater
    3. A zoning variance of the neighbor's property for commercial use
    4. Warped doors

36. A salesperson would like to be classified as an independent contractor by his broker. What percentage of his income must be based on sales production for him to qualify for independent-contractor status?
    1. 60 percent
    2. 70 percent
    3. 80 percent
    4. 90 percent

37. A couple is interested in buying a property located in an economically distressed section of town. Although the couple has an excellent credit history, they have been refused a loan by three different lenders. The MOST LIKELY statement regarding these lenders is that they are
    1. engaging in illegal redlining.
    2. violating antitrust laws by all making the same decision.
    3. violating the requirements of the Equal Credit Opportunity Act (ECOA).
    4. not engaging in illegal activities as the rejections are based on independently made economic-based property reviews.

38. You have listed a property. The seller told you that he must net at least $14,000 after all fees and expenses are paid. You estimate the seller's closing cost to be $3,500 and he must pay off an existing loan of $108,750. In addition you are going to charge 7 percent commission on the sale. What is the least amount that the property can sell for to return the seller's desired net?
    1. $126,250
    2. $134,310
    3. $135,088
    4. None of the above

39. Which approach to value is an appraiser most likely to emphasize in the appraisal of a single-family home?
    1. Cost approach
    2. Gross income multiplier approach
    3. Income capitalization approach
    4. Sales comparison approach

40. Which of the following installment sales amounts is NOT covered by the imputed interest law?
    1. $2,000
    2. $4,000
    3. $9,000
    4. $10,000

41. The tax on the profit realized from an exchange of property is
    1. ordinary income in the year of the exchange.
    2. deferred.
    3. eliminated.
    4. None of the above

42. You own an apartment building that provides you a gross income of $40,000 a year. Your annual expenses are $10,000 a year. The value of your real estate if you need a 12 percent return on your investment is
    1. $83,333.   3. $333,333.
    2. $250,000.   4. $444,444.

43. Which of the following statements does NOT correctly describe joint tenancy?
    1. It is a form of co-ownership.
    2. Owners have the right of survivorship.
    3. Owners must be husband and wife.
    4. Owners may partition the property.

44. Which of the following statements does NOT correctly describe radon gas?
    1. As radon is released from the rocks, it finds its way to the surface and usually is released into the atmosphere.
    2. Radon enters a house through the roof vents.
    3. Radon can become concentrated in the crawl space.
    4. Long-term exposure to radon gas is said to cause lung cancer.

45. Strict liability under Superfund means that
    1. each individual owner is personally responsible for the damages in whole.
    2. the owner is responsible to the injured party without excuse.
    3. the liability is not limited to the person who currently owns the property but also includes people who have owned the site in the past.
    4. anyone who has been involved in the transaction will be liable for damages.

46. Which of the following may NOT be governed by deed restrictions?
    1. Height of a building
    2. Ethnicity of tenants
    3. Use of a residence as a business
    4. Types of pets that can be housed within the subdivision

47. The business ownership structure of an S corporation provides which of the following benefits over the standard corporation structure?
    1. Profits are not taxed.
    2. The requirements for incorporation are simpler.
    3. The liability of individual owners for losses is removed.
    4. The investor's membership list does not have to be disclosed to the Internal Revenue Service (IRS).

48. The rent on a house is $400 a month or $4,800 a year, and the house recently sold for $52,000. The gross rent multiplier on the house was
    1. 10.8.   3. 130.
    2. 108.   4. 130.8.

49. The rate of return an investor will require to invest in real estate is called a(n)
    1. gross rent multiplier.
    2. gross income multiplier.
    3. capitalization rate.
    4. assemblage.

50. National advertising and economies of volume purchasing are advantages for
    1. franchises.
    2. quasi-franchises.
    3. broker cooperatives.
    4. broker associations.

51. A broker requires that all budgeted costs for the planning period be justified each time a new budget is developed. This requirement reflects
    1. the cash method of keeping financial records.
    2. the concept of cash flow.
    3. the concept of desk cost.
    4. the concept of zero-base budgeting.

52. Which of the following statements does NOT correctly describe the independent-contractor relationship?
    1. The salesperson contracts with a broker to produce specific outcomes such as commission.
    2. The broker may not tell salespeople how to sell real estate.
    3. The broker must provide a pension plan.
    4. The salesperson must pay his or her board dues.

53. A salesperson works for a broker. The salesperson may
    1. work for the broker as an independent contractor.
    2. place an ad without identifying the broker.
    3. receive a commission directly from a seller.
    4. receive a commission directly from another broker.

54. A broker has listed a home. The broker generally will earn her commission when
    1. she submits an offer to purchase to the seller.
    2. the seller indicates that he thinks an offer to purchase is acceptable.
    3. she finds a "buyer ready, willing, and able" to buy on the terms of the listing.
    4. the closing takes place.

55. A Hispanic buyer has asked a broker to show her homes in a white neighborhood. The broker's response to the buyer should be
    1. "I think you would be happier in a neighborhood with people of similar background."
    2. "I don't think you would be comfortable with the people in that neighborhood because they do not welcome outsiders."
    3. "I'll be happy to show you homes in that neighborhood but I think you could do better than that."
    4. "I'll be happy to show you homes in that neighborhood or any other neighborhood."

56. During a listing presentation, the seller tells the broker that she will not sell to Hispanics. Should the broker follow the seller's instructions?
    1. Yes. The owner has a right to choose prospective buyers.
    2. Yes. The broker is the seller's agent and must honor his fiduciary responsibility.
    3. No. The broker might lose any commission by limiting potential buyers.
    4. No. The broker should not accept the listing.

57. You are preparing a Competitive Market Analysis (CMA) on a two-story, three-bedroom house with one bathroom on the first floor and all of the bedrooms on the second floor. The appraisal term that BEST identifies how this affects the list price is
    1. physical deterioration.
    2. deferred maintenance.
    3. functional obsolescence.
    4. economic obsolescence.

58. Which of the following is NOT an example of real property?
    1. A neighbor's strawberry bush, which she calls "fructus naturales"
    2. Percolating water
    3. Unexcavated clay
    4. The clay bricks that you will use to build your patio wall

59. A listing broker acting as a single agent in the course of selling the property would be in violation of the broker's fiduciary duties to the seller by
    1. telling a prospective buyer the lowest price the seller will accept below the list price.
    2. paying for a property appraisal during the course of helping the owner set the list price.
    3. accepting a commission that is lower than usual for marketing similar properties in the area.
    4. allowing prospective buyers to prepare and submit offers through buyer-brokers instead of sub-agents of the seller.

60. A CORRECT statement about a Competitive Market Analysis (CMA) is that it
    1. must be performed by a licensed appraiser.
    2. must be reviewed by an employing broker in order to be valid.
    3. is based on the sales comparison (market data) approach to value.
    4. will develop a final assessment of value by averaging three bank appraisals.

61. Which of the following forms of ownership is characterized by double taxation?
    1. Corporation
    2. Sole proprietorship
    3. S corporation
    4. General proprietorship

62. A man wants to know how much money he owes on his mortgage loan. He knows that the interest part of the last monthly payment was $608.52. If he was paying interest at the rate of 10 percent, what was the outstanding balance of his loan before that last payment was made?
    1. $60,852.20   3. $73,022.40
    2. $66,937.20   4. $77,942.26

63. Your aunt bought her house one year ago for $62,400. Property in her neighborhood is said to be increasing at a rate of 7 percent annually. If this is true, what is the current market value of your aunt's real estate?
    1. $65,520   3. $66,768
    2. $66,144   4. $66,971

64. Your home is valued at $104,000. Property in your city is assessed at 70 percent of its value, and the local tax rate is $3.35 per $100. What is the amount of your monthly taxes?
    1. $192.86   3. $290.33
    2. $203.23   4. $331.64

65. In the cost approach, an appraiser makes use of which of the following?
    1. Sales prices of similar properties
    2. The owner's original cost of construction
    3. An estimate of the building's replacement cost
    4. Multiplying the net income by the capitalization rate

66. An appraisal of a church probably would be based on the
    1. market/data approach.
    2. cost approach.
    3. income approach.
    4. capitalization approach.

67. With an FHA loan, the buyer will NOT be required to
    1. pay a 20 percent down payment.
    2. find an approved lender willing to make the loan.
    3. buy a house that meets minimum FHA credit standards.
    4. buy mortgage insurance to protect the lender.

68. Which of the following statements regarding points is true?
    1. Points must be charged to the seller.
    2. One point equals 1 percent of the loan.
    3. Points must be charged to the buyer.
    4. One point equals ¼ percent of the loan.

69. X, who works for broker Y on a 50-50 basis, sold a house listed by broker Z for $167.750. The seller agreed to pay a 7 percent commission, but stipulated in the listing that 65 percent was to go to the selling broker. How much commission will X make on the sale (to the nearest dollar)?
    1. $2,054   3. $4,110
    2. $3,816   4. $7,633

70. The net spendable income from an investment is known as the
    1. budget.
    2. cash flow.
    3. company dollar.
    4. gross income.

71. A broker has calculated the amount of income remaining after deducting all of the firm's commissions from the firm's gross income. The broker has calculated the
    1. budget.
    2. cash flow.
    3. company dollar.
    4. desk cost.

72. A broker has an annual overhead of $200,000; there are ten desks, each accommodating two salespeople. The broker's desk cost is
    1. $5,000.   3. $15,000.
    2. $10,000.   4. $20,000.

73. The discriminatory practice of guiding ethnic minorities toward available housing in neighborhoods made up of residents of the same ethnic group is referred to as
    1. puffing.
    2. steering.
    3. redlining
    4. blockbusting.

74. Which of the following statements does NOT apply to both purchase money mortgages and land contracts?
    1. The seller is financing the transaction.
    2. The buyer takes possession when the contract is executed.
    3. The buyer gives the seller a down payment.
    4. The buyer has equitable title during the life of the contract.

75. Which of the following is covered by Regulation Z?
    1. A personal property credit transaction for $20,000
    2. A loan with three installments
    3. A real estate purchase agreement
    4. An agricultural loan for $29,000

76. Which of the following is exempted from the federal fair housing law?
    1. The rental of rooms in an owner-occupied, four-family dwelling
    2. The rental of rooms in an owner-occupied, five-family dwelling
    3. The rental of a single-family home when a broker is used
    4. The lodgings of a private club when the lodgings are operated commercially

77. You purchased a residence and neither took possession nor recorded the deed. Which of the following statements BEST describes the status of your property ownership?
    1. You have given actual notice of ownership.
    2. You do not have a valid deed from the previous owner.
    3. You have not provided constructive notice of ownership.
    4. You will have to go to court to assert your ownership rights prior to reselling the property.

78. The relationship of the broker to the listing owner who hired him or her is that of a(n)
    1. attorney-in-fact.   3. trustee.
    2. strawman.   4. fiduciary.

79. Which of the following would NOT be deposited in your trust account?
    1. The commission you earn on the transaction
    2. Earnest money received on a transaction
    3. The down payment for a land contract transaction
    4. An amount sufficient to cover the bank service charges on the account

80. Which of the following statements does NOT correctly describe a limited liability company?
    1. It offers the single-level taxation of a partnership.
    2. It may not be directly managed by members.
    3. It offers the limited liability of a corporation.
    4. It must have at least one member.

81. In order to represent legally all parties in the same real estate transaction, a licensee MUST
    1. hold a securities license.
    2. agree to receive compensation from only one of the principles.
    3. ensure that all documents that the licensee signs are notarized.
    4. obtain the informed consent to dual agency from all principals.

82. You are working as an agent for a prospective buyer. The buyer buys a house listed on the multiple-listing service (MLS) of which you are a member. Which of the following statements does NOT correctly describe the situation?
    1. You acted as a disclosed dual agent.
    2. You will be entitled to a commission from the buyer.
    3. You could be paid by the seller if the parties agree.
    4. The listing broker is an agent of the seller.

83. Tenancy in common is distinguished by which of the following characteristics?
    1. The co-owners have right of survivorship.
    2. Ownership interests must be equal.
    3. A co-owner cannot will his or her interest in a property.
    4. Each co-owner's interest may be conveyed separately.

84. A plumbing company installed a new furnace and filed a lien for nonpayment immediately on completion. This was most likely a
    1. voluntary lien.   3. novation.
    2. general lien.   4. specific lien.

85. Which of the following is NOT an example of functional obsolescence?
    1. A five-bedroom house with one bathroom
    2. Outdated plumbing fixtures
    3. A roof that leaks
    4. A poor floor plan

86. A broker listed and sold a seller's home. The broker most likely earned her commission when
    1. the transaction was closed.
    2. she found a buyer "ready, willing, and able" to buy on the terms of the listing.
    3. the buyer's financing contingency was removed from the offer to purchase.
    4. the buyer's check cleared the bank after closing.

87. A salesperson has taken a four-month exclusive right-to-sell listing on a house. Prior to the expiration of the listing, the salesperson leaves the state and inactivates her license. Which of the following correctly describes the status of the listing?
    1. The listing automatically terminates when the salesperson leaves the state and inactivates her license.
    2. The seller may terminate the listing once the salesperson has left the state.
    3. The broker will have to negotiate with the seller to retain the listing.
    4. The listing will continue as a valid contract between the seller and the broker.

88. A parcel of property that measures ⅛ mile by ⅛ mile is equal to
    1. 10 acres.
    2. 40 acres.
    3. 160 acres.
    4. 320 acres.

89. Which of the following is NOT an advantage of the FHA-insured loan?
    1. Low down payment
    2. Buyer protection with FHA insurance
    3. Enables cash-short buyers to enter real estate market
    4. Protects lender with FHA insurance.

90. Which of the following is NOT a legal requirement of an option?
    1. A purchase price and how it will be determined
    2. Consideration
    3. The date on which the option will expire
    4. The exercise of the option by the optionee

91. A 300-acre farm is divided into house lots. The streets require one-eighth of the whole farm and there are 280 lots. How many square feet are in each lot?
    1. 38,115
    2. 40,838
    3. 46,671
    4. None of the above

92. The process of reviewing the various approaches to value in order to arrive at a final estimate of market value is called
    1. assemblage.
    2. capitalization.
    3. balance.
    4. reconciliation.

93. A broker and a seller have just signed a listing contract for the sale of the seller's house. Which of the following statements does NOT correctly describe their situation?
    1. A fiduciary relationship now exists between the broker and seller.
    2. The broker has become a general agent for the seller.
    3. The broker is an agent and the seller is the principal.
    4. The broker has become a special agent for the seller.

94. The Americans with Disabilities Act (ADA) requires that certain employers. . .an employer with a MINIMUM of how many employees must comply with the ADA requirements?
    1. 3
    2. 5
    3. 10
    4. 15

95. You have just listed a property and the owner has informed you that the roof leaks and the fourth bedroom was added without a building permit being issued. Which of the following best describes the type of disclosure you should make to potential buyers?
    1. You should disclose that the roof leaks.
    2. You do not have to disclose that the bedroom was added without a permit because the project has already been completed.
    3. You do not have to disclose either unless you are instructed to do so by the seller.
    4. You must disclose both the roof leak and the lack of a building permit.

96. *A* agreed to lease *D*'s house on a month-to-month basis. This lease is an example of a(n)
    1. tenancy at will.
    2. estate for years.
    3. tenancy at sufferance.
    4. periodic estate.

97. According to the federal fair housing laws, parties who feel that they have been aggrieved by a discriminatory housing practice have a MAXIMUM of how long after the event to file a complaint?
1. Thirty days   3. Six months
2. Sixty days   4. One year

98. You lease the 36 apartments in your building for a total monthly rental of $8,000. If this figure represents an 8 percent annual return on your investment, what was the original cost of the property?
1. $100,000   3. $1,200,000
2. $236,000   4. $2,360,000

99. P bought a house for $160,000 five years ago. His mortgage was for $128,000. Today P's house is valued at $200,000 and his mortgage balance is $123,000. What is P's equity in the property?
1. $32,000   3. $72,000
2. $37,000   4. $77,000

100. The county zoo holds title to the land that includes a condition that the zoo will hold title so long as it does not charge an admission fee. This is an example of a
1. fee simple estate.
2. defeasible fee estate.
3. conventional life estate.
4. tenancy at will.

ANSWER KEY WITH EXPLANATIONS

NOTE: The number in parentheses at the end of each explanation refers to the page number and the outline reference where this material is discussed.

1. **(2)** A leasehold estate, chattels, and trade fixtures are classified as personal property. (27)
2. **(2)** When a person dies intestate, the descendant's real estate and personal property pass on to her heirs according to statute. (99)
3. **(2)** Rural development makes and guarantees loans to low-income people in rural areas. FHLMC is a warehousing agency in the secondary mortgage market. FHA insures home mortgages. Farm Service Agency makes and guarantees loans to farmers and ranchers. (66)
4. **(4)** The words *as long as* are key to the creation of a determinable fee, sometimes referred to as a qualified fee, conditional fee, or base fee estate. (30)
5. **(2)** Under an open listing, if the seller personally sells the property without the aid of any broker, the seller is not obligated to pay the commission. (90)
6. **(3)** NAR is the REALTOR® trade association. EEOC deals with discrimination in employment, while ARELLO works with license law issues. (109)
7. **(3)** $80,300 × .08 = $6,424 annual interest
$6,424 ÷ 12 = $535.333 interest for one month
$653.00 P&I − $535.333 = $117.67 principal payoff
$80,300 − $117.67 = $80,182.33 balance after next payment (120)
8. **(2)** $804.65 ($121,000 × 6.65) (127–28)
9. **(4)** $804.65 × 360 months =
$289,674   Total P&I
−121.000   Loan
$168,674   total interest (127–28)
10. **(4)** A conventional mortgage is neither insured nor guaranteed by the government. A down payment generally is higher than with insured and guaranteed loans. (65)
11. **(1)** $92,000 × 70% (0.70) = $64,400, assessed value ÷ 100 = $644
$644 × $3.40 = $2,189.60 annual tax
Divided by 2 to get the semiannual tax
$2,189.60 ÷ 2 = $1,094.80 (121)

12. **(4)** The broker is not entitled to a commission because he had no contractual agreement with the buyer or the seller. (76)

13. **(3)** The loan amount cannot exceed the DVA appraisal on a DVA loan. The veteran must pay the difference between the appraised value and the purchase price in cash. (66)

14. **(4)** Payments on an amortized mortgage include principal and interest. A purchase money mortgage involves seller financing while a graduated payment mortgage has low initial payments that increase over time. (63)

15. **(1)** Attachment refers to the act of taking a person's property into legal custody or placing a lien thereon by court or judicial order to hold it available for application to that person's debt to a creditor. An easement is the right to use the land of another for a specific purpose. An appurtenance is a right, privilege or improvement that belongs to and passes with the transfer of the property but is not necessarily a part of the real property. (29)

16. **(1)** The relationship of the buyer to the listing licensee is of no concern to the selling licensee. Showing a property to a customer does not create an express agency. Introducing the property to the buyer does not necessarily entitle the listing licensee to a portion of the selling licensee's compensation. (76)

17. **(4)** Brokers must report details of a closing to the IRS on Form 1099S; Section 1031 of the Internal Revenue Code deals with a tax-deferred exchange. (104)

18. **(4)** A reverse annuity mortgage becomes due on a specific date, the sale of the property, or the death of the borrower. (67)

19. **(1)** A graduated lease provides for rent increase at set future dates, while a percentage lease provides for minimum fixed rent plus a percentage of the business income. Under a net lease, the tenant pays rent plus all or part of the property charges. (135)

20. **(4)** The vendee (buyer) takes possession when the contract is executed. (92–93)

21. **(1)** Leverage is using other people's money to finance an investment. Arbitrage refers to buying and selling credit instruments to profit from differences in prices. Novation occurs when a new obligation is substituted for an old one. (69)

22. **(4)** The listing broker is required to prepare as well as submit all offers unless otherwise instructed. The broker does not have the authority to accept or reject those offers for the seller. (76)

23. **(3)** The dominant tenement owner may terminate the easement right but does not pay the real estate taxes on the servient tenement. The dominant tenement owner may acquire his or her rights under an easement appurtenant by means other than by prescription. (29)

24. **(1)** Tenants by the entirety must be husband and wife. Joint tenancy requires the interest to be equal. (31)

25. **(3)** The different types of buyer brokerage agreements are discussed on page 91.

26. **(4)** A mortgage is a voluntary act, not involuntary. (99)

27. **(3)** $70,000 (first investor) + $40,000 (second investor) = $110,000
$200,000 - $110,000 = $90,000, third investor's contribution

$$\frac{\text{Part}}{\text{Total}} = \text{Percent}$$

$90,000 ÷ $200,000 = 0.45 or 45% (120)

28. **(4)** The broker is responsible for disclosing physical defects in the house but to disclose that the seller would take less than the list price would be a violation of the broker's fiduciary responsibilities to the seller. (75)

29. **(4)** The key to this answer is being able to prove that fraud occurred. (76)

30. **(2)** If the air-conditioning system is installed because of saleability it would be contribution. In this case, the installation was due to the market availability of air-conditioned space. (54)

31. **(3)** Neither A's knowledge of B's making a loan nor the size of such a loan would affect the priority of claims. The court could not rule in favor of B if B had signed a satisfaction. A subordination clause is a clause in which the mortgagee (A) permits a subsequent mortgage (B's loan) to take priority. (64)

32. **(3)** $2,380 ÷ 12 months = $198.333 per month
$198.33 ÷ 30 days = $6.611 per day
$198.33 × 6 months = $1,189.98
$6.611 × 29 days = $197.719
$1,189.88 + $191.719 = $1,381.699 or $,381.70
The taxes for the year have not been paid, and when they are, the buyer will be in possession and have to pay the bill. The seller, therefore, must pay (be debited) for the portion of the year that he occupied the property. The buyer receives a credit for the same amount. (125–26)

33. **(1)** $4,100 − $600 salary = $3,500, commission sales
$3,500 ÷ 3.5% (0.035) = $100,000 value of property sold (120)

34. **(4)** The broker may serve as an agent of the seller or any of the buyers. The broker could even represent a buyer and a seller in the same transaction, provided that he or she had the knowledge and consent of all parties involved. (75)

35. **(3)** A zoning variance for commercial use is economic or locational obsolescence, which would be incurable. (55)

36. **(4)** An individual must also have a current real estate license and have a written contract with the broker that states that the individual will not be treated as an employee for tax purposes. (104)

37. **(4)** What is described in the question could be looked on as "legal" redlining. The lenders refused to loan because of the depressed economic conditions of the neighborhood, not because of the racial or ethnic makeup of the area. (111)

38. **(4)** Start by adding the desired net $14,000 PLUS existing loan payoff of $108,750 and closing costs of $3,500 = $126,250, the minimum that the seller must receive. If the selling price is 100 percent, the commission is 7 percent and the net to the seller is 93 percent. $125,250 is 93 percent of the selling price.
Therefore, $126,250 ÷ 93% (0.93) = selling price of $135,752.69, which is not one of the answer options. (120)

39. **(4)** The sales comparison approach is considered the most reliable of the three approaches in appraising residential property. (55)

40. **(1)** Installment sales of less than $3,000 are not covered by the imputed interest law. (104)

41. **(2)** Under Section 1031 of the Internal Revenue Code, real estate investors can defer taxation of capital gains by making a property exchange. Property involved in the exchange must be of like kind—real estate for real estate. (105)

42. **(2)** $40,000 gross income − $10,000 expenses = $30,000 net annual income
$30,000 net annual income ÷ 12% (0.12) = $250,000 value of real estate (124–25)

43. **(3)** The owners must be husband and wife in tenancy by the entirety. (4-V) (31–32)

44. **(2)** Radon generally enters the house through the foundation or basement as well as through the crawl space. (44)

45. **(2)** Liability under the Superfund is also considered to be retroactive, meaning that the liability is not limited to the current owner but includes previous owners of the site. (46–47)

46. **(2)** Deed restrictions (private land use controls) may not be used to discriminate against members of protected classes; they may be terminated by a quitclaim deed executed by the necessary parties. (47)

47. **(1)** There is no double taxation as in a corporation. In other words, income losses and capital gains are passed directly to the shareholders. (144–45)

48. **(3)** The gross rent multiplier (GRM) relates to *monthly* income, not annual.
$52,000 sale price ÷ $400 monthly rent = 130 gross multiplier (8) (55)

49. **(3)** The gross rent and gross income multipliers are used as substitutes for the income approach. Assemblage is the joining of two or more properties. (9-IV) (55)

50. **(1)** Other advantages of a franchise include management expertise and a client referral system. Disadvantages include loss of individual identity and high initial fees and franchise fees. (145–46)

51. **(4)** Cash flow refers to net spendable income while company dollar is the amount of income that remains after subtracting all the commissions from the gross income. The cash method records income as received and expenses when actually paid. (150)

52. **(3)** The broker may not provide fringe benefits such as health insurance. In addition, the broker may not withhold federal and state income taxes, social security taxes, or state unemployment insurance from commissions. (146–47)

53. **(1)** A salesperson cannot place blind ads. The salesperson may not receive monetary compensation for a real estate transaction from anyone other than the broker for whom he or she is working. (77)

54. **(3)** It is important to distinguish between earning and receiving a commission. (76)

55. **(4)** The broker must not restrict the buyer's freedom of choice. (111)

56. **(4)** It is illegal under the federal fair housing law to accept a listing that involves discrimination, such as refusing to sell to members of a protected class. (109)

57. **(3)** Functional obsolescence is a loss in value due to a deficiency in the floor plan or design of the house. (55)

58. **(4)** Real property refers to physical land and appurtenances, including easements, water rights, mineral rights, and fixtures. Strawberry bushes are perennial plants and would be considered real property. Percolating water and unexcavated clay would also be considered real property. Personal property refers to anything that can be moved. (27)

59. **(1)** Disclosing the lowest price that the seller will accept is a violation of the fiduciary relationship. (75)

60. **(3)** A competitive market analysis is based on the sales comparison approach to value. (53)

61. **(1)** Double taxation is a primary disadvantage of the corporation form of ownership. (144)

62. **(3)** $608.52 × 12 = $7,302.24
$7,302.24 ÷ 10% (0.10) = $73,022.40
$62,400 + $4,368 = $66,768 (120)

63. **(3)** $62,400 × 7% (0.07) = $4,368, or
$62,400 × 107% (1.07) = $66,768
$62,400 + $4,368 = $66,768 (120)

64. **(2)** $104,000 × 70% (0.70) = $72,800 assessed value
Divide by 100 because the tax rate is stated per $100
$72,800 ÷ 100 = $728
$728 × $3.35 = $2,438.80 annual taxes
Divide by 12 to get monthly payments
$2,438.80 ÷ 12 = $203.23 (121)

65. **(3)** Sales prices of similar properties are used in the market/data approach. The net income and capitalization rate are used in the income approach. The owner's original cost of construction would be irrelevant, because in the cost approach the appraiser is concerned with the current replacement cost of the structure. (54)

66. **(2)** The market/data approach is considered most reliable when appraising a single-family home. The income approach and capitalization approach are stressed in appraising commercial and industrial properties. (55)

67. **(1)** The buyer's down payment on an FHA loan is 3 percent of the first $25,000 and 5 percent of any amount more than $25,000. (65)

68. **(2)** One point equals 1 percent of the loan. (65)

69. **(2)** $167,750 sales price × 7% (0.07) = $11,742.50 broker's commission
$11,742.50 × 65% = $7,632.63 × 0.50 = $3,816 selling salesperson's commission (120)

70. **(2)** The budget is the quantified business plan, while company dollars is the amount of income remaining after subtracting all the commissions from the gross income. Gross income is the revenue earned from all the sources in a brokerage firm such as sales and management fees. (150)

71. **(3)** Budget and company dollar were defined previously. Desk cost is the cost of providing the opportunity for salespeople to conduct their business. (150)

72. **(2)** $200,000 annual overhead ÷ 20 (10 desks × 2 salespeople each) = $10,000 desk cost (150)

73. **(2)** Puffing is sales psychology. Redlining is selecting specific areas and choosing not to make loans in that area; the areas generally are composed of members of protected classes. Blockbusting is panic peddling. (111)

74. **(4)** The vendee in a land contract holds equitable title until the land contract is paid in full, while the mortgagor receives legal title at closing. (93)

75. **(1)** Loans with five or more installments would be covered. An agricultural loan for less than $25,000 would also be covered. (113)

76. **(1)** Rental of rooms in an owner-occupied dwelling of five units or more is not exempted. (111)

77. **(3)** An unrecorded deed is valid between the parties, but constructive notice must be given to protect against subsequent buyers of the property. (102)

78. **(4)** An attorney-in-fact is a competent, disinterested person authorized by another person to act in his or her place. A strawman is one who buys property for someone else to conceal the identity of the real buyer. A trustee holds property in trust for another to secure the performance of an obligation. (75)

79. **(1)** A broker may not commingle his personal funds with those of clients in a trust account. (76)

80. **(2)** Limited liability companies may be directly managed by members or responsibility may be delegated to a property manager. (145)

81. **(4)** Brokers generally are prohibited from representing and collecting

compensations from both parties to a transaction unless both parties receive prior knowledge and give mutual consent. (85)

82. **(1)** In this situation you are the agent of the buyer and the listing broker is the agent of the seller. (75)

83. **(4)** Answers 1, 2, and 3 are all characteristics of joint tenancy. (31)

84. **(4)** A voluntary lien is a mortgage lien such as a lien created by an owner who obtains a mortgage loan. A general lien usually affects all the property of a debtor, both real and personal. A specific lien usually is secured by a specific property. (29)

85. **(3)** A roof that leaks would be an example of physical deterioration. (55)

86. **(2)** The broker is entitled to a commission when she is employed by the seller and finds a "ready, willing, and able" buyer. (76)

87. **(4)** The salesperson is an agent of the broker. When the salesperson no longer is employed by the broker, the broker retains any unsold or unexpired listings. The status of the listings remains unchanged. (91–92)

88. **(1)** $\frac{1}{8} \times \frac{1}{8} = \frac{1}{64}$ sq. mile
$\frac{1}{64} \times 640$ acres per sq. mile = 10 acres (28)

89. **(2)** FHA insurance is provided as protection for the lender. (65)

90. **(4)** When an option is given, the optionee gives the optionor consideration, the price is determined, and the time is set. The optionee does not have to exercise the option. (92)

91. **(2)** 43,560 square feet per acre × 300 acres = 13,068,000 square feet
13,068,000 square feet × (0.125) = 1,633,500 square feet for streets
13,068,000 − 1,633,500 = 11,434,400 sq. ft. for lots
11,434,500 square feet ÷ 280 lots = 40,838 square feet per lot (28)

92. **(4)** Reconciliation is the next-to-last step in the appraisal process. (57)

93. **(2)** The listing agreement is an employment contract. The broker is "employed" to do only one thing and that is to find a "ready, willing, and able" buyer. The broker, therefore, is a special agent, not a general agent. (75–76)

94. **(4)** ADA requires that any employer with 15 or more employees must adopt nondiscriminatory employment procedures and make reasonable accommodations to enable an individual with a disability to perform in his or her employment. (112)

95. **(4)** The broker is obligated to disclose to the buyer the material facts relating to property. (85)

96. **(4)** An estate for years is a lease for a definite duration whereas a periodic estate has an indefinite duration. (135)

97. **(4)** The statute of limitations for initiating administrative proceedings is one year after the alleged discriminatory housing practice. (111)

98. **(3)** $8,000 × 12 = $96,000 annual return
$96,000 ÷ 8% (0.08) = $1,200,000 original cost of property (8) (124–25)

99. **(4)** $200,000 current value - $123,000 current mortgage = $77,000 equity. (69)

100. **(2)** A defeasible fee estate continues for an indefinite period. The period of ownership may be based on either a certain or uncertain event. The words "so long as" indicate that the estate will be extinguished on the occurrence of the designated event; the charging of admission to the zoo, for example. (30)

BROKER EXAMINATION II

1. You have hauled your heavy farm equipment across some vacant land of your neighbor's for years with your neighbor's knowledge, but not permission. Now your neighbor wants to make improvements on the property and tells you to stop using it. Assuming you meet the required statutory period for having used the property, you may be able to get the courts to grant you the right to continue using the land, even if it means your neighbor's plans have to be abandoned. Which of the following terms BEST identifies the right described above?
   1. License
   2. Adverse possession
   3. An easement appurtenant
   4. An easement by prescription

2. The basic reason for choosing among a warranty, a special warranty, or a quitclaim deed is to
   1. avoid the need for a habendum clause.
   2. verify the kind of estate the grantee will receive.
   3. explain any restrictions or limitations on the title.
   4. define the covenants by which the grantor is bound.

3. Under their mother's will, a woman and her brother inherited title to a house as tenants in common. The woman married and had title to her share put in joint tenancy with her husband. Her brother is now
   1. a joint tenant with his sister and her husband.
   2. sole owner of the property.
   3. a tenant in common, owning an undivided ⅓ interest.
   4. a tenant in common, owning an undivided ½ interest.

4. You received a monthly salary of $900 plus 3.5 percent commission on all your listings that you sell and 3 percent on all of your sales. None of the listings that you took sold last month, but you receive $4,800 salary and commission. What was the value of the property you sold?
   1. $130,000
   2. $160,000
   3. $111,428
   4. None of the above

5. You are taking a listing on a property and notice that a neighboring building appears to have a roof overhang encroaching on the property line. The seller has never noticed this, even though the building has been there for several decades. Which of the following statements BEST identifies this situation?
   1. The seller must record a party wall easement prior to transferring title.
   2. The seller must perform a title search to discover if this represents a cloud on the title.
   3. The neighbor may be entitled to a prescription easement guaranteeing the right to leave the building as is.
   4. The neighbor may claim ownership of the property under the roof under the doctrine of prior appropriation.

6. Broker *C* is renting apartments for landlord *M*. *C* shows an apartment to a black couple and prior to informing the couple that they may have the apartment he receives a call from the landlord who asks about the race of the prospective tenants. Which of the following statements correctly describes how C should respond to *M*'s question concerning the race of the prospective tenants?
   1. *C* should tell the owner that the prospective tenants are black.
   2. *C* should tell the landlord that he cannot answer that question.
   3. *C* should state he will answer the question only if the owner promises to keep the information confidential.
   4. *C* should provide the race of the prospects only if he tells the landlord it is illegal but he must respond because he owes loyalty to the landlord.

7. The state needs your farm to build a highway. You have rejected their offer. The state may obtain your property by exercising its right of
   1. adverse possession.
   2. eminent domain.
   3. escheat.
   4. police power.

8. Keeping which of the following types of funds in a broker's trust account is MOST likely to be illegal?
   1. Rents on an apartment building you are managing
   2. Earnest money deposits
   3. Commission earned on previous sales
   4. Security deposits on properties you are managing

9. *X* owns a life estate and *Y* hold the future interest in the life estate. When *X* dies,
   1. *X*'s wife will become the owner under her dower interest.
   2. *X*'s life estate will pass to his heirs according to the terms of his will.
   3. *X* and *Y* will hold title as tenants in common.
   4. *Y* will hold title to the property.

10. *A* has had an offer to purchase accepted by *B*. Prior to closing, *A* will hold
    1. fee simple title.
    2. defeasible title.
    3. legal title.
    4. equitable title.

11. A zoning ordinance would not regulate
    1. land use.
    2. height of the building.
    3. use of the building.
    4. construction standards.

12. When the owner of a property sold for back taxes or mortgage default is granted a period of time after the sale to buy the property back, this is referred to as the owner's
    1. lien priority.
    2. homestead rights.
    3. right of redemption.
    4. deed in lieu of foreclosure.

13. You have pledged your home as security for a mortgage without giving up possession. This is called
    1. hypothecation.
    2. abstract.
    3. subordination.
    4. release of mortgage.

14. Which of the following statements does NOT correctly describe the relationship of a salesperson working for a broker as an employee?
    1. The broker may choose to provide fringe benefits.
    2. The broker may not tell salespeople how to list property.
    3. The broker may require attendance at sales meetings.
    4. The broker is required to withhold federal and state income taxes from commissions.

15. The rent on a house is $900 a month, or $10,800 a year, and the house recently sold for $126,000. The gross rent multiplier on the house was
    1. 11.67.   3. 111.7.
    2. 14.   4. 140.

16. A broker has been found guilty of discrimination under the federal fair housing law for the third time in the past seven years. The broker will be subject to a civil penalty not exceeding
    1. $10,000.   3. $50,000.
    2. $25,000.   4. $100,000.

17. An earthquake tore away some of the land on your farm recently. This is an example of
    1. accession.   3. avulsion
    2. accretion.   4. erosion.

18. Which of the following practices does NOT constitute a discriminatory act under the federal fair housing law?
    1. The owner-occupant of a duplex refuses to rent to a family with children.
    2. A lender uses one type of application for whites and another for blacks.
    3. A white broker refers Hispanic prospects only to Hispanic brokers.
    4. A property manager requires a higher security deposit for blacks than whites.

19. In the sales comparison approach to value, if a feature in the comparable property is inferior to that of the subject property a
    1. plus adjustment must be made to the price of the subject.
    2. minus adjustment must be made to the price of the comparable.
    3. plus adjustment must be made to the price of the comparable.
    4. minus adjustment must be made to the price of the subject.

20. If you give your land to your brother for the balance of his life and at his death the land is to go to your sister, his interest or estate is called a
    1. reversion.   3. base fee.
    2. curtesy.   4. life estate.

21. Buyer *A* purchased a home for $148,000 with the help of a mortgage for 90 percent of the selling price. Four years later, the balance of the mortgage was $129,000. An appraisal of the house at that same time estimated the value of *A*'s home at $163,000. *A*'s equity in the home is
    1. $14,800.
    2. $19,000.
    3. $34,000.
    4. None of the above

22. A property manager renting units for an apartment owner is an example of a
    1. special agent.   3. subagent.
    2. general agent.   4. dual agent.

23. Which of the following situations would NOT be prohibited under the federal fair housing law?
    1. A broker makes a profit by inducing owners to sell because of prospective entry of minorities into the neighborhood.
    2. A broker encourages minorities to live in areas of minorities.
    3. A lender refuses to make mortgage loans in a minority neighborhood.
    4. A broker refuses to show a house to a potential buyer based on the buyer's sexual orientation.

24. The relationship of trust and confidence that a broker has with a client is a(n)
    1. escrow relationship.
    2. subordination agreement.
    3. fiduciary relationship.
    4. trustee relationship.

25. A salesperson may legally accept a cash bonus directly from
    1. a seller for whom she did an excellent job.
    2. an appreciative buyer.
    3. a grateful title company.
    4. a broker/employer.

26. A broker knowingly misled a potential buyer on the boundary lines of a property. The buyer discovered the problem after buying the property. Is the broker guilty of misrepresenting the property?
    1. Yes, because the broker should have had the property surveyed before commenting on the property boundary lines.
    2. Yes, because the broker intentionally misled the buyer.
    3. No, because the broker is not a surveyor.
    4. No, because the broker did not provide any misrepresentation in writing.

27. You own a defeasible fee estate and sell it on a land contract. Until the land contract has been paid in full, the buyer will hold a(n)
    1. leasehold estate.
    2. life estate.
    3. equitable title.
    4. fee simple title.

28. A broker sold a home for $183,000. The broker charged the owner a 7 percent commission and will pay 30 percent of that amount to the listing salesperson and 25 percent to the selling salesperson. What amount of commission will the listing salesperson receive from the sale?
    1. $3,202.50
    2. $3,843
    3. $4,483.50
    4. $12,810

29. A seller asks a listing licensee to drop the price of the property to $105,000 from $120,000 in order to spur a quick sale. The licensee then prepares a new Competitive Market Analysis (CMA), which indicates the property may be worth $115,000. In this situation, the licensee's BEST course as a fiduciary for the seller is to
    1. offer to buy the property for $105,000.
    2. follow instructions and drop the price immediately.
    3. encourage the seller to hold the price up for negotiation room.
    4. disclose to the seller that the home is worth $115,000 before proceeding with a list-price change.

30. You have just given an option to buy your house to your friend. Which of the following statements does NOT correctly describe your agreement?
    1. Your friend is the optionee.
    2. Your friend is not obligated to buy your house.
    3. You are the optionor.
    4. You will have to return the fee for the option right to your friend if he chooses not to buy your house.

31. Which of the following facts would not need to be disclosed by a broker?
    1. There is water in the basement.
    2. There is an underground storage tank in the backyard.
    3. There is asbestos wrap on the heating pipes.
    4. The seller has AIDS.

32. A broker was listing a man's house for sale when the man informed him that he was Catholic and could not sell the house to anyone who was not Catholic. The broker should
   1. take the listing but state that he could not promise that he could get a Catholic buyer.
   2. get the request in writing on the listing contract and then attempt to find a Catholic buyer.
   3. take the listing but tell the owner that he would have to check with the state licensing board to make sure it was appropriate.
   4. not take the listing.

33. A broker has entered into a listing contract with a client in which the broker will receive a commission regardless of who sells the property during the term of the listing contract. The broker's listing is a(n)
   1. exclusive right-to-sell listing.
   2. net listing.
   3. open listing.
   4. exclusive-agency listing

34. Three investors decided to pool their savings and buy an office building for $250,000. If one invested $80,000 and the second investor contributed $50,000, what percentage of ownership was left for the third investor?
   1. 20 percent
   2. 32 percent
   3. 48 percent
   4. None of the above

35. You own an apartment building that provides you with a gross income of $50,000 a year. Your annual expenses are $12,000. The value of your real estate if you receive a 14 percent return on your investment is
   1. $85,714.   3. $271,429.
   2. $170,928.   4. $325,143.

36. A buyer's broker has entered into an agreement with a client in which the broker is assured of buyer loyalty relative to any other agents. The buyer, however, may purchase property on his own without the assistance of an agent and thus without commission being due to the buyer's agent. This arrangement is known as
   1. dual agency.
   2. open buyer agency.
   3. exclusive buyer agency.
   4. exclusive-agency buyer agency.

37. K owns his home in fee simple. This means that K has
   1. a legal life estate.
   2. a personal property interest.
   3. a tenancy by the entirety.
   4. the highest type of interest in real estate.

38. Your home is valued at $143,000. Property in your city is assessed at 80 percent of its value, and the local tax rate is $3.65 per $100. What is the amount of your monthly taxes?
   1. $319.37.   3. $352.73
   2. $347.96   4. $357.50

39. Which of the following represents the MOST likely recourse for a lender who has foreclosed on a property and does not recover enough from the sale to cover the outstanding loan amount due?
   1. Sue the borrower for a deficiency judgment.
   2. Apply to the appropriate federal agency for the difference.
   3. Seek compensation from the borrower's title insurance company.
   4. Initiate proceedings to recover the difference from homestead exemption funds.

40. You own a home on a block that is zoned residential; however, there is a retail store on the lot next door to you. The retail store
    1. is an example of downzoning.
    2. is a nonconforming use.
    3. will have to close if you file a complaint with the planning commission.
    4. is a buffer zone.

41. Which of the following statements is CORRECT about an exclusive agency listing in that it authorizes
    1. the listing agent to sign offers on behalf of the seller.
    2. the listing agent to be the only licensee to show the property.
    3. the seller to find a buyer and not be obligated to pay a sales commission.
    4. the seller to demand that the listing firm purchase the property if it remains unsold at the end of the listing period.

42. A doctor built a $400,000 home in a neighborhood of $200,000 homes. This situation reflects the principle of
    1. competition.   3. progression.
    2. conformity.   4. regression.

43. You purchased a home with an FHA-insured loan. At closing, the seller was charged the five discount points for the loan. This money will be paid to
    1. the broker.
    2. the lending institution.
    3. the FHA.
    4. you.

44. A doctrine of law that gives title to property to a buyer under a binding offer to purchase under certain conditions is known as
    1. accession.
    2. equitable conversion.
    3. laches.
    4. partition.

45. You have just purchased a business including the inventory and equipment. Title to the inventory and equipment will be transferred to you by means of a
    1. bargain and sale deed.
    2. bill of sale.
    3. quitclaim deed.
    4. warranty deed.

46. You have listed a property. The seller told you that he must net at least $18,000 after all fees and expenses are paid. You estimate the seller's closing costs to be $5,200 and he must pay off an existing loan of $104,600. In addition you are going to charge a 6 percent commission on the sale. What is the least amount that the property can sell for to return the seller's desired net?
    1. $111,277
    2. $130,425
    3. $137,419
    4. None of the above

47. Six months after a real estate transaction closes, one of the parties discovers information about the transaction that raises the possibility of having been the victim of fraud. Which of the following terms BEST identifies the legal principle governing whether or not the aggrieved party can still bring a lawsuit this long after closing?
    1. Laches.
    2. Equity of redemption.
    3. Statute of frauds.
    4. Statute of limitations.

48. A term loan is MOST likely to use which of the following repayment schedules?
    1. Monthly interest payments with a final balloon payment of the original principal
    2. Monthly principal payments with a final balloon payment of remaining principal and interest
    3. Periodic payments of principal and interest that increase according to an agreed-upon amortization schedule
    4. No payments at all during the loan period with the entire balance of principle and accrued interest due on a specified future date

49. X, who works for broker Y on a 50-50 basis, sold a house listed by broker Z for $192,900. The seller agreed to pay 6 percent commission but stipulated in the listing that 60 percent was to go to the selling broker. How much commission will X make on this sale (to the nearest dollar)?
    1. $2,083   3. $4,630
    2. $3,472   4. $6,944

50. Which of the following responsibilities would NOT be considered part of the licensee's fiduciary duties to a client?
    1. Procuring a buyer for a seller-client
    2. Presenting all offers promptly to the client
    3. Advising a buyer-client how to take title to the property
    4. Ensuring that earnest monies are placed in a trust account

51. Standing timber is legally considered to be
    1. emblements.
    2. personal property.
    3. real property.
    4. trade fixtures.

52. Which of the following governs the disclosures required when advertising financing terms for real estate?
    1. Regulation Z
    2. Sherman Antitrust Act
    3. Equal Credit Opportunity Act (ECOA)
    4. Real Estate Settlement Procedures Act (RESPA)

53. Title of the land and building in a cooperative is held by a
    1. corporation.
    2. general partnership.
    3. homeowners association.
    4. syndicate.

54. Which of the following would be required for a deed to be valid?
    1. The grantee must sign the deed.
    2. The deed must be recorded by the grantor.
    3. The grantor must sign the deed.
    4. The deed must be recorded by the grantee.

55. A broker has an accepted offer to purchase a property and would like to change the language to reflect the desire of the buyer and seller to revise the contract. The broker will accomplish this by means of a(n)
    1. addendum.
    2. amendment.
    3. counteroffer.
    4. recission.

56. The major employer in your city has decided to relocate to another state, resulting in a substantial decline in housing prices. This would be an example of
    1. the principle of regression.
    2. functional obsolescence.
    3. physical deterioration.
    4. economic obsolescence.

57. Which of the following is a physical characteristic of land?
    1. Scarcity
    2. Situs
    3. Immobility
    4. Improvements

58. What is the actual value of your property, if the annual taxes are $3,940 and real estate is assessed at 40 percent of actual value? (Figure a level of 35 mills per $1 of assessed value.)
    1. $98,500
    2. $112,571
    3. $281,429
    4. None of the above

59. A correct statement about an easement in gross is that it
    1. benefits the dominant tenement.
    2. has only a dominant tenement.
    3. has only a servient tenement.
    4. has both a dominant and a servient tenement.

60. Ownership is freely transferable in all of the following forms of ownership EXCEPT
    1. a sole proprietorship.
    2. a corporation.
    3. an S corporation.
    4. a general partnership.

61. Using the mortgage factor chart on page 127, what is the monthly payment for $129,000 at 8 percent for 30 years?
    1. $923,64   3. $968.79
    2. $946.86   4. $99.01

62. Using the numbers in question 61, what is the total interest paid over the life of the loan?
    1. $209,975.88   3. $211,869.60
    2. $210,922.74   4. $212,816.46

63. You and your brother have purchased an apartment building as joint tenants. Which of the following statements does NOT correctly describe your situation?
    1. You and your brother hold the right of survivorship.
    2. Owners must be related in order to own joint tenancy.
    3. The unities of title, time, interest, and possession are required to create a valid joint tenancy.
    4. Either you or your brother may partition the land.

64. You and your husband live in a community property state. Which of the following assets owned by you would be considered community property?
    1. A car given to you after your marriage.
    2. A duplex that you and your husband purchased after your marriage.
    3. Stock inherited by your husband after your marriage.
    4. A house which you owned before you were married.

65. Limited liability companies must have a MINIMUM of how many members?
    1. 1 member   3. 35 members
    2. 10 members   4. 75 members

66. You have listed a property. The seller told you that he must net at least $26,000 after all fees and expenses are paid. You estimate the seller's closing cost to be $5,000 and he must pay off an existing loan of $119,600. In addition, you are going to charge 6 percent commission on the sale. What is the least amount that the property can sell for to return the seller's desired net?
    1. $127,234
    2. $154,893
    3. $169,825
    4. None of the above

67. The use of lead-based paint in residential properties was banned for health reasons in which of the following years?
    1. 1972
    2. 1978
    3. 1977
    4. 1991

68. A father wants to know how much money his daughter owes on her mortgage loan. The father knows that the interest part of the last monthly payment was $526.49. If his daughter is paying interest at 8 percent, what was the outstanding balance of the loan before the last payment was made?
    1. $70,198.67
    2. $78,973.50
    3. $90,255.42
    4. None of the above

69. A difference between an individual's ownership interest in a cooperative and a condominium is that in a cooperative, the owner
    1. is not subject to real estate taxes.
    2. holds fee simple title whereas a condominium owner holds a proprietary lease.
    3. is not responsible for unpaid real estate taxes of other owners whereas a condominium owner is.
    4. holds a personal property interest whereas a condominium owner holds a real property interest.

70. A CORRECT statement about agency relationships when a salesperson lists a property is that
    1. the licensee becomes a principal.
    2. the licensee's broker becomes the agent of the seller.
    3. the seller is entitled to subagency from all licensees who show the property.
    4. the seller must sign a dual agency relationship agreement with all prospective buyers.

71. The denial of a loan by a lender is a violation of the federal fair housing law if such denial is based on
    1. lack of income.
    2. familial status.
    3. public beliefs.
    4. sexual preference.

72. Which of the following does NOT represent a pair of individuals in which the first person has fiduciary responsibilities to the second?
    1. Listing broker to seller
    2. Buyer broker to buyer
    3. Mortgagor to mortgagee
    4. Appraiser to client.

73. A married couple owned their home as tenants by the entirety. They then separated, and the husband continued to live in the house. If the husband decides to sell the home, can he do so without the wife's consent?
    1. Yes, because the wife relinquished her interest when she moved out of the house.
    2. Yes, because under tenancy by the entirety either party may sell the house without the consent of the other party.
    3. No, because the wife holds a dower interest that will not be extinguished upon the sale of the house.
    4. No, because under tenancy by the entirety title may be conveyed only by a deed signed by both parties.

74. A salesperson working as an independent contractor
    1. is required to attend sales meetings.
    2. may not be required to follow any set work schedule.
    3. is not responsible for transportation expenses.
    4. may receive fringe benefits if the broker agrees.

75. A broker has met with a customer and declined to work with the person in finding a home. It is legal for the broker to decline the opportunity, if the decision is based on the customer's
    1. familial status.   3. race.
    2. income.   4. religion.

76. A borrower's three-day right of rescission for a residential real estate loan transaction is based on the provisions of
    1. Regulation Z.
    2. the Fair Housing Laws.
    3. the Equal Credit Opportunity Act (ECOA).
    4. the Real Estate Settlement Procedures Act (RESPA).

77. You have listed your house with only one licensed broker but reserved the right to sell the property yourself without owing a commission. This relationship is called a(n)
    1. net listing.
    2. open listing.
    3. exclusive-agency listing.
    4. exclusive right-to-sell listing.

78. A woman owns a four-unit apartment building but does not live there. She is currently advertising for Lutheran tenants only. Is her advertising policy legal?
    1. Yes, because the property contains four units.
    2. Yes, because no real estate agent is involved in the marketing of the property.
    3. No, because four-unit properties are not exempted from the Federal Fair Housing Law.
    4. No, because she is not living in the apartment building.

79. The civil penalty for a first violation of the American with Disabilities Act (ADA) is up to
    1. $10,000.   3. $50,000.
    2. $25,000.   4. $100,000.

80. You own an apartment building in which one of your tenants subsequent to his lease expiring has continued to live in his unit without a new lease. However, the tenant has continued to pay rent and you have accepted it. This type of tenancy is a(n)
    1. estate for years.
    2. estate from year to year.
    3. tenancy at will.
    4. tenancy at sufferance.

ANSWER KEY WITH EXPLANATIONS

1. **(4)** A license may be canceled by the licensor. Adverse possession would result in a change of ownership. An easement appurtenant requires a dominant tenement. (29)

2. **(4)** The habendum clause follows the granting clause when it is necessary to define the ownership to be enjoyed by the grantee. Any type of deed should explain any restrictions and limitations on the title. (100–101)

3. **(4)** The sister and her husband jointly own an undivided one-half interest as tenants in common with the brother. (31)

4. **(1)** $4,800 - $900 salary = $3,900 commission on sales
   $3,900 ÷ 3% (0.03) = $130,000 value of property sold (120)

5. **(3)** A title search would not reveal the existence of an encroachment. Prior appropriation relates to water rights. A party wall easement would be appropriate if that was the case and could be negotiated with the neighbor. (29)

6. **(2)** A broker may not disclose that a prospective tenant is a member of a protected class. (110)

7. **(2)** Eminent domain is the right of the government to acquire private property for public use

while paying just compensation to the owner. (41)

8. **(3)** A broker may not commingle his funds with those of his clients in his trust account. (76)

9. **(4)** When the life tenant dies, the life estate is terminated. On the death of the life estate owner, full ownership will pass to the owner of the future interest. (30–31)

10. **(4)** After both the buyer and the seller have executed the offer to purchase contract, the buyer acquires equitable title. (92)

11. **(4)** Construction standards are regulated by building codes. (42)

12. **(3)** Lien priority refers to the rights of creditors as does homestead rights. A deed in lieu of foreclosure is an alternative to a process of foreclosure. (64)

13. **(1)** Hypothecation is pledging of property as security for a loan without losing possession of it. Arbitrage, subordination, and release of mortgage were discussed above. (70)

14. **(2)** The broker may guide activities and maintain standards of conduct for a salesperson working as an employee. (146–47)

15. **(4)** The gross rent multiplier (GRM) relates to monthly rental income, not annual.
$126,000 sale price ÷ $900 monthly rent = 140 gross multiplier (55)

16. **(3)** Specific penalties under the federal fair housing law are discussed in Part 12. (111)

17. **(3)** Erosion is the gradual wearing away of land by the action of natural forces. Accession and accretion were discussed above. (47–48)

18. **(1)** Treating people differently because they are members of a protected class is a violation of the federal fair housing laws. There is, however, an exemption covering rentals if the rooms or units are in an owner-occupied one-family to four-family dwelling. (111)

19. **(3)** You should use the three steps for making adjustments in the value comparison approach to value.
1. Always work from the price of the comparable to the subject property.
2. C.B.S.—comparable better subtract.
3. S.B.A.—subject better add. (55)

20. **(4)** Your brother's interest is a life estate because it is limited to your brother's life. A reversion would exist only if the land reverted to you. A base fee may be inherited. Curtesy refers to the life estate of a husband. (30–31)

21. **(3)** $163,000 (Current appraised value) – $129,000 (Current mortgage balance) = $34,000 A's equity in the home (69)

22. **(2)** A broker employed to sell an owner's home would be a special agent. Cooperating brokers under a multiple-listing service (MLS) would be subagents. Dual agency occurs when a broker represents both the seller and the buyer in a transaction. (76)

23. **(4)** Sexual orientation is not a protected class under the federal fair housing law. (109)

24. **(3)** An escrow relationship refers to a third party agreement such as an escrow agent who does a closing for the buyer and seller. A subordination agreement changes the order of lien priority between the two creditors. A trustee acts as an agent and is generally responsible for handling money or holding title to land. (75)

25. **(4)** A salesperson may accept financial compensation for completing a real estate transaction only from her employing broker. (77)

26. **(2)** This is clearly a case of intentional misrepresentation. (77)

27. **(3)** The fact that you own a defeasible fee estate does not affect the vendee's interest of equitable title in the estate. (92–93)
28. **(2)** $183,000 sales price × 7% (0.07) = $12,810 × 0.30 = $3,843 (120)
29. **(4)** The broker has a fiduciary responsibility to the seller, which requires that she disclose her fair opinion of value to the principal. (75)
30. **(4)** The fee for the option right belongs to the owner (optionor) regardless of the outcome of the transaction. (92)
31. **(4)** Persons who have AIDS are protected under the federal fair housing laws. (109)
32. **(4)** Religion is a protected class under the federal fair housing laws. (109)
33. **(1)** In an exclusive-agency or open listing, the sellers have the right to sell their property on their own without having to pay the broker a commission. A net listing is based on the net price the seller will receive if the property is sold; the broker receives any amount received above the net price. The net listing is prohibited or discouraged in most states. (90)
34. **(3)** $80,000 (first investor) + $50,000 (second investor) = $130,000
$250,000 − $130,000 = $120,000 third investor's contribution

$$\frac{\text{Part}}{\text{Percent}} = \text{Total}$$

$120,000 ÷ $250,000 = 0.48 or 48% (120)
35. **(3)** $50,000 gross income − $12,000 expenses = $38,000 net annual income
$38,000 net annual income ÷ 14% (0.14) = $271,429 value of real estate (124–25)
36. **(4)** A dual agent would have an agency agreement with the buyer and seller. In an exclusive buyer agency agreement the broker is entitled to payment regardless of whether the broker locates the property; the agent will be paid even if the buyer finds the property without the agent's help. The open buyer agency agreement allows the buyer to enter into similar agreements with other brokers. Only the broker who locates the property will be compensated. (91)
37. **(4)** A fee simple is a real property interest, while a legal life estate is a spouse's estate in all the inheritable real estate of the deceased spouse. Tenancy by the entirety is a unit form of ownership in which the owners must be husband and wife. (30)
38. **(2)** $143,000 × 80% (0.80) = $140,000 assessed value
Divided by 100 because the tax rate is stated per $100
$1,144 × $3.65 = $4,175.60 annual taxes
Divide by 12 to get monthly taxes $4,175.60 ÷ 12 = $347.96 (121)
39. **(1)** Deficiency judgments may be obtained for any deficiency. (65)
40. **(2)** Downzoning refers to a situation where the zoning for a parcel of land is changed from a dense to a less dense usage. The planning commission cannot close the retail store. A nonconforming use generally is removed if it suffers 50 percent or more damage and is not rebuilt within one year. A buffer zone is a land area that separates one land use from another. (41–42)
41. **(3)** Only one broker is authorized to act as an exclusive agent of the seller, but the sellers may sell the property themselves. Brokers generally enter into exclusive-right-to-sell listings. (90)
42. **(4)** The principle of regression states that the value of the better property is affected adversely by the

presence of the lesser quality properties. (54)

43. **(2)** Discount points usually are charged by and paid to the lender when the FHA interest rate is less than the conventional, or market, rate of interest. (65)

44. **(2)** Accession refers to a way in which personal property can become real property. Laches and partition are described above. (102)

45. **(2)** Inventory and equipment are considered to be personal property. (137)

46. **(4)** Add the desired net, $18,000 plus the existing loan payoff, $104,600 and the closing costs $5,200. $127,800 is the minimum that the seller must receive. The correct answer is $127,800 ÷ .94 (100% − 6%) = $135,957. (120)

47. **(4)** Laches is a doctrine whereby one is unable to assert a legal right because of waiting too long to enforce it. Equity of redemption refers to the time period for foreclosure which the buyer may redeem his property. The statute of frauds requires certain contracts to be in writing in order to be enforceable. (33)

48. **(1)** Straight or term loans are generally used for home improvements and second mortgages. (63)

49. **(2)** $192,900 × 0.06 = $11,574 broker's commission.
$11,574 × 60% = $6,944.40 × .05 = $3,472.20 selling salesperson's commission (120)

50. **(3)** A broker may not offer legal advice; only a licensed attorney may do so. (75)

51. **(3)** All of the alternative answers refer to personal property. (140)

52. **(1)** Regulation Z required disclosure of cost in a credit transaction as well as the advertising of financing terms. The Sherman Antitrust Act deals with antitrust violations such as boycotting. ECOA prohibits discrimination against

protected classes with regard to loan applications. (113–14)

53. **(1)** Each buyer in the cooperative becomes a shareholder and receives a proprietary lease. (136)

54. **(3)** The grantee must be identified in the deed. Unrecorded deeds are valid between the parties. However, the deed should be recorded in order to provide constructive notice. (101)

55. **(2)** An amendment changes the language of a contract; an addendum adds additional terms. (93)

56. **(4)** Functional obsolescence and physical deterioration are losses in value that occur within the property, while economic obsolescence occurs outside the property. The principle of regression was discussed above. (55)

57. **(3)** Scarcity, situs, and improvements are economic characteristics of land. (27–28)

58. **(3)** $3,940 ÷ 0.035 = $112,571 assessed value
$112,571 ÷ 40% (0.40) = $281,429 market value (121)

59. **(3)** An easement in gross does not have a dominant tenement. (29)

60. **(4)** A general partnership also is exposed to the problems arising from the health or bankruptcy of the partner(s). (144)

61. **(2)** $946.86 ($129,000 × 7.34) (126–28)

62. **(3)** $946.86 × 360 months =

$340,869.60   Total P&I
− $129,000.00   Loan
$211,869.60   Total interest
(126–28)

63. **(2)** Owners in joint tenancy do not have to be related. (31–32)

64. **(2)** Community property includes real and personal property acquired by either spouse during the marriage. Separate property (real or personal) is that owned individually by either spouse before the marriage. Separate property also includes any

arate property also includes any property acquired by inheritance or gift during the marriage or purchased with separate funds during the marriage. (32)

65. **(1)** Members of limited liability companies may be individuals, corporations, trusts, general or limited partnerships, or foreign persons. (145)

66. **(4)** Add the desire net, $26,000, plus the existing loan payoff, $119.600, and the closing cost, $5,000. $150,600 is the minimum that the seller must receive.

If the selling price is 100 percent the commission is 6 percent, the net to seller is 94 percent.

$150,600 is 94 percent of the selling price.

Therefore, $150,600 ÷ 94% (0.94) = selling price of $160,212.76, which is not one of the options. (120)

67. **(2)** You should be aware that licensees involved in the sales, financing, appraisal or management of properties built prior to 1978 face potential liability for any personal injury suffered by occupants resulting from exposure to lead-based paint. (45)

68. **(2)** $526.49 × 12 = $6,317.88 annual interest

Part ÷ percent = total

$6,317.88 ÷ 8% (0.08) = $78,973.50 (120)

69. **(4)** Each buyer receives a proprietary lease and becomes a stockholder. However, a cooperative is converted to a real estate interest in those states that have adopted the Common Interest Ownership Act. (136)

70. **(2)** The broker is the agent of the seller. The salesperson is the agent of the broker and subagent (not agent) of the seller. (75)

71. **(2)** Familial status was added in 1988. (109)

72. **(3)** Mortgagees have a fiduciary relationship with investors who place money in their lending institutions. (63)

73. **(4)** Tenancy by the entirety is a unit ownership of the property. (32)

74. **(2)** Independent contractors work under limited supervision from the broker. (147)

75. **(2)** Familial status, race, and religion are protected classes under the federal fair housing law. (109)

76. **(1)** The three day right of recession covers a home equity loan or the refinancing of a home mortgage. It does not cover owner-occupied residential purchase-money as first mortgage or deed of trust loans. (113)

77. **(3)** A net listing is based on the amount of money the seller will receive if the property is sold. In the open listing, the seller retains the right to employ any number of brokers to act as his or her agents. In an exclusive right-to-sell listing, the seller gives up the right to sell the property himself or herself and thus avoids paying the broker's commission (90)

78. **(4)** The federal fair housing law exempts the rental of units in an owner-occupied one-family to four-family dwelling. (111)

79. **(3)** A penalty of up to $100,000 may be assessed for any subsequent violation of ADA. (113)

80. **(2)** A periodic estate is a lease for an indefinite period of time without a specific expiration date; notice must be given to terminate. (135)

abandonment The voluntary and permanent cessation of use or enjoyment with no intention to resume or reclaim one's possession or interest. May pertain to an easement of a property.

abstract of title A condensed version of the history of a title to a particular parcel of real estate as recorded in the county clerk's records; consists of a summary of the original grant and all subsequent conveyances and encumbrances affecting the property.

abutting The joining, reaching, or touching of adjoining land. Abutting parcels of land have a common boundary.

accelerated depreciation A method of calculating for tax purposes the depreciation of income property at a faster rate than would be achieved using the straight-line method. Note that any depreciation taken in excess of what would be claimed using the straight-line rate is subject to **recapture** as ordinary income to the extent of the gain resulting from the sale. *See also STRAIGHT-LINE METHOD.*

acceleration clause A provision in a written mortgage, note, bond, or conditional sales contract that in the event of default, the whole amount of the principal and the interest may be declared due and payable at once.

accession Title to improvements or additions to real property is acquired as a result of the accretion of alluvial deposits along the banks of streams or as a result of the annexation of fixtures.

accretion An increase or addition to land by the deposit of sand or soil washed up naturally from a river, lake, or sea.

accrued depreciation The actual depreciation that has occurred to a property at any given date; the difference between the cost of replacement new (as of the date of the appraisal) and the present appraised value.

acknowledgment A declaration made by a person to a notary public or other public official authorized to take acknowledgments that an instrument was executed by him or her as a free and voluntary act.

actual eviction The result of legal action originated by a lessor, by which a defaulted tenant is physically ousted from the rented property pursuant to a court order. *See also EVICTION.*

actual notice Express information or fact; that which is known; actual knowledge.

administrator The party appointed by the county court to settle the estate of a deceased person who died without leaving a will.

ad valorem tax A tax levied according to value; generally used to refer to real estate tax. Also called **general tax.**

adverse possession The actual, visible, hostile, notorious, exclusive and continuous possession of another's land under a claim to title. Possession for a statutory period may be a means of acquiring title.

affidavit A written statement signed and sworn to before a person authorized to administer an oath.

agent One who represents or has the power to act for another person (called the principal). The authorization may be express, implied, or apparent. A fiduciary relationship is created under the **law of agency** when a property owner, as the principal, executes a listing agreement or management contract authorizing a licensed real estate broker to be her or his agent.

agreement of sale A written agreement by which the purchaser agrees to buy certain real estate and the seller agrees to sell, on the terms and conditions set forth in the agreement.

air lot A designated airspace over a piece of land. Air lots, like surface property, may be transferred.

air rights The right to use the open space above a property, generally allowing the surface to be used for another purpose.

alienation The act of transferring property to another. Alienation may be voluntary, such as by gift or sale, or involuntary, such as through eminent domain or adverse possession.

alienation clause (due-on-sale clause) The clause in a mortgage or deed of trust that states that the balance of the secured debt becomes immediately due and payable at the mortgagee's option if the title is transferred or the property is sold. In effect, this clause prevents the mortgagor from assigning the debt without the mortgagee's approval.

alluvion The actual soil increase resulting from accretion.

amenities The tangible and intangible features that increase the value or desirability of real estate.

Americans with Disabilities Act (ADA) A federal law, effective in 1992, designed to eliminate discrimination against individuals with disabilities.

amortization The liquidation of a financial burden by installment payments, which include principal and interest.

amortized loan A loan in which the principal and interest are payable in monthly or other periodic installments over the term of the loan.

antitrust laws The laws designed to preserve the free enterprise of the open marketplace by making illegal certain private conspiracies and combinations formed to minimize competition. Violation of antitrust laws in the real estate business generally involves either **price fixing** (brokers conspiring to set fixed compensation rates) or allocation of customers or markets (brokers agreeing to limit their trades or dealings to certain areas or properties).

appraisal An estimate of the quantity, quality, or value of something. The process through which conclusions about property value are obtained; also refers to the report that sets forth the process of estimation and conclusion of value.

appraised value An estimate of a property's present worth.

appreciation An increase in the worth or value of a property, due to economic or related causes, which may prove to be either temporary or permanent; opposite of depreciation.

appurtenant Belonging to; incident to; annexed to. For example, a garage is appurtenant to a house, and the common interest in the common elements of a condominium

is appurtenant to each apartment. Appurtenances pass with the land when the property is transferred.

arbitration A means of settling a controversy between two parties through the medium of an impartial third party whose decision on the controversy (if agreed upon) will be final and binding.

assessment The imposition of a tax, charge, or levy, usually according to established rates.

assignment The transfer in writing of rights or interest in a bond, mortgage, lease, or other instrument.

assumed name statute (fictitious name statute) The law, in effect in most states, that stipulates that no person shall conduct a business under any name other than his or her own individual name, unless such person files the desired name with the county clerk in each county where the business is conducted. In the case of brokers and salespeople, statement of such filing should be submitted to the state's real estate commission.

assumption of mortgage The transfer of title to property to a grantee, by which the grantee assumes liability for payment of an existing note secured by a mortgage against the property. Should the mortgage be foreclosed and the property sold for a lesser amount than that due, the grantee/purchaser who has assumed and agreed to pay the debt secured by the mortgage is personally liable for the deficiency. Before a seller may be relieved of liability under the existing mortgage, the lender must accept the transfer of liability for payment of the note.

attachment The method by which a debtor's property is placed in the custody of the law and held as security, pending the outcome of a creditor's suit.

attorney-in-fact The holder of a power of attorney.

attorney's opinion of title An instrument written and signed by the attorney who examines the title, stating her or his opinion as to whether a seller may convey good title.

automatic extension A clause in a listing agreement that states that the agreement will continue automatically for a certain time period after its expiration date. In many states, use of this clause is discouraged or prohibited.

avulsion A sudden tearing away of land by the action of natural forces.

balloon payment The final payment of a mortgage loan that is considerably larger than the required periodic payments because the loan amount was not fully amortized.

bargain and sale deed A deed that carries with it no warranties against liens or other encumbrances but that does imply the grantor has the right to convey title. Note that the grantor may add warranties to the deed at his or her discretion.

base fee A determinable fee estate that may be inherited.

base line One of a set of imaginary lines running east and west and crossing a principal meridian at a definite point. Base lines are used by surveyors for reference in locating and describing land under the rectangular survey system (or government survey method) of property description.

benchmark A permanent reference mark or point established for use by surveyors when measuring differences in elevation.

beneficiary 1. The person for whom a trust operates or in whose behalf the income from a trust estate is drawn. 2. A lender who lends money on real estate and takes back a note and deed of trust from the borrower.

bequest A provision in a will providing for the distribution of personal property.

bilateral contract A contract in which each party promises to perform an act in exchange for the other party's promise to perform.

bill of sale A written instrument given to pass title to personal property.

binder An agreement that may accompany an earnest money deposit for the purchase of real property as evidence of the purchaser's good faith and intent to complete the transaction.

blanket mortgage A mortgage that covers more than one parcel of real estate and provides for each parcel's partial release from the mortgage lien on repayment of a definite portion of the debt.

blockbusting The illegal practice of inducing homeowners to sell their properties by making representations regarding the entry or prospective entry of minority persons into the neighborhood.

blue-sky laws The common name for state and federal laws that regulate the registration and sale of investment securities.

boycotting Two or more businesses conspire against other businesses to reduce competition.

branch office A secondary place of business apart from the principal or main office from which real estate business is conducted. A branch office generally must be run by a licensed real estate broker, broker salesperson or associate broker working on behalf of the broker operating the principal office.

breach of contract The failure, without legal excuse, of one of the parties to a contract to perform according to the contract.

broker One who buys and sells for another for a commission. *See also* REAL ESTATE BROKER.

brokerage The business of buying and selling for another for a commission.

broker/salesperson A person who has passed the broker's licensing examination but is licensed to work only on behalf of a licensed broker and who may be allowed to manage an office. In many states, known as (licensed as) associate broker or broker/associate.

budget loan A loan in which the monthly payments made by the borrower cover not only interest and a payment on the principal but also 1/12 of such expenses as taxes, insurance, assessments, private mortgage insurance premiums and similar charges.

buffer zone A strip of land that separates one land use from another.

building code An ordinance specifying minimum standards of construction of buildings for the protection of public safety and health.

building line A line fixed at a certain distance from the front and/or sides of a lot beyond which no structure can project; a setback line used to ensure a degree of uniformity in the appearance of buildings and unobstructed light, air, and view.

building restrictions The limitations on the size or type of property improvements established by zoning acts or by deed or lease restrictions. Building restrictions are considered encumbrances, and violations render the title unmarketable.

bundle of legal rights The theory that land ownership involves ownership of all legal rights to the land, such as possession, control within the law and enjoyment, rather than ownership of the land itself.

business plan A three-year to five-year blueprint for an organizational or individual real estate practitioner.

canvassing The practice of making telephone calls or visiting from door to door to seek prospective buyers or sellers; in the real estate business, generally associated with acquired listings in a given area.

capacity of parties The legal ability of persons to enter into a valid contract. Most persons have full capacity to contract and are said to be **competent parties.**

capital gain Profit earned from the sale of an asset.

capital investment The initial capital and the long-term expenditures made to establish and maintain a business or investment property.

capitalization The process of converting into present value (or obtaining the present worth of) a series of anticipated future periodic installments of net income. In real estate appraisal, it usually takes the form of discounting. The formula is expressed as

$$\frac{\text{Income}}{\text{Rate}} = \text{Value}$$

capitalization rate The rate of return a property will produce on the owner's investment.

cash flow The net spendable income from an investment, determined by deducting all operating and fixed expenses from the gross income. If expenses exceed income, a negative cash flow is the result.

casualty insurance A type of insurance policy that protects a property owner or other person from loss or injury sustained as a result of theft, vandalism, or similar occurrences.

caveat emptor A Latin phrase meaning, "Let the buyer beware."

certificate of sale The document generally given to a purchaser at a tax foreclosure sale. A certificate of sale does not convey title; generally, it is an instrument certifying that the holder may receive title to the property after the redemption period has passed and that the holder paid the property taxes for that interim period.

certificate of title The statement of opinion on the status of the title to a parcel of real property, based on an examination of specified public records.

chain of title The succession of conveyances from some accepted starting point by which the present holder of real property derives her or his title.

chattels Personal property.

city planning commission A local governmental organization designed to direct and control the development of land within a municipality.

cloud on title A claim or encumbrance that may affect the title to land.

codicil A testamentary disposition subsequent to a will that alters, explains, adds to, or confirms the will, but does not revoke it.

coinsurance clause A clause in insurance policies covering real property that requires the policyholder to maintain fire insurance coverage generally equal to at least 80 percent of the property's actual replacement cost.

collateral Something of value given or pledged to a lender as a security for a debt or obligation.

commercial property A classification of real estate that includes income-producing property such as office buildings, restaurants, shopping centers, hotels, and stores.

commingled property Property of a married couple that is so mixed or commingled that it is difficult to determine whether it is separate or community property. Commingled property becomes community property.

commingling The illegal act of a real estate broker who mixes the money of other people with that of his or her own; brokers are required by law to maintain a separate trust account for other parties' funds held temporarily by the broker.

commission The payment made to a broker for services rendered, such as in the sale or purchase of real property; usually a percentage of the selling price of the property.

common elements The parts of a property that are necessary or convenient to the existence, maintenance, and safety of a condominium or that are normally in common use by all of the condominium residents. All condominium owners have an undivided ownership interest in the common elements.

common law A body of law based on custom, usage and court decisions.

community property A system of property ownership based on the theory that each spouse has an equal interest in the property acquired by the efforts of either spouse during marriage.

comparables The properties listed in an appraisal report that are substantially equivalent to the subject property.

competent parties Persons who are recognized by law as being able to contract with others; usually those of legal age and sound mind. *See also CAPACITY OF PARTIES.*

composite depreciation A method of determining the depreciation of a multibuilding property using the average rate at which all the buildings are depreciating.

condemnation A judicial or administrative proceeding or process to exercise the power of **eminent domain.**

condominium The absolute ownership of an apartment or a unit, generally in a multiunit building, based on a legal description of the airspace the unit actually occupies, plus an undivided interest in the ownership of the common elements, which are owned together with the other condominium unit owners. The entire tract of real estate included in a condominium development is called a *parcel* or *development parcel.* One apartment or space in a condominium or a part of a property intended for independent use and having lawful access to the public way is called a unit. Ownership of one unit also includes a definite undivided interest in the common elements.

conformity *See PRINCIPLE OF CONFORMITY.*

consideration Something of value that induces one to enter into a contract. Consideration may be "valuable" (money or commodity) or "good" (love and affection). Also, an act of forbearance, or the promise thereof, given by one party in exchange for something from the other. Forbearance is a promise *not* to do something.

constructive eviction 1. Acts by the landlord that so materially disturb or impair the tenant's enjoyment of the leased premises that the tenant is effectively forced to move out and terminate the lease without liability for any further rent. 2. A purchaser's inability to obtain clear title.

constructive notice Notice given to the world by recorded documents. All persons are charged with knowledge of such documents and their contents, whether or not they have actually examined them. Possession of property also is considered constructive notice that the person in possession has an interest in the property.

contract An agreement entered into by two or more legally competent parties by the terms of which one or more of the parties, for a consideration, undertakes to do or to refrain from doing some legal act or acts. A contract may be either **unilateral,** where only one party is bound to act, or **bilateral,** where all parties to the instrument are legally bound to act as prescribed.

contract for deed A contract for the sale of real estate under which the sale price is paid in periodic installments by the purchaser, who is in possession and holds equitable title although actual title is retained by the seller until final payment. Also called an **installment contract** or **land contract.**

contract for exchange of real estate A contract for sale of real estate in which the consideration is paid wholly or partly in property.

conventional loan A loan that is not insured or guaranteed by a government agency.

conveyance A written instrument that evidences transfer of some interest in real property from one person to another.

cooperative A residential multiunit building whose title is held by a trust or corporation that is owned by and operated for the benefit of persons living within the building. These persons are the beneficial owners of the trust or the shareholders of the corporation, each having a proprietary lease.

corporation An entity or organization created by operation of law whose rights of doing business are essentially the same as those of an individual. The entity has continuous existence until dissolved according to legal procedures.

correction lines The provisions in the rectangular survey system (government survey method) made to compensate for the curvature of the earth's surface. Every fourth township line (at 24-mile intervals) is used as a correction line on which the intervals between the north and south range lines are remeasured and corrected to a full six miles.

cost approach The process of estimating the value of a property by adding the appraiser's estimate of the reproduction or replacement cost of the building, less depreciation, to the estimated land value.

counseling The business of providing people with expert advice on a subject, based on the counselor's extensive, expert knowledge of the subject.

counteroffer A new offer made as a reply to an offer received, having the effect of rejecting the original offer. The original offer cannot be accepted thereafter unless revived by the offeror's repeating it.

cul-de-sac A dead-end street that widens sufficiently at the end to permit an automobile to make a U-turn.

curtesy A life estate, usually a fractional interest, given by some states to the surviving husband in real estate owned by his deceased wife. Most states have abolished curtesy.

cycle A recurring sequence of events that regularly follow one another, generally within a fixed interval of time.

datum A horizontal plane from which heights and depths are measured.

dba Doing business as.

debenture A note or bond given as evidence of debt and issued without security.

debt Something owed to another; an obligation to pay or return something.

declining balance method An accounting method of calculating depreciation for tax purposes designed to provide large deductions in the early years of ownership. *See also ACCELERATED DEPRECIATION.*

decreasing returns *See DIMINISHING RETURNS.*

deed A written instrument that when executed and delivered conveys title to or an interest in real estate.

deed in lieu of foreclosure A process by which the mortgagor can avoid foreclosure. Mortgagor gives a deed to mortgagee when mortgagor is in default according to terms of mortgage.

deed of reconveyance The instrument used to reconvey title to a trustor under a deed of trust once the debt has been satisfied.

deed of trust An instrument used to create a mortgage lien by which the mortgagor conveys her or his title to a trustee, who holds it as security for the benefit of the noteholder (the lender); also called a **trust deed.**

deed restrictions The clauses in a deed limiting the future uses of the property. Deed restrictions may impose a variety of limitations and conditions, such as limiting the density of buildings, dictating the types of structures that can be erected, and preventing buildings from being used for specific purposes or from being used at all.

default The nonperformance of a duty, whether arising under a contract or otherwise; failure to meet an obligation when due.

defeasance clause A clause used in leases or mortgages that cancels a specified right on the occurrence of a certain condition, such as cancellation of a mortgage on repayment of the mortgage loan.

deficiency judgment A personal judgment levied against the mortgagor when a foreclosure sale does not produce sufficient funds to pay the mortgage debt in full.

delinquent taxes Unpaid taxes that are past due.

delivery The legal act of transferring ownership. Documents such as deeds and mortgages must be delivered and accepted to be valid.

delivery in escrow Delivery of a deed to a third person until the performance of some act or condition by one of the parties.

demand The willingness of persons to buy available goods at a given price; often coupled with **supply.**

density zoning The zoning ordinances that restrict the average maximum number of houses per acre that may be built within a particular area, generally a subdivision.

depreciation 1. In appraisal, a loss of value in property due to all causes, including physical deterioration, functional obsolescence, and economic obsolescence. 2. In real estate investment, an expense deduction for tax purposes taken over the period of ownership of the income property.

descent The hereditary succession of an heir to the property of a relative who dies intestate.

determinable fee estate A fee simple estate in which the property automatically reverts to the grantor on the occurrence of a specified event or condition.

devise A transfer of real estate by will or last testament. The donor is the devisor and the recipient is the devisee.

diminishing returns The principle that applies when a given parcel of land reaches its maximum percentage return on investment and further expenditures for improving the property yield a decreasing return.

discount points An added loan fee charged by a lender to make the yield on a lower-than-market-value loan competitive with higher-interest loans. *See also POINT.*

discount rate The rate of interest a commercial bank must pay when it borrows from its federal reserve bank. Consequently, the discount rate is the rate of interest the banking system carries within its own framework. Member banks may take certain promissory notes that they have received from customers and sell them to their district federal reserve bank for less than face value. With the funds received, the banks can make further loans. Changes in the discount rate may cause banks and other lenders to reexamine credit policies and conditions.

dispossess To oust from land by legal process.

dominant tenement A property that includes in its ownership the appurtenant right to use an easement over another's property for a specific purpose.

dower The legal right or interest recognized in some states that a wife acquires in the property her husband held or acquired during their marriage. During the lifetime of the husband, the right is only a possibility of an interest; on his death it can become an interest in land.

duress The use of unlawful constraint that forces action or inaction against a person's will.

DVA loan A mortgage loan on approved property made to a qualified veteran by an authorized lender and guaranteed by the Department of Veterans Affairs to limit possible loss by the lender. Also called a **GI-guaranteed mortgage.**

earnest money deposit An amount of money deposited by a buyer under the terms of a contract.

easement A right to use the land of another for a specific purpose, such as for a right-of-way or utilities; an incorporeal interest in land. An easement appurtenant passes with the land when conveyed.

easement by necessity An easement allowed by law as necessary for the full enjoyment of a parcel of real estate; for example, a right of ingress and egress over a grantor's land.

easement by prescription An easement acquired by continuous, open, uninterrupted, exclusive and adverse use of the property for the period of time prescribed by state law.

easement in gross An easement that is not created for the benefit of any land owned by the owner of the easement but that attaches personally to the easement owner. For example, the right to an easement granted by *A* to *B* to use a portion of *A*'s property for the rest of *B*'s life would be an easement in gross.

economic life The period of time over which an improved property will earn an income adequate to justify its continued existence.

economic obsolescence The impairment of desirability or useful life arising from factors external to the property, such as economic forces or environmental changes, that affect supply-demand relationships in the market. Loss in the use and value of a property arising from the factors of economic obsolescence is to be distinguished from loss in value from physical deterioration and functional obsolescence, both of which are inherent in the property. Also referred to as locational obsolescence or environmental obsolescence.

emblements Growing crops that are produced annually through the tenant's own care and labor and that she or he is entitled to take away after the tenancy is ended. Emblements are regarded as personal property even prior to harvest, so if the landlord terminates the lease, the tenant still may reenter the land and remove such crops. If the tenant terminates the tenancy voluntarily; however, he or she generally is not entitled to the emblements.

eminent domain The right of a government or municipal quasi-public body to acquire property for public use through a court action called **condemnation,** in which the court determines that the use is a public use and determines the price or compensation to be paid to the owner.

employee status The status of one who works as a direct employee of an employer. An employer is obligated to withhold income taxes and Social Security taxes from the compensation of his or her employees. *See also INDEPENDENT CONTRACTOR.*

employment contract A document evidencing formal employment between the employer and the employee or between the principal and the agent. In the real estate business, this generally takes the form of a listing or management agreement.

encroachment A fixture or structure, such as a wall or fence, that invades a portion of a property belonging to another.

encumbrance Any lien—such as a mortgage, tax or judgment lien; easement; restriction on the use of the land; or an outstanding dower right—that may diminish the value of the property.

endorsement The act of writing one's name, either with or without additional words, on a negotiable instrument or on a paper attached to such instrument.

equalization The raising or lowering of assessed values for tax purposes in a particular county or taxing district to make them equal to assessments in other counties or districts.

equitable title The interest held by a vendee under a contract for deed or an installment contract; the equitable right to obtain absolute ownership to property when legal title is held in another's name.

equity The interest or value that an owner has in a property over and above any mortgage indebtedness.

erosion The gradual wearing away of land by water, wind, and general weather conditions; the diminishing of property caused by the elements.

escheat The reversion of property to the state in the event its owner dies without leaving a will and has no heirs to whom the property may pass by lawful descent.

escrow The closing of a transaction through a third party called an escrow agent, or *escrowee*, who receives certain funds and documents to be delivered on the performance of certain conditions in the escrow agreement.

estate for years An interest for a certain, exact period of time in property leased for a specified consideration.

estate in land The degree, quantity, nature, and extent of interest that a person has in real property.

estate in severalty An estate owned by one person.

estoppel certificate A legal instrument executed by a mortgagor showing the amount of the unpaid balance due on a mortgage and stating that the mortgagor has no defenses or offsets against the mortgagee at the time of execution of the certificate. Also called a *certificate of no defense.*

estovers Legally allowed necessities such as the right of a tenant to use timber on leased property to support a minimum need for fuel or repairs.

ethical Conforming to professional standards of conduct.

et ux The Latin abbreviation for *et uxor,* meaning "and wife."

eviction A legal process to oust a person from possession of real estate.

evidence of title A proof of ownership of property, which is commonly a certificate of title, a title insurance policy, an abstract of title with lawyer's opinion or a Torrens registration certificate. *See also TORRENS SYSTEM.*

exchange A transaction in which all or part of the consideration for the purchase of real property is the transfer of like-kind property (that is, real estate for real estate).

exclusive-agency listing A listing contract under which the owner appoints a real estate broker as his or her exclusive agent for a designated period of time to sell the property on the owner's stated terms for a commission. The owner, however, reserves the right to sell without paying anyone a commission by selling to a prospect who has not been introduced or claimed by the broker.

exclusive-right-to-sell listing A listing contract under which the owner appoints a real estate broker as his or her exclusive agent for a designated period of time to sell the property on the owner's stated terms and agrees to pay the broker a commission when the property is sold, whether by the broker, the owner, or another broker.

executed contract A contract in which all parties have fulfilled their promises and thus performed the contract.

execution The signing and delivery of an instrument. Also, a legal order directing an official to enforce a judgment against the property of a debtor.

executor The male person designated in a will to handle the state of the deceased. The probate court must approve any sale of property by the executor. A female is called the *executrix.*

executory contract A contract under which something remains to be done by one or more of the parties.

expenses The short-term costs that are deducted from an investment property's income, such as minor repairs, regular maintenance, and renting costs.

expressed contract An oral or written contract in which the parties state its terms and express their intentions in words.

Fair Housing Act of 1968 The term for Title VIII of the Civil Rights Act of 1968 as amended, which prohibits discrimination based on race, color, sex, religion, national origin, handicaps, and familial status in the sale and rental of residential property.

Federal Home Loan Mortgage Corporation (FHLMC) A federally chartered corporation created to provide a secondary mortgage market for conventional loans (Freddie Mac).

Federal Housing Administration (FHA) A federal administrative body created by the National Housing Act in 1934 to encourage improvement in housing standards and conditions, to provide an adequate home-financing system through the insurance of housing mortgages and credit, and to exert a stabilizing influence on the mortgage market.

federal income tax An annual tax based on income, including monies derived from the lease, use or operation of real estate.

Federal National Mortgage Association (FNMA) "Fannie Mae" is the popular name for this federally chartered corporation, which creates a secondary market for existing mortgages. FNMA does not loan money directly, but rather buys DVA, FHA, and conventional loans.

fee simple estate The maximum possible estate or right of ownership of real property continuing forever. Sometimes called a *fee* or *fee simple absolute*.

FHA appraisal An FHA evaluation of a property as security for a loan. Includes the study of the physical characteristics of the property and surroundings, and the location of the property.

FHA loan A loan insured by the FHA and made by an approved lender in accordance with FHA regulations.

fiduciary relationship A relationship of trust and confidence, as between trustee and beneficiary, attorney and client, principal, and agent.

financing statement *See UNIFORM COMMERCIAL CODE.*

first mortgage A mortgage that creates a superior voluntary lien on the property mortgaged relative to other charges or encumbrances against the property.

fiscal policy The government's policy in regard to taxation and spending programs. The balance between these two areas determines the amount of money the government will withdraw or feed into the economy in an attempt to counter economic peaks and slumps.

fixture An article that was once personal property but has been so affixed to real estate that it has become real property.

forcible entry and detainer A summary proceeding for restoring to possession of land one who is wrongfully kept out or has been wrongfully deprived of the possession.

foreclosure A legal procedure by which property used as security for a debt is sold to satisfy the debt in the event of default in payment of the mortgage note or default of other terms in the mortgage document. The foreclosure procedure brings the rights of all parties to a conclusion and passes the title in the mortgaged property either to the holder of the mortgage or to a third party who may purchase the realty at the foreclosure sale, free of all encumbrances affecting the property subsequent to the mortgage.

foreign acknowledgment An acknowledgment taken outside of the state in which the land lies.

franchise A private contractual agreement to run a business using a designated trade name and operating procedures.

fraud A misstatement of a material fact made with intent to deceive or made with reckless disregard of the truth and that actually does deceive.

freehold estate An estate in land in which ownership is for an indeterminate length of time, in contrast to a **leasehold estate.**

functional obsolescence The impairment of functional capacity or efficiency. Functional obsolescence reflects the loss in value brought about by factors that affect the property, such as overcapacity, inadequacy, or changes in the art. The inability of a structure to perform adequately the function for which it currently is employed.

future interest A person's present right to an interest in real property that will not result in possession or enjoyment until some time in the future, such as a **reversion** or right of reentry.

gap A defect in the chain of title of a particular parcel of real estate; a missing document, or conveyance that raises doubt as to the present ownership of the land.

general contractor A construction specialist who enters into a formal construction contract with a landowner or master lessee to construct a real estate building or project. The general contractor often contracts with several **subcontractors** specializing in various aspects of the building process to perform individual jobs.

general lien A lien on all real and personal property owned by a debtor.

general partnership *See PARTNERSHIP.*

general tax *See AD VALOREM TAX.*

general warranty deed A deed that states that the title conveyed therein is good from the sovereignty of the soil to the grantee therein and that no one else can successfully claim the property. This type of deed contains several specific warranties sometimes referred to as the English Covenants of Title.

GI-guaranteed mortgage *See DVA LOAN.*

government lots Fractional sections in the rectangular survey system (government survey method) that are less than one full quarter-section in area.

Government National Mortgage Association (GNMA) "Ginnie Mae," a federal agency and division of HUD that operates special assistance aspects of federally aided housing programs and participates in the secondary market through its mortgage-backed securities pools.

graduated lease Lease that provides for rent increases at set future dates.

graduated payment mortgage A mortgage loan for which the initial payments are low but increase over the life of the loan.

grant The act of conveying or transferring title to real property.

grant deed A type of deed that includes three basic warranties: (1) the owner warrants that she or he has the right to convey the property; (2) the owner warrants that the property is not encumbered other than with those encumbrances listed in the deed; and (3) the owner promises to convey any after-acquired title to the property. Grant deeds are popular in states that rely heavily on title insurance.

grantee A person to whom real estate is conveyed; the buyer.

grantor A person who conveys real estate by deed; the seller.

gross lease A lease or property under which a landlord pays all property charges regularly incurred through ownership, such as repairs, taxes, insurance, and operating expenses. Most residential leases are gross leases.

gross national product The total value of all goods and services produced in the United States in a year.

gross rent multiplier A figure used as a multiplier of the gross monthly rental income of a property to produce an estimate of the property's value.

ground lease A lease of land only, on which the tenant usually owns a building or is required to build her or his own building as specified in the lease. Such leases are usually long-term net leases; a tenant's rights and obligations continue until the lease expires or is terminated through default.

guaranteed sale plan An agreement between the broker and the seller that if the seller's real property is not sold before a certain date, the broker will purchase it for a specified price.

guardian One who guards or cares for another person's rights and properties. A guardian has legal custody of the affairs of a minor or a person incapable of taking care of his or her own interests, called a *ward.*

habendum clause The deed clause beginning "to have and to hold," which defines or limits the extent of ownership in the estate granted by the deed.

heir One who might inherit or succeed to an interest in land under the state law of descent when the owner dies without leaving a valid will.

hereditaments Every kind of inheritable property, including personal, real corporeal, and incorporeal.

highest and best use The possible use of land that will produce the greatest net income and thus develop the highest land value.

holdover tenancy A tenancy by which a lessee retains possession of leased property after her or his lease has expired and the landlord, by continuing to accept rent from the tenant, agrees to the tenant's continued occupancy as defined by state law.

holographic will A will that is written, dated, and signed in the handwriting of the maker.

homeowner's insurance policy A standardized package insurance policy that covers a residential real estate owner against financial loss from fire, theft, public liability, and other common risks.

homeowner's warranty program An insurance program offered to buyers by some brokerages, warranting the property against certain defects for a specified period of time.

homestead The land and the improvements thereon designated by the owner as his or her homestead and, therefore, protected by state law, either in whole or in part, from forced sale by certain creditors of the owner.

HUD The Department of Housing and Urban Development; regulates FHA and GNMA.

hypothecation The pledge of property as security of a loan in which the borrower maintains possession of the property while it is pledged as security.

implied contract A contract under which the agreement of the parties is demonstrated by their acts and conduct.

implied grant A method of creating as easement. One party may be using another's property for the benefit of both parties—for example, a sewer on a property that serves two or more properties.

improvement 1. Improvements *on* land: any structure, usually privately owned, erected on a site to enhance the value of the property; for example, buildings, fences and driveways. 2. Improvements *to* land: usually a publicly owned structure, such as a curb, sidewalk, or sewer.

inchoate right Incomplete right, such as a wife's dower interest in her husband's property during his life.

income approach The process of estimating the value of an income-producing property by capitalization of the annual net income expected to be produced by the property during its remaining useful life.

incorporeal right A nonpossessory right in real estate; for example, an **easement** or right-of-way.

increasing returns The principle that applies when increased expenditures for improvements to a given parcel of land yield an increasing percentage return on investment.

independent contractor One who is retained to perform a certain act but who is subject to the control and direction of another only as to the end result, and not as to how he or she performs the act. Unlike an employee, an independent contractor pays all of his or her expenses, pays his or her income and Social Security taxes, and receives no employee benefits. Many real estate salespeople are independent contractors.

index lease Lease that allows the rent to be increased or decreased periodically, based on changes in a selected economic index, such as the Consumer Price Index.

industrial property All land and buildings used or suited for use in the production, storage, or distribution of tangible goods.

installment contract *See CONTRACT FOR DEED.*

installment sale A method of reporting gain received from the sale of real estate when the sale price is paid in two or more installments over two or more years. If the sale meets cer-

tain requirements, a taxpayer can spread recognition of the reportable gain over more than one year, which may result in tax savings.

insurable title A title to land that a title company will insure.

insurance The indemnification against loss from a specific hazard or peril through a contract (called a policy) and for a consideration (called a premium).

interest A charge made by a lender for the use of money.

interim financing A short-term loan usually made during the construction phase of a building project, often referred to as a *construction loan.*

intestate The condition of a property owner who dies without leaving a will. Title to such property passes to his or her heirs as provided in the state law of descent.

invalid Having no force or effect.

invalidate To render null and void.

investment Money directed toward the purchase, improvement, and development of an asset in expectation of income or profits. A good financial investment has the following characteristics: safety, regularity of yield, marketability, acceptable denominations, valuable collateral, acceptable duration, required attention, and potential appreciation.

joint tenancy The ownership of real estate by two or more parties who have been named in one conveyance as joint tenants. On the death of a joint tenant, her or his interest passes to the surviving joint tenant or tenants by the right of survivorship.

joint venture The joining of two or more people to conduct a specific business enterprise. A joint venture is *similar* to a partnership in that it must be created by agreement between the parties to share in the losses and profits of the venture. It is *unlike* a partnership in that the venture is for one specific project only, rather than for a continuing business relationship.

judgment The official and authentic decision of a court on the respective rights and claims of the parties to an action or suit. When a judgment is entered and recorded with the county recorder, it usually becomes a general lien on the property of the defendant for a ten-year period.

judgment clause A provision that may be included in notes, leases, and contracts by which the debtor, lessee, or obligor authorizes any attorney to go into court to confess a judgment against him or her for a default in payment. Also called a *cognovit*.

laches An equitable doctrine used by the courts to bar a legal claim or prevent the assertion of a right because of undue delay, negligence or failure to assert the claim or right.

land The earth's surface extending downward to the center of the earth and upward infinitely into space.

land contract *See CONTRACT FOR DEED.*

law of agency *See AGENT.*

lawyer's opinion of title *See ATTORNEY'S OPINION OF TITLE.*

lease A contract between a landlord (the lessor) and a tenant (the lessee) transferring the right to exclusive possession and use of the landlord's real property to the lessee for a specified period of time and for a stated consideration (rent). By state law, leases for longer than a certain period of time (generally one year) must be in writing to be enforceable.

leasehold estate A tenant's right to occupy real estate during the term of a lease, generally considered to be a personal property interest.

legacy A disposition of money or personal property by will.

legal description A description of a specific parcel of real estate sufficient for an independent surveyor to locate and identify it. The most common forms of legal description are **rectangular survey, metes and bounds,** and subdivision **lot and block (plat).**

legality of object An element that must be present in a valid contract. All contracts that have for their object an act that violates the laws of the United States or the laws of a state to which the parties are subject are illegal, invalid, and not recognized by the courts.

lessee The tenant who leases a property.

lessor One who leases property to a tenant.

leverage The use of borrowed money to finance the bulk of an investment.

levy To assess, seize, or collect. To levy a tax is to assess a property and set the rate of taxation. To levy an execution is to seize officially the property of a person to satisfy an obligation.

license 1. A privilege or right granted to a person by a state to operate as a real estate broker or salesperson. 2. The revocable permission for a temporary use of land—a personal right that cannot be sold.

lien A right given by law to certain creditors to have their debt paid out of the property of a defaulting debtor, usually by means of a court sale.

life estate An interest in real or personal property that is limited in duration to the lifetime of its owner or some other designated person.

life tenant A person in possession of a life estate.

liquidity The ability to sell an asset and convert it into cash at a price close to its true value.

lis pendens A public notice that a lawsuit affecting title to or possession, use, and enjoyment of a parcel of real estate has been filed in either a state or federal court.

listing agreement A contract between a landowner (as principal) and a licensed real estate broker (as agent) by which the broker is employed as agent to sell real estate on the owner's terms within a given time, for which service the landowner agrees to pay a commission.

listing broker The broker in a multiple-listing situation from whose office a listing agreement is initiated, as opposed to the **selling broker,** from whose office negotiations leading to a sale are initiated. The listing broker and the selling broker may, of course, be the same person. *See also MULTIPLE LISTING.*

littoral rights 1. A landowner's claim to use water in large lakes and oceans adjacent to her or his property. 2. The ownership rights to land bordering these bodies of water up to the high-water mark.

lot and block description A description of real property that identifies a parcel of land by reference to lot and block numbers within a subdivision, as identified on a subdivided **plat** duly recorded in the county recorder's office.

management agreement A contract between the owner of income property and a management firm or individual property manager outlining the scope of the manager's authority.

marginal lease A lease agreement that barely covers the costs of operation for the property.

marginal real estate Land that barely covers the costs of operation.

marketable title A good or clear salable title reasonably free from risk of litigation over possible defects; also called a *merchantable title.*

market/data approach A method of appraising or evaluating real property based on the proposition that an informed purchaser would pay no more for a property than the cost to him or her of acquiring an existing property with the same utility. This approach is applicable when an active market provides sufficient quantities of reliable data that can be verified from authoritative sources. The approach is relatively unreliable in an inactive market or in estimating the value of properties for which no real comparable sales data are available. It is also questionable when sales data cannot be verified with principals to the transaction. Also referred to as the *market comparison* or *direct sales comparison approach.*

market price The actual selling price of a property.

market value The most profitable price a property will bring in a competitive and open market under all conditions requisite to a fair sale. The price at which a buyer would buy and a seller would sell, each acting prudently and knowledgeably, and assuming the price is not affected by undue stimulus.

mechanic's lien A statutory lien created in favor of contractors, laborers, and materialmen or material suppliers who have performed work or furnished materials in improving real property.

metes-and-bounds description A legal description of a parcel of land that begins at a well-marked point and follows the boundaries, using direction and distances around the tract, back to the **point of beginning.**

mill One-tenth of one cent. Some states use a mill rate to compute real estate taxes; for example, a rate of 52 mills would be 5.2 cents tax for each dollar of assessed valuation of a property.

millage rate A property tax rate obtained by dividing the total assessed value of all the property in the tax district into the total amount of revenue needed by the taxing district. This millage rate then is applied to the assessed value of each property in the district to determine individual taxes.

misrepresentation To represent falsely; to give an untrue idea of a property. May be accomplished by omission or concealment of a material fact.

monetary policy The government regulation of the amount of money in circulation through such institutions as the Federal Reserve Board.

money judgment A court judgment ordering payment of money rather than specific performance of a certain action. *See also JUDGMENT.*

money market Those institutions, such as banks, savings-and-loan associations and life insurance companies, who supply money and credit to borrowers.

month-to-month tenancy A periodic tenancy—the tenant rents for one period at a time. In the absence of a rental agreement (oral or written), a tenancy generally is considered to be from month to month.

monument A fixed natural or artificial object used to establish real estate boundaries for a metes-and-bounds description.

mortgage A conditional transfer or pledge of real estate as security for a loan. Also, the document creating a **mortgage lien.**

mortgage lien A lien or charge on a mortgagor's property that secures the underlying debt obligations.

mortgagor One who, having all or part of title to property, pledges that property as security for a debt; the borrower.

multiple listing An exclusive listing (generally, an exclusive right to sell) with the additional authority and obligation on the part of the listing broker to distribute the listing to other brokers in the multiple-listing organization.

municipal ordinances The laws, regulations, and codes enacted by the governing body of a municipality.

mutual rescission The act of putting an end to a contract by mutual agreement of the parties.

negligence Carelessness and inattentiveness resulting in violation of trust. Failure to do what is required.

net income The gross income of the property minus the operating expenses (not including debt service).

net lease A lease requiring the tenant to pay not only rent but also costs incurred in maintaining the property, including taxes, insurance, utilities, and repairs.

nonconforming use A use of property that is permitted to continue after a zoning ordinance prohibiting it has been established for the area.

nonhomogeneity A lack of uniformity; dissimilarity. Because no two parcels of land are exactly alike, real estate is said to be nonhomogeneous or heterogeneous.

notarize To certify or attest to a document, as by a **notary public.**

notary public A public official authorized to certify and attest to documents, take affidavits, take acknowledgments, administer oaths, and perform other such acts.

note An instrument of credit given to attest a debt.

novation Acceptance by parties to an agreement to replace an old debtor with a new one. A novation releases liability.

offer and acceptance The two components of a valid contract; a "meeting of the minds."

officer's deed A deed by sheriffs, trustees, guardians, etc.

one hundred percent commission plan A salesperson compensation plan by which the salesperson pays his or her broker a monthly service charge to cover the costs of office expenses and receives 100 percent of the commissions from the sales that he or she negotiates.

open-end mortgage A mortgage loan expandable by increments up to a maximum dollar amount, all of which is secured by the same original mortgage.

open listing A listing contract under which the broker's commission is contingent on the broker's producing a **"ready, willing and able"** buyer before the property is sold by the seller or another broker; the principal (owner) reserves the right to list the property with other brokers.

option The right to purchase property within a definite time at a specified price. No obligation to purchase exists, but the seller is obligated to sell if the option holder exercises the right to purchase.

optionee The party that receives and holds an option.

optionor The party that grants or gives an option.

ownership The exclusive right to hold, possess or control, and dispose of a tangible or intangible thing. Ownerships may be held by a person, corporation or governmental entity.

package mortgage A method of financing in which the loan that finances the purchase of a home also finances the purchase of certain items of personal property, such as a washer, dryer, refrigerator, stove or other specified appliances.

parol evidence rule Law that states that no prior or contemporary oral or extraneously written agreement can change the terms of a contract.

partial eviction A case in which the landlord's negligence deprives the tenant of the use of all or part of the premises.

participation financing A mortgage in which the lender participates in the income of the mortgaged venture beyond a fixed return, or receives a yield on the loan in addition to the straight interest rate.

partition The division of cotenants' interests in real property when the parties do not all voluntarily agree to terminate the co-ownership; takes place through court procedures.

partnership An association of two or more individuals who carry on a continuing business for profit as co-owners. Under the law, a partnership is regarded as a group of individuals rather than as a single entity. A **general partnership** is a typical form of joint venture in which each general partner shares in the administration, profits and losses of the operation. A limited partnership is a business arrangement by which the operation is administered by one or more general partners and funded by limited or silent partners, who are by law responsible for losses only to the extent of their investment.

party wall A wall that is located on or at a boundary line between two adjoining parcels for the use of the owners of both properties.

payee The party that receives payment.

payor The party that makes payment to another.

percentage lease A lease commonly used for retail property in which the rental is based on the tenant's gross sales at the premises; often stipulates a base monthly rental plus a percentage of any gross sales above a certain amount.

performance bond A binding agreement, often accompanied by surety and usually posted by one who is to perform work for another, that assures that a project or undertaking will be completed as per the agreement or contract.

periodic estate An interest in leased property that continues from period to period—week to week, month to month, or year to year.

personal assistant An individual working for a broker or salesperson who handles non-sales-related aspects of real estate transactions.

personal property Items, called **chattels,** that do not fit into the definition of real property; movable objects.

physical deterioration A reduction in utility resulting from an impairment of physical condition. For purposes of appraisal analysis, it is most common and convenient to divide physical deterioration into curable and incurable components.

plat A map of a town, section, or subdivision indicating the location and boundaries of individual properties.

plat book A record of recorded subdivisions of land.

point A unit of measurement used for various loan charges; one point equals 1 percent of the amount of the loan. *See also DISCOUNT POINTS.*

point of beginning The starting point of the survey situated in one corner of the parcel in a **metes-and-bounds legal description.** All metes-and-bounds descriptions must follow the boundaries of the parcel back to the point of beginning.

police power The government's right to impose laws, statutes, and ordinances to protect the public health, safety, and welfare, including zoning ordinances and building codes.

power of attorney A written instrument authorizing a person (the attorney-in-fact) to act on behalf of the maker to the extent indicated in the instrument.

premises The specific section of a deed that states the names of the parties, recital of consideration, operative words of conveyance, legal property description, and appurtenance provisions.

prepayment clause In a mortgage, the statement of the terms on which the mortgagor may pay the entire or stated amount of the mortgage principal at some time prior to the due date.

prepayment penalty A charge imposed on a borrower by a lender for early payment of the loan principal to compensate the lender for interest and other charges that would otherwise be lost.

price fixing *See ANTITRUST LAWS.*

primary mortgage market *See SECONDARY MORTGAGE MARKET.*

principal 1. A sum lent or employed as a fund or investment, as distinguished from its income or profits. 2. The original amount (as in a loan) of the total due and payable at a certain date. 3. A main party to a transaction—the person for whom the agent works.

principal meridian One of 35 north and south survey lines established and defined as part of the rectangular survey system (government survey method).

principle of conformity The appraisal theory stating that buildings that are similar in design, construction, and age to other buildings in the area have a higher value than they would have in a neighborhood of dissimilar buildings.

priority The order of position or time. The priority of liens generally is determined by the chronological order in which the lien documents are recorded; tax liens, however, have priority, even over previously recorded liens.

probate The formal judicial proceeding to prove or confirm the validity of a will or proof of heirship and to settle the affairs of the deceased.

procuring cause The effort that brings about the desired result. Under an open listing, the broker who is the procuring cause of the sale receives the commission.

property management The operation of the property of another for compensation. Includes marketing space; advertising and rental activities; collection, recording and remitting rents; maintenance of the property; tenant relations; hiring employees; keeping proper accounts; and rendering periodic reports to the owner.

property tax Taxes levied by the government against either real or personal property. The right to tax real property in the United States rests exclusively with the states, not with the federal government.

proration The proportional division or distribution of expenses of property ownership between two or more parties. Closing statement prorations generally include taxes, rents, insurance, interest charges, and assessments.

prospectus A printed advertisement, usually in pamphlet form, presenting a new development, subdivision, business venture or stock issue.

public utility easement A right granted by a property owner to a public utility company to erect and maintain poles, wires and conduits on, across or under her or his land for telephone, electric power, gas, water or sewer installation.

pur autre vie A Latin term meaning "for the life of another." A life estate pur autre vie is a life estate measured by the life of a person other than the grantee. Also spelled per autrie vie.

purchase-money mortgage A note secured by a mortgage or deed of trust given by a buyer, as a mortgagor, to a seller, as a mortgagee, as part of the purchase price of the real estate.

qualification The act of determining the prospect's needs, abilities, and urgency to buy and then matching these with available properties.

quitclaim deed A conveyance by which the grantor transfers whatever interest he or she has in the real estate without warranties or obligations.

range A strip of land six miles wide, extending north and south and numbered east and west according to its distance from the principal meridians in the rectangular survey system (government survey method) of land description.

"ready, willing and able" buyer One who is prepared to buy property on the seller's terms and is ready to take positive steps to consummate the transaction.

real estate Land; a portion of the earth's surface extending downward to the center of the earth and upward infinitely into space, including all things permanently attached thereto, whether by nature or by man.

real estate broker Any person, partnership, association or corporation that sells (or offers to sell), buys (or offers to buy), or negotiates the purchase, sale or exchange of real estate, or that leases (or offers to lease) or rents (or offers to rent) any real estate or the improvements thereon for others and for a compensation or valuable consideration. A real estate broker may not conduct business without a real estate broker's license.

Real Estate Settlement Procedures Act (RESPA) The federal law ensuring that the buyer and seller in a real estate transaction have knowledge of all the settlement costs when the purchase of a one-family to four-family residential dwelling is financed by a federally related mortgage loan. Federally related loans include those made by savings-and-loan associations, insured by the FHA or DVA, administered by HUD, or intended to

be sold by the lenders to an agency. Prohibits kickbacks.

reality of consent An element of all valid contracts. Offer and acceptance in a contract usually are taken to mean that reality of consent also is present. This is not the case, however, if any of the following are present: mistake, misrepresentation, fraud, undue influence, or duress.

real property Real property consists of land, anything affixed to it so as to be regarded as a permanent part of the land, that which is appurtenant to the land, and that which is immovable by law, including all rights and interests.

REALTOR® A registered trademark term reserved for the sole use of active members of local REALTORS® boards affiliated with the National Association of REALTORS®.

recapture See ACCELERATED DEPRECIATION.

receiver The court-appointed custodian of property involved in litigation, pending final disposition of the matter before the court.

reconciliation The final step in the appraisal process in which the appraiser reconciles the estimates of value received from the market/data, cost, and income approaches to arrive at a final estimate of market value for the subject property.

recording The act of entering or recording documents affecting or conveying interests in real estate in the recorder's office established in each county. Until recorded, a deed or mortgage generally is not effective against subsequent purchases or mortgage liens.

recovery fund A fund established in some states from real estate license funds to cover claims of aggrieved parties who have suffered monetary damage through the actions of a real estate licensee.

rectangular survey system A system established in 1785 by the federal government, which provides for surveying and describing land by reference to principal meridians and base lines.

redemption period A period of time established by state law during which a property owner has the right to redeem her or his real estate from a foreclosure or tax sale by paying the sales price, interest, and costs. Many states do not have mortgage redemption laws.

redlining The illegal practice of denying loans or restricting their number for certain areas of a community.

Regulation Z A regulation of the Federal Reserve Board designed to ensure that borrowers and customers in need of consumer credit are given meaningful information with respect to the cost of credit.

release To relinquish an interest in or claim to a parcel of property.

relocation service An organization that aids a person in selling a property in one area and buying another property in another area.

remainder The remnant of an estate that has been conveyed to take effect and be enjoyed after the termination of a prior estate, such as when an owner conveys a life estate to one party and the remainder to another.

renegotiable rate mortgage A mortgage loan that is granted for a term of 3 to 5 years and secured by a long-term mortgage of up to 30 years with the interest rate being renegotiated or adjusted each period.

rent A fixed, periodic payment made by a tenant of a property to the owner for possession and use, usually by prior agreement of the parties.

rent schedule A statement of proposed rental rates, determined by the owner or the property manager or both, based on a building's estimated expenses, market supply and demand, and the owner's long-range goals for the property.

replacement cost The cost of construction at current prices of a building having utility equivalent to the building being appraised but built with modern materials and according to current standards, designs, and layout.

reproduction cost The cost of construction at current prices of an exact duplicate or replica using the same materials, construction standards, design, layout, and quality of workmanship and embodying all the deficiencies, superadequacies, and obsolescences of the subject building.

rescission The termination of a contract by mutual agreement of the parties.

reservation in a deed The creation by a deed to property of a new right in favor of the grantor. Usually involves an **easement,** a **life estate,** or a mineral interest.

restriction A limitation on the use of real property, generally originated by the owner or subdivider in a deed.

reverse annuity mortgage A mortgage loan that allows the owner to receive periodic payments based on the equity in the home.

reversion The remnant of an estate that the grantor holds after he or she has granted a life estate to another person; the estate will return or revert to the grantor. Also called a *reverter.*

reversionary right An owner's right to regain possession of leased property on termination of the lease agreement.

rezoning The process involved in changing the existing zoning of a property or area.

right of first refusal A person's right to have the first opportunity to either lease or purchase real property.

right of survivorship *See JOINT TENANCY.*

riparian rights An owner's rights in land that borders flowing water such as a stream or river. These rights include access to and use of the water.

Rural Development A federal agency of the U.S. Department of Agriculture that channels credit to farmers and rural residents and communities; formerly known as the Farm Service Agency and Farmer's Home Administration (FmHA).

sale and leaseback A transaction in which an owner sells her or his improved property and, as part of the same transaction, signs a long-term lease to remain in possession of the premises.

sales contract A contract containing the complete terms of the agreement between buyer and seller for the sale of a particular parcel or parcels of real estate.

salesperson A person who performs real estate activities while employed by or associated with a licensed real estate broker.

satisfaction A document acknowledging the payment of a debt.

secondary mortgage market A market for the purchase and sale of existing mortgages, designed to provide greater liquidity for mortgages; also called the secondary money market. Mortgages are originated in the *primary mortgage market.*

section A portion of a township under the rectangular survey system (government survey method). A township is divided into 36 sections numbered 1 to 36. A section is a square with mile-long sides and an area of one square mile, or 640 acres.

self-proving will A will in which the witnesses give their testimony at the time of signing.

This testimony is preserved in a notarized affidavit to eliminate the problem of finding the witnesses at the maker's death and to assist in the probating procedure.

selling broker *See LISTING BROKER.*

separate property The real property owned by a husband or wife prior to their marriage.

servient tenement The land on which an easement exists in favor of an adjacent property (called a *dominant estate* or *tenement*) also called a *servient estate.*

setback The amount of space local zoning regulations require between a lot line and a building line.

severalty The ownership of real property by one person only, also called **sole ownership.**

situs The personal preference of people for one area over another, not necessarily based on objective facts and knowledge.

sole ownership *See SEVERALTY.*

sovereignty of the soil The beginning of the record of ownership of land by conveyance from the sovereign or the state.

special assessment A tax or levy customarily imposed against only those specific parcels of real estate that will benefit from a proposed public improvement, such as a street or sewer.

special warranty deed A deed in which the grantor warrants or guarantees the title only against defects arising during the period of his or her tenure and ownership of the property and not against defects existing before that time, generally using the language, "by, through, or under the grantor but not otherwise."

specific lien A lien affecting or attaching only to a certain, specific parcel of land or piece of property.

specific performance suit A legal action brought in a court of equity in special cases to compel a party to carry out the terms of a contract. The basis for an equity court's jurisdiction in breach of a real estate contract is the fact that land is unique, and mere legal damages would not adequately compensate the buyer for the seller's breach.

sponsoring broker A duly licensed real estate broker who employs a salesperson. Under law, the broker is responsible for the acts of her or his salespeople.

squatter's rights Those rights acquired through adverse possession. By "squatting" on land for a certain statutory period under prescribed conditions, one may acquire title by limitations. If an **easement** only is acquired, instead of the title to the land itself, one has title by prescription, or **easement by prescription.**

statute of frauds The part of a state law that requires certain instruments such as deeds, real estate sales contracts, and certain leases to be in writing to be legally enforceable.

statute of limitations That law pertaining to the period of time within which certain actions must be brought to court.

statutory lien A lien imposed on property by statute, for example, a tax lien, in contrast to a voluntary lien, which an owner places on his or her own real estate, for example, a mortgage lien.

steering The illegal practice of channeling home seekers to particular areas or avoiding specific areas, either to maintain or to change the character of an area, or to create a speculative situation.

straight-line method A method of calculating depreciation for tax purposes computed by dividing the adjusted basis of a property less its estimated salvage value by the estimated number of years of remaining useful life.

subcontractor *See GENERAL CONTRACTOR.*

subdivision A tract of land divided by the owner, known as the subdivider, into blocks, building lots, and streets according to a recorded subdivision plat that must comply with local ordinances and regulations.

subletting The leasing of premises by a lessee to a third party for part of the lessee's remaining term. *See also ASSIGNMENT.*

subordination A relegation to a lesser position, usually in respect to a right or security.

subordination agreement An agreement that changes the order of priority of liens between two creditors.

subrogation The substitution of one creditor for another, with the substituted person succeeding to the legal rights and claims of the original claimant. Subrogation is used by title insurers to acquire the right to sue from the injured party to recover any claims they have paid.

substitution An appraisal principle stating that the maximum value of a property tends to be set by the cost of purchasing an equally desirable and valuable substitute property, assuming that no costly delay is encountered in making the substitution.

suit for possession A court suit initiated by a landlord to evict a tenant from leased premises after the tenant has breached one of the terms of the lease or has held possession of the property after the lease's expiration.

suit for specific performance A legal action brought by either a buyer or a seller to enforce performance of the terms of a contract.

suit (bill) to quiet title A legal action intended to establish or settle the title to a particular property, especially when there is a cloud on the title.

summation appraisal An approach under which value equals estimated land value plus reproduction costs of any improvements after depreciation has been subtracted.

supply The amount of goods available in the market to be sold at a given price. The term often is coupled with **demand.**

surety bond An agreement by an insurance or bonding company to be responsible for certain possible defaults, debts or obligations contracted for by an insured party; in essence, a policy insuring one's personal and/or financial integrity. In the real estate business, a surety bond generally is used to ensure that a particular project will be completed at a certain date or that a contract will be performed as stated.

survey The process by which boundaries are measured and land areas are determined; the on-site measurement of lot lines, dimensions, and positions of buildings on a lot, including the determination of any existing **encroachments** or **easements.**

syndicate A combination of two or more persons or firms to accomplish a joint venture of mutual interest. Syndicates dissolve when the specific purpose for which they were created has been accomplished.

taxation The process by which a government or municipal quasi-public body raises monies to fund its operation.

tax lien A charge against property created by the operation of law. Tax liens and assessments take priority over all other liens.

tax rate The rate at which real property is taxed in a tax district or county. For example, in a certain county, real property may be taxed at a rate of 56 mills (or 0.056) per dollar of assessed valuation.

tax sale A court-ordered sale of real property to raise money to cover delinquent taxes.

tenancy at sufferance The tenancy of a lessee who lawfully comes into possession of a landlord's real estate but who continues to occupy the premises improperly after her or his lease rights have expired.

tenancy at will An estate that gives the lessee the right to possession until the estate is terminated by either party; the term of this estate is indefinite.

tenancy by the entirety The joint ownership, recognized in some states, of property acquired by husband and wife during marriage. On the death of one spouse, the survivor becomes the owner of the property.

tenancy in common A form of co-ownership by which each owner holds an undivided interest in real property as if he or she were the sole owner. Each individual has the right to partition. Unlike a joint tenancy, there is no right of survivorship between tenants in common, and owners may have unequal interests.

tenant One who holds or possesses lands or tenements by any kind of right of title.

tenement Everything that may be occupied under a lease by a tenant.

termination (lease) The cancellation of a lease by the action of either party. A lease may be terminated by expiration of the term; surrender and acceptance; constructive eviction by lessor; or option when provided in the lease for breach of covenants.

termination (listing) The cancellation of a broker-principal employment contract. A listing may be terminated by death or insanity of either party, expiration of listing period, mutual agreement, sufficient written notice, or the completion of performance under the agreement.

testate Having made and left a valid will.

testator A male will maker.

testatrix A female will maker.

time is of the essence A phrase in a contract that requires the performance of a certain act within a stated period of time.

title insurance Insurance designed to indemnify the holder for loss sustained by reason of defects in a title, up to and including the policy limits.

Torrens system A method of evidencing title by registration with the proper public authority, generally called the registrar. Named for its founder, Sir Robert Torrens.

township The principal unit of the rectangular survey system (government survey method). A township is a square with six-mile sides and an area of 36 square miles.

township lines The lines running at six-mile intervals parallel to the base lines in the rectangular survey system (government survey method).

trade fixtures The articles installed by a tenant under the terms of a lease and removable by the tenant before the lease expires.

trust A fiduciary arrangement by which property is conveyed to a person or institution, called a trustee, and held and administered on behalf of another person, called a beneficiary.

trust deed An instrument used to create a mortgage lien by which the mortgagor conveys his or her title to a trustee, who holds it as security for the benefit of the note holder (the lender); also called a **deed of trust.**

trustee One who as agent for others handles money or holds title to their land.

trustee's deed A deed executed by a trustee conveying land held in a trust.

undivided interest *See TENANCY IN COMMON.*

unearned increment An increase in the value of a property caused by increased population, development and demand for which the owner is not responsible.

Uniform Commercial Code A codification of commercial law, adopted in most states, that attempts to make uniform laws relating to commercial transactions, including chattel mortgages and bulk transfers. Security interests in chattels are created by an instrument known as a security agreement. Article 6 of the code regulates bulk transfers, that is, the sale of a business as a whole, including all fixtures, chattels, and merchandise.

unilateral contract A one-sided contract by which one party makes a promise to induce a second party to do something. The second party is not legally bound to perform; if the second party does comply, however, the first party is obligated to keep the promise.

unity of ownership The four unities traditionally needed to create a joint tenancy—unity of title, unity of time, unity of interest, unity of possession.

urban renewal The acquisition of run-down city areas for purposes of redevelopment.

useful life In real estate investment, the number of years a property will be useful to the investors.

usury The practice of charging more than the rate of interest allowed by law.

valid contract A contract that complies with all the essential elements of a contract and is binding and enforceable on all parties to it.

valid lease An enforceable lease that has the following essential parts: lessor and lessee with contractual capacity, offer and acceptance, legality of object, description of the premises, consideration, signatures, and delivery. Leases for more than one year also must be in writing.

value The present worth of future benefits arising from the ownership of real property. To have value, a property must have utility, scarcity, effective demand, and transferability.

variable rate mortgage A mortgage loan that contains an interest rate provision related to a selected index. Under this provision, the interest rate may be adjusted annually either up or down.

variance An exception from the zoning ordinances; permission granted by zoning authorities to build a structure or conduct a use which is expressly prohibited by zoning ordinance.